Praise for *ENDGAME*

"In *Endgame* two leaders with vast and relevant training and experience—one Catholic and the other Protestant—masterfully reveal the serious marital, relational, and familial problems plaguing believers and their churches today, undermining our welfare and our cultural witness. They do a lot more though—mapping strategies which, if faithfully applied, have been demonstrated through careful research to be effective in supporting sound marriage and family life in Christian churches as well as reaching out to and uplifting the communities these churches serve. The book masterfully and accurately pulls together the best and most up-to-date social science studies out there, making the complex understandable and applicable in describing our current problems and their deepest causes, as well as solutions that are within the reach of every church and community. A copy of this book should be on the shelf of every pastor and priest in the United States, and in the library of every church, seminary, and religious college. I cannot possibly recommend a book on this topic more highly."

> David J. Ayers, Ph.D.
> Professor of Sociology at Grove City College, Fellow for Marriage and Family with the Institute for Faith and Freedom
> Author of *Christian Marriage: A Comprehensive Introduction* and *After the Revolution: Sex and the Single Evangelical*

"*Endgame* is the book that every bishop, priest and lay family minister needs to read. This book is for all those overwhelmed by the "bad news" about marriage and family life in America. *Endgame* provides a way forward that completely sidesteps political divisions and the culture wars. The book marries pathbreaking empirical research with the efforts of a powerful, ecumenical network of churches. Communio can make you hope again."

> Helen Alvare
> Professor of Law at George Mason University and legal scholar on the Family
> Member of the Vatican's Dicastery for Laity, Family, and Life

"*Endgame* is the marriage and family manifesto the church needs to heed. Van Epp and De Gance offer proven strategies and practical skills for seasoned ministry leaders as well as those just getting started. I had many "Ah-ha" moments while reading this book. Everything about this book points couples to thriving Christ-centered marriages. I'm thrilled to have this as a resource to recommend to church and community leaders."

Ted Cunningham
Pastor, Woodland Hills Family Church, Branson, MO
Author of *Fun Loving You*

"*Endgame* is the long-awaited resource the church needs to seize its opportunity and responsibility to strategically serve the needs of relational health in our local churches, communities, and our nation. Van Epp and De Gance are a powerful team with invaluable life training and experiences to competently guide you through the necessary understanding and solutions to the breakdown of faith and family in America today. Their commitment to an integrated approach of historical Christian orthodoxy, psychological and sociological research, and current field testing of best practices for individual and systemic change puts this book in a class of its own. I'll be using it in my seminary classes, and I commend it to churches and seminaries across America."

C. Gary Barnes, Ph.D.
Professor of Biblical Counseling, Dallas Theological Seminary
Ordained Anglican Priest and Licensed Psychologist.

"As someone who has worked to help churches help marriages for the past 20 years, I want every church leader to read, *Endgame*. Van Epp and De Gance do a masterful job of leveraging the harsh reality of the current state of marriage to illuminate the opportunity the church has to save the day."

Ted Lowe
Executive Director of Marriage Strategies, Orange
Co-Author of *Married People, How Your Church Can Build Marriages That Last*

"John Paul II famously said 'As the family goes, so goes the nation.' JP De Gance and John Van Epp build on this, with impeccable data and countless real life examples, that as the family goes, so goes the Church. The reality is that family formation and family stability play an outsized and underappreciated role in the passing on of the faith--and the Church needs to focus more on what it can do to help foster healthy family life. JP and John have written the book that every pastor needs to read."

Ryan T. Anderson, Ph.D.
President of the Ethics and Public Policy Center

"*Endgame* is a book for anyone serious about evangelization and sharing the Gospel. JP De Gance and John Van Epp identify arguably the biggest 21st century barrier to faith in Jesus. They also provide a set of real solutions and strategies for churches and Christians to begin breaking down this barrier."

Craig Springer
Executive Director of Alpha USA
Author of *How to Follow Jesus* and *How to Revive Evangelism*

"By their design, Christian churches should be at the forefront of providing healing for relationships, both within and outside their congregation. *Endgame* puts a focus on America's family and relationship crisis, which we've all caught glimpses of, and then provides a current model for how Christians can address it. I recommend this book as a valuable tool to anyone who wants to mobilize their church to heal relationships in their community."

Greg Gianforte
Governor of Montana

"Married couples learning to truly be 'subject to one another out of reverence for Christ,' (Ephesians 5:21) will be at the heart of the renewal of our Church and the world. As Pope St. John Paul II said, 'as the family goes, so goes the nation and so goes the whole world in which we live.' I commend this book's important contribution in laying out a vision, principles, and strategies for local churches to assist couples in developing strong, healthy, fruitful relationships. I am also grateful to Communio for the work they have already done in parishes throughout the Archdiocese of Denver and the fruit it has born."

Archbishop Samuel Aquila
Archdiocese of Denver

"After pastoring a large church for over 35 years I have come to believe that as the family goes... so goes the church. I also believe that is the message behind this book, *Endgame* by John Van Epp and JP De Gance. There is a great line in the book that says, 'Healthy marriage relationships are the bricks that lay the foundation of both society and the Church itself.' Not only do I believe that churches hold the key to addressing broken marriages, but I also believe that healthy marriages hold the key to strengthening the church! Which is why I think every pastor and church leader should read this book. I've known John Van Epp for several years and his work on building strong marriages is some of the best I have ever read."

Steve Poe
Senior Pastor Northview Church
Author of *Creatures of Habit*

"Finally, a practical and productive way for the church to leave the building and bring the core of family transformation to the community. Wherever the church thinks it should be headed post-covid, this is the clear Macedonian call from our culture to help in the ways the church can really flourish. You can now read a theology and ecclesiology of relationships that is backed by eye-opening data that gives our nation's families a door of hope in the valley of trouble. *Endgame* is an epic milestone publication!"

Dr. Joseph Umidi
Executive Vice President for Student Life, Regent University
Founder/President of Lifeforming Leadership Coaching, Inc.

"*Endgame* is a timely work with serious implications that warrant careful consideration. This is not just another work about relationships or relational ministry that we hear so much about. There is serious research behind this and an emphasis on actual relational skills and integrative biblical principles that are true and timeless. This is a call to do some serious and necessary work within the body of Christ."

Todd J. Williams, Ph.D.
President, Cairn University

"You need this book, *Endgame*. This is THE book for our day as the Christian church. If the church can capture a strong vision for marriage and family ministry from this book- we have a real shot at changing the church and the culture. The authors have written a book easily accessible to anyone, all types of leaders in churches. But it is chock full of some of the most interesting research and well- developed and researched theories on marriage. They integrate Christian principles for marriage that are like fresh bread at the family dinner table. And as if that weren't enough, there are then practical suggestions that any church could use for effective ministries tomorrow."

Jennifer Ripley, Ph.D.
Rosemarie S. Hughes Endowed Chair of Christian Thought in
Mental Health Practice at Regent University

"People without belief in God will soon be the American majority. JP De Gance and John Van Epp identify a central cause -- the demise of our marriages and families. If we care deeply about the well-being of future generations, we must invest in strengthening marriage and families. Here are actionable tools for the church that change the trajectory."

Cheryl Bachelder
Former President and CEO of Popeyes
Author of *Dare to Serve*

"While reading *Endgame*, three words came to mind. **Strategic**. Sound. Sensible. It's hard to imagine a more Strategic book for our time and place. The Christian faith is all about relationships. From our One God, who is a community of three, to humankind's broken and restored relationship with God depicted in the imagery of John's Revelation, the Bible shouts the centrality of relationships. We live in a culture of superficial and broken relationships. A culture largely indifferent to the sanctity of marriage vows and where 'social media' has become toxic to healthy, life-giving relationships. Endgame is a sound and sensible guide, helping churches address our culture's relationship crisis. **Sound** because it's grounded in reliable research and Biblical truth. **Sensible**, because it goes beyond articulating the problem and introduces a workable plan. *Endgame* is a "must-read" for serious church leaders.

William Hoyt, D.Min.
President NexStep Coaching and Consulting

"The collapse of marriage in America is making our society more and more fragile. *Endgame* synthesizes and presents a vast quantity of research on the resulting social crisis. De Gance and Van Epp go beyond defining the problem, providing concrete proposals that have been robustly tested. This book is for anyone hoping to see faith and family renewed in American life."

Seth Kaplan, Ph.D.
Lecturer, SAIS/Johns Hopkins University
Senior Adviser, Institute for Integrated Transitions (IFIT)

"Few questions are as urgent or important as what we can do to strengthen marriage. In *Endgame*, JP De Gance and John Van Epp show that the Church has a vital role to play, one that the Church must play for it's own well-being as well as for the good of the larger society. The data they present and the arguments they advance deserve a wide hearing."

Robert P. George, J.D., Ph.D.
McCormick Professor of Jurisprudence, Princeton University

ENDGAME

The Church's Strategic Move to Save Faith and Family in America

God bless,

TRINITY

TRINITY

ENDGAME: The Church's Strategic Move to Save Faith and Family in America

Love Thinks, LLC
555 N. El Camino Real, Suite A272
San Clemente, CA 92672

Communio
5901 Kingstowne Village Parkway, Suite 102
Alexandria, VA 22315

For information regarding purchasing, bulk pricing, and additional resources, please go to www.ENDGAMEbook.org.

Cover Design: Rachel Boland
Interior Design: Kelly Martin and Michael Gorfido
Edited by Iain Bernhoft

Unless otherwise indicated, Scripture quotations are taken from the New International Version (NIV) © 1973, 1978, 1984, International Bible Society. Used by permission of Zondervan Bible Publishers.
Other Scripture quotations are taken from the Holy Bible, King James Version (KJV)—Public Domain.

Library of Congress

Van Epp, John and De Gance, J.P.
ENDGAME: The Church's Strategic Move to Save Faith and Family in America / John Van Epp and J.P. DeGance
Includes bibliographical references (p. 255 – 266) and subject and Scripture indexes.
ISBN 978-1-7375656-0-4 (paperback)
ISBN 978-1-7375656-1-1 (audio)

Printed in the United States of America

Contents

Acknowledgments xi

Foreword xv

Chapter 1 – The Church's 21st Century Opportunity
and Responsibility 1

***

**Section I: The Crisis of Relationships
and the Decline of Christianity**.................. 23

Chapter 2 – Fighting the Smoke Instead of the Fire 25

Chapter 3 – The Decoupling Effect 41

Chapter 4 – The Decoupling of Sex from Marriage 47

Chapter 5 – The Decoupling of Romantic Partnerships
from Marriage 63

Chapter 6 – The Decoupling of Parenting from Marriage 75

Chapter 7 – The Flight from Marriage Produces Bad
Fruit for the World and the Church 87

***

**Section II: The Qualities of Healthy Relationships
and the Growth of Christianity**.................. 99

Chapter 8 – The Church's Twenty-First Century Mission:
Relationship Health to Evangelize the World 101

Chapter 9 – Healthy Relationships Require Intentional
Management 117

Chapter 10 – Healthy Relationships Consist of Strong
Bonds 129

Chapter 11 –   Healthy Relationships Express the Virtues
                of Agape Love   147

Chapter 12 –   Healthy Relationships Engage with Proficient
                Skills   161

★ ★ ★

**Section III: The Plan for Prioritizing Relationship
                 Ministries and Outreaches**   179

Chapter 13 –   Key Ingredients for an Effective Relationship
                Ministry   181

Chapter 14 –   Growing the Church through Relationship
                Ministry: The Data-Informed, Full-Circle
                Relationships Ministry®   209

Chapter 15 –   Going on Mission: The Ministry Engagement
                Ladder®   223

Chapter 16 –   A Model Church for Prioritizing the Mission
                of Relationship Health   237

Chapter 17 –   The Endgame for the Church in America   249

                Chapter Notes –   255

                Subject Index –   267

                Scripture Index –   273

Acknowledgements

This book is the result of the influence and impact of many on my (JP's) life. First, my parents, Joseph and Jackie De Gance, and their marriage of more than fifty years is the best place to start. Their faithfulness brought six kids and twenty-one grandkids into the world. They modeled a great marriage and cultivated within me faith in our Lord. My bride, Christina, is so much better than I deserve. She has relentlessly supported me and did so in the face of a questionable career move out of policy and into a focus on strengthening marriage.

My sister, Danielle, I want to thank for letting me share her story and for trusting my wife and me to love and take care of her kids. To say she suffered immensely would be a vast understatement. Her decision changed my life, my family's life, and ignited all of the work that led to this book. I also want to express my gratitude and love for each of my eight kids—John-Paul, Luke, Anastasia, Cecilia, Matthew, Perpetua, Ignatius, and Lucy. They each inspire me to be a better dad.

Three others played an essential role—Sean Fieler, Toby Neugebauer, and John Stanley. Sean and Toby are two board members who stood with me at a critical moment and made Communio happen. I will be forever grateful to them. At a critical moment in my journey, John made a phone call to me that set the foundation for all Communio's work to happen—including this book.

This book is also the result of either the support, encouragement, or partnership of many others: Adam Meyerson, Mike Leven, Joseph Moser and his wife Jillian, Will Hild, Christina Tenney, Sarah Miller, Regina Truslow, Richard Albertson, Dennis Stoica, Jad Levi, Mark Regnerus, Brad Wilcox, Wendy Wang, Luke Nelson, Isaiah Contu, Simone Loel, David Travis, Charlie Kenney, Matthew De Gance, Chris De Gance, Wayne Lanier, Chad Moore, David Ashcraft, Tim Ahlman, Dale Brown, Paul Vitz, Greg and Susan Gianforte, Julie Baumgardner, Julia Ceravalo, and Steve Moore.

There was a group of generous business leaders who knew me and my work in public policy and came along on this journey. They supported the vision of strengthening our country by improving the health of our marriages and families. I do not name them here, but each should know how much their generosity has changed the family legacies of tens of thousands. Their leadership made this book a reality.

JP and I (John) know that we stand on the shoulders of many, many authors, pastors, relationship experts, social scientists, and pioneers within the marriage movement who have come before us, and many who continue to this day. But neither of us would have been able to write this book without the transforming love we have experienced in our marriages and families.

Shirley and I will be celebrating forty-two years as husband and wife, and she continues to be the one who breathes inspiration and confidence into my life and work. I marvel at her grace, wisdom, and deep love, which bless our two daughters, their spouses, and our three (soon to be four) grandchildren. She read and reread each draft, providing grammatical edits and invaluable suggestions on content. Our daughters and their spouses, Morgan and Chad, and Jessica and Patrick, engaged with me in thoughtful discussions about *Endgame*, for which I am incredibly grateful. Both JP and I cannot express strongly enough our immense appreciation for the heroic efforts of Michael Gorfido and his countless hours with completing the internal design of this book.

I am especially thankful for the wonderful opportunity to work with my daughter, Dr. Morgan Cutlip, for over fifteen years—she is a kindred spirit and a phenomenal creator of healthy relationship content, which she shares daily with over 100,000 followers on the MyLoveThinks Instagram page.

In many ways, this book is the culmination of my entire career, beginning with a vision I had for providing marriage and family resources to our congregation and community shortly after planting an Evangelical church in northern Ohio. That vision was tabled as I completed my doctoral studies and left the pastoral ministry for a twenty-five-year counseling practice. But first, let me meander back in time and thank those couples from the leadership of that church plant who lovingly shaped a newlywed couple and twenty-two-year old "wet-behind-the-ears" founding pastor—Russ and Andrea Gifford, Gary and Karen Gifford, Dick and Helen Stephens, Bob and Lee Ellenberger, Fred and Jean Gale, Jim and Dawn Imig, and Tim and Robbie Collins, along with our "family" in the Medina Community Church.

My education was greatly shaped by the late Richard Dobbins, who was a master at integrating theology with psychology, while always holding fast to the inerrancy of Scripture. I also learned much from the clients and families I was honored to work with during my twenty-five-year private practice.

A major turning point in my career occurred when I began attending the Smart Marriage Conference in 1997. Diane Sollee spearheaded the Community Marriage Education movement over those years, providing me with endless opportunities, introductions, encouragement, and direction. There are so many colleagues I have learned from and worked with during this movement—but one couple that must be acknowledged is Mike and Harriet McManus and their work through Marriage Savers. They were pioneers in bringing marriage education to churches throughout the United States and Canada.

I am also indebted to Julie Baumgardner and the leadership of the National Association of Relationship and Marriage Education (NARME) Conference. Together, the NARME and the Smart Marriage conferences showcased my evidence-based relationship courses and created the platforms for me to engage with the majority of those who labor in the marriage and healthy relationship movement. In addition, I greatly appreciate the lead pastor, Steve Poe, and the groups pastor, Derek Irvin, from the Northview Church, who helped shape the RAM Series® messages and small-group resources from our existing evidence-based courses, and lead pastor at LCBC, David Ashcraft, and his amazing staff, who contributed to the development of the RAM Series elementary resources.

Finally, I have had the honor of knowing and serving thousands of chaplains from all branches of the military, and I am especially grateful to the past and present chaplain leaders in the Army Strong Bonds, the Air Force Strong Bonds, and the Navy who tirelessly worked to help singles, couples, and families develop healthier relationships. I am hesitant to begin mentioning names— too many will be left out—so please know how indebted I feel to all of you, especially those with whom I have had the privilege of sharing many hours of engaging and inspiring conversations.

Foreword

In Pursuit of Happiness:
Why Faith and Family Matter More Than Ever

One of the central ironies of American life today is this: faith and family life have hit record lows even as the science continues to mount telling us how much they matter for the welfare of men, women, and children. Recent data from Gallup tell us, for instance, that church membership in the United States fell to a record low in 2020: 47%. Likewise, marriage and fertility rates in the United States hit lows never seen before in 2020. Data from the Centers for Disease Control indicate our total fertility rate was 1.64 children per woman in 2020. This is a level well below the replacement rate, 2.1 children per woman, needed to keep our society's population stable over the long term. What all this means is that faith and family life are playing a smaller role in lives of ordinary Americans than ever before.

This is ironic because Gallup also found in 2020 that two groups of Americans were especially resilient in the face of COVID's myriad health, economic, and social trials: churchgoing and married Americans. Men and women who kept attending church in 2020 were 58% more likely to report their mental health as "excellent," compared to those rarely or never attended. Likewise, married Americans were 51% more likely to say their mental health was "excellent," compared to their fellow countrymen and women who were not married.

None of this would surprise Emile Durkheim, the great 19th century French sociologist. "The believer who has communicated with his god," Durkheim wrote, "is not merely a man who sees new truths of which the unbeliever is ignorant; he is a man who is stronger. He feels within him more force, either to endure the trials of existence, or to conquer them." Durkheim fully appreciated and anticipated the ways in which strong families and faith traditions afford men and women a sense of meaning, direction, and social support, all of which make them stronger. Today, a large body of research indicates churchgoing and marriage are linked to significantly lower rates of suicide and depression, and to higher rates of longevity and happiness.

Endgame fully appreciates all the ways in which strong families and faith communities are vital to the health of contemporary men, women, and especially children. More importantly, this new book by JP DeGance and John Van Epp points us to a path forward to renewal for our families and churches. Not only do they explore all the ways that faith makes marriage and family life stronger, as well as all the ways that strong families boost church membership and attendance, they also provide clear, actionable steps that churches and ministries can take to strengthen and stabilize the families already in their pews and to attract more families into their pews. DeGance and Van Epp are pointing us to the path to reverse the falling fortunes of family and faith in the twenty-first century.

Endgame is a book that is needed more than ever. It builds on the foundation that in America today, the "pursuit of happiness" is most likely to be realized by men, women, and children in strong families and vital faith communities.

~ W. Bradford Wilcox, Ph.D.

Director of the National Marriage Project and Professor of Sociology at the University of Virginia

Senior Fellow of the Institute for Family Studies

CHAPTER 1

The Church's 21st Century Opportunity and Responsibility

A Picture of a Failing Marriage

The two had met as high schoolers, but never dated back then. By the time they got together as adults, they both bore relational and emotional scars.

Lee had a rough childhood. His sometimes severe father kept things uncertain. Mom had been distant. Then Dad unexpectedly died, and Mom was shattered. He enlisted in the Navy after high school, perhaps to make a clean break with the unhealthy home life of his childhood.

When Danielle reconnected with Lee, she was emerging with two children from a marriage that had ended badly. Her first husband spent much of his free time at bars and playing pool. She tolerated that, but not when he almost killed her eldest child in a DUI incident.

During their courtship, Lee would drive down to South Florida from Jacksonville on days off to visit Danielle. He proposed prior to his next overseas deployment. While the couple persevered through the physical separation, Danielle began to have her doubts about Lee, even calling off the wedding at one point. Encouraged by her parents, she put the wedding back on again, hoping that marriage would resolve into happily ever after. The young family moved to follow Lee's new Navy appointment to Virginia Beach, and within two years the family had grown in size to six with the births of two more children.

But it was far from happily ever after. As relationship challenges from Lee's family of origin began to metastasize, arguments became common. Then violent. The first time Lee became physical with Danielle was during her first pregnancy with him. He slapped her ear so hard that her eardrum ruptured, causing a temporary loss of hearing. Another time, Lee body-slammed Danielle onto a concrete floor. The resulting injury immobilized her and required back surgery. The couple hid the true cause of the injury, allowing Lee to stay employed and appear to outsiders like a great husband caring for his ailing wife.

The children suffered too. Lee had adopted Danielle's older pair of children but withheld from them the affection he showed his own children (unless other people were around). He grew jealous of Danielle's oldest son, causing the boy to withdraw to his room to spend hours alone on his computer. And when Lee one day overheard Danielle's younger daughter and mistook her playing with dolls for scolding her half-sister, he picked the four-year-old up by her throat and slammed her head into a wall so hard that it left a hole in the dry wall. He lied about the cause of the damage for years, until the daughter grew old enough to recount the exchange to Danielle.

This dysfunctional home life led Danielle into depression. While she had been raised in an actively Christian home, the family stopped attending church. Near the end of the marriage, home-cooked meals became scarce, and the kids grew accustomed to cereal or fast food for dinner. Meanwhile, Lee wasn't advancing through the ranks in the Navy, and often found himself in conflict with his chain of command. He was supposed to go on an extended deployment, giving the family some promise of space and stability. But as the deployment approached, Lee grew more and more agitated.

One night, a marital flare-up turned redhot. With the children home, Lee pinned Danielle against the wall and began to choke and strike her. When one of the kids recounted the incident to a counselor, the Navy launched an investigation that put Lee in the brig. Danielle wouldn't testify and so he was never convicted, but she sought and received a protective order against him through civil authorities.

It is impossible to underestimate the compounding impact of years of such an unhealthy and volatile relationship. Danielle's mental health had severely deteriorated, and the four kids had suffered years of stress and uncertainty. Her family tried to help, but the combative life she had endured triggered paranoia and survival instincts. She soon left her family in South Florida, attempting to reset her life by moving with all four kids back to Virginia Beach, the last place she had felt healthy and safe.

Crisis ensued. Despite the prior physical abuse and the protective order, Danielle moved back in with Lee, who had enough money from his Navy-provided transitional income to get a place to rent. When his income and her temp job ended, Danielle had nowhere to go. The nearby shelter would only take in Danielle and her kids if she sent her eldest son elsewhere—he was fifteen and thus ineligible to stay with them. Unwilling to break up her children, she met a single dad through MySpace and temporarily moved in with him.

It had now been more than a year since Danielle had spoken with anyone in her family. But she had a brother who lived just 150 miles away in Northern Virginia. One July afternoon, she called her brother and asked him to take in his nieces and nephews for a time. It was the single most painful event in her life. But Danielle wasn't mentally well. The traumatic cycle of domestic violence was triggering irrational phobias and a manic state—and, it later became clear, a very severe case of post-traumatic stress disorder. To her great credit, she recognized this reality and how badly she needed help.

Danielle's brother was reluctant to take in her children. He and his wife had recently started their own family: two kids and one on the way. They had been married just four years and had recently moved into their first single-family home. Taking in four older kids—two boys and two girls ages fifteen, fourteen, eleven, and ten—seemed too much. But after the phone call, while he was hesitating, his wife, Christina, was purchasing train tickets. Soon, a devastated Danielle placed her children on an Amtrak train bound for Quantico, nearly all their possessions fitting in three bags.

In the days and months that followed, it was clear that the children carried tremendous wounds. All four began to meet with therapists. The youngest daughter had become easily startled by any loud voices and would avoid conflict at all costs. Because it had now been years since they had anything like a family meal, the younger two had little table etiquette. The kids had rarely attended church and had little familiarity with Jesus.

The fallout of this failed marriage was profound. It would take years until Danielle would become renewed in her health. But God is good. Danielle had a reversion to faith in Jesus Christ. She reunited with her children as they finished school in Northern Virginia. Today, she is an amazing woman and mom.

* * *

I tell you Danielle's story not simply because it manifests the physical, mental, social, and spiritual toll of an unhealthy marriage. I begin here because, in so many ways, Danielle's journey is really my own (JP).

Her path led me on a journey that took me away from a life in politics to a life in ministry, and to co-authoring the book you are reading right now. You see, Danielle is my sister. And it was my wife, Christina, who picked up those four children from the Quantico train station that surreal July day. My wife and I experienced in a deeply personal way what happens to children when families fail. God used this experience to redirect my career and life mission.

I wish I could tell you that I didn't hesitate, but I did. I was twenty-eight, and I felt overwhelmed by the challenges of parenting deeply wounded teenagers. More than once, I wanted to give up. My bride refused. She constantly reassured me that God had called us to this work. But despite her pushing, I wanted to bail.

One night on the back patio of our home, I was talking to a close friend who had served as a lead pastor at multiple Evangelical churches. I confided in him my doubt about our decision to take the kids in, hoping he would agree with me. He rebuked me instead: "JP, you know you are the only chance these kids have. This is your cross. Those kids need you."

Political Insights

At the time these events took place, I had been working in the political world. Like many, I had come to Washington, D.C., motivated by the idea of saving the country. Fresh out of college, I jumped into the machinery of our electoral and public policy process with grand hopes of producing change.

I learned much in those years. My first mentor was Morton Blackwell, who hired me at the Leadership Institute right after I worked to re-elect Jeb Bush in 2002. From Morton I learned the importance of mastering political technology and applying consistent principles and sound methodology. In 2006, another professional mentor, Kevin Gentry, recruited me to work for Charles Koch on his special projects team at Koch Industries. Much of my work focused on advancing economic freedom through issue advocacy, and I learned the importance of beginning any work with the end in mind. Eventually, this led to me becoming vice president of external affairs at Americans for Prosperity (AFP), where in just over two years we quadrupled fundraising revenue to more than $120 million annually.

In short, from 2006 until 2013 I worked on the biggest state and national public policy battles in collaboration with leading communications and messaging firms, polling companies, and some of the nation's top political strategists. The binary outcomes of policy fights meant there was a clear winner and clear loser. This sort of high-stakes clarity produces a relentless focus on constant improvement and innovation. If you lose one battle, you do a rigorous post-mortem to understand why. You then redesign your strategy and techniques to produce a better result next time.

This work also brought me into close collaboration with some of the nation's top business leaders—billionaires and centimillionaires, amazing men and women like the late Rich DeVos. Men like him expected rigorous execution and candor about what worked and what did not work. They knew setbacks occur in their own businesses. In real life, failures happen; savvy businesspeople strive to understand why.

I recall one particular conversation with a billionaire—he called me because he wanted me to know AFP had misspelled his wife's name on a letter. We had never met his wife. She had a very challenging name to spell, and when her name was entered into the database, it was spelled phonetically, which is to say, incorrectly. He was a six-figure donor to our work.

"You know, JP, I want you to know that I'm not like this at all," the businessman said before pausing for effect. "But some major donors who see their wife's name misspelled on a letter might say to themselves, 'If the organization can't spell my wife's name correctly on a letter, they probably have much bigger problems in their ability to execute their mission.'"

All this professional education shaped me. Strategy. Focus. Discipline. Flawless execution. Rigorous self-assessment and improvement. These were critical in the high-stakes realm of public policy.

So let me ask you a question: Do we as Christians see our work as less important than public policy? Surely it is *more* important—the stakes have eternal consequences. And yet how frequently we approach ministry work without the same focus, the same attention to strategy or testing and improvement. Why

Do we as Christians see our work as less important than public policy?

don't the People of God put all these principles to work in building up the Kingdom? Is prayer and faithfulness to the Holy Spirit somehow incompatible with a high level of rigor and discipline?

These questions started to haunt me, both professionally and personally. As I evaluated what was happening in the public policy world, I began to conclude that there were things of far more profound significance and national impact than regulation, energy, or health care policy.

And the journey I was undergoing in my home with my nieces and nephews—now five years later—made me ask existential questions about what truly mattered. I had come to Washington to help save the country. But what if the best way for me to contribute to "saving the country" didn't involve Washington at all? It was becoming more and more clear that what occurred in the homes and families of my fellow Americans had a far more profound impact than what happened inside the Beltway. Public policy is important, sure, but I saw that family life is much more integral to the health of our country than I had previously realized.

In the final five years of my political life, my wife and I were friends with four practicing Christian couples who divorced. One couple's divorce particularly shook us. The husband came to the men's group. They were active in our parish. They had all the right "externals." They had five children. One was a child with special needs.

Then, one day, he just didn't come home.

He had been having an affair. Several of our friends tried to intervene to draw him back, to get him to repent and to be faithful to his vows. Nothing worked, and divorce soon followed. The new single mom moved away to be closer to family. Priests from our parish tried to meet with the husband. But our parish had no marriage ministry. It had nothing to support couples as couples—no parish-based skills ministry, no mentoring ministry.

I looked at my two nephews and thought about this couple's sons. I thought of their daughter with special needs. It made me fearful for their future. What could I do? Our Lord kept working on my heart.

The Culture of Freedom Initiative

In the days that followed Election Day 2012, I started to consider what it would look like to take everything I had learned professionally about strategy, measurement, discipline, and execution, and apply it to something more edifying than politics: renewing marriage and the family.

What would it look like, I wondered, if churches worked to strengthen marriage in their communities with the same focus on results and strategy employed in the public policy world? What if we treated the collapse of marriage with the same sense of urgency and the same relentless focus as we show the next presidential election? It certainly holds far more importance than the next election. Why should we put less effort there?

As these thoughts reverberated in my mind, I received a phone call from an old colleague who was recruiting her replacement at The Philanthropy Roundtable—an organization that worked with philanthropists on helping them strengthen America's free and civil society. She had been the organization's chief operating officer, and she was going on sabbatical. Did I know anyone interested in the role?

The Roundtable was a perfect fit for exploring these ideas. Adam Meyerson, the organization's president, knew strong marriages and families were a core ingredient to a healthy civil society, and he gave me tremendous latitude to develop a test project in which philanthropists could invest—one that applied the skills and practices of public policy to strengthening marriages in America.

We called it the Culture of Freedom Initiative. The funders I had personally known had a deep love for our nation and the American experiment in freedom and self-government. I made the case to them that if you truly care about America, then you need to focus on strengthening the preconditions for what allows a nation to be free and self-governing: strong marriages, families, and churches.

So in 2013 and 2014, I began to speak to business leaders and philanthropists interested in doing just that. We convened our first planning meeting at George Washington's Mount Vernon on November 14, 2014. A group of eleven high-net-worth business leaders joined our initial task force, and they in turn invited a larger group of their peers to test strategies that might measurably improve marriage outcomes and grow church attendance. In March of 2015, we held our first large-donor convening in Dallas: the Culture of Freedom Summit. No privately-funded initiative had successfully shifted marriage outcomes on the scale of a large US city. Most doubted that it was possible.

Before launching, the Culture of Freedom Initiative spent a year analyzing existing efforts in marriage ministry, community marriage support, and relationship health to understand what did and did not work. We hired an insider from the federal marriage program to do a post-mortem on why that secular effort appeared to produce mediocre or mixed results.

In that year it became clear to us that there was already an abundance of content and programs. The real issue was that great content (particularly relationship health content) does not get to those who most need it. We needed to find a way to encourage people to encounter and adopt this life-changing content. And we recognized that the only way to shift marriage dynamics on the large scale was by focusing on the small scale—by increasing the personal relationships within a community.

Our approach began with the Biblical centrality of relationships: We believe that life changes most powerfully through personal relationships—none more profoundly life-changing than the relationship with Jesus Christ. Personal relationships form the path toward true discipleship; ultimately, healthy marriage relationships are the bricks that lay the foundation of both society and the Church itself. For this reason, impersonal programs are bound to fail—no matter how well-intentioned. Only through the arm of churches reaching into communities with sound relationship skills, vision, and community can there ever be major changes in families' lives.

> We believe that life changes most powerfully through personal relationships—none more profoundly life-changing than the relationship with Jesus Christ.

So the Culture of Freedom Initiative took

shape in helping churches and local nonprofits enlarge the number of life-changing relationships that could occur in a specific community. Within these life-changing relationships, we would help people use proven relationship education content to improve marriage and relationship health.

* * *

During a three-year test period that officially began on January 1, 2016, and ended December 31, 2018, we raised and deployed more than $20 million in risk capital. We helped churches in three different pilot markets—Phoenix, Jacksonville, and Dayton—move individuals through more than 200,000 individual relationship health programs of four hours or longer.[1]

This donor-led project partnered with content creators, church leaders, community marriage leaders, and scholars. We brought techniques and strategies to ministry that are not often deployed there. We contracted with the Right Brain People, a behavioral-based psychological research firm that seeks to understand the underlying emotional motivations behind consumer decisions. They looked at the underlying emotional drivers of why young people choose to go to church, get married, cohabit, and divorce.

In 2015, the Culture of Freedom Initiative (COFI) was the first to apply consumer product data modeling to the realm of ministry in order to help improve digital outreach and invitation. We asked data scientists to model marriages that recently ended in divorce, and then applied that model to currently married individuals to assess the risk of divorce. Those who fit this model—we labeled them "marriages with a high propensity for divorce"—were then invited to programs at participating churches and nonprofits. No one had done this before.

We learned incredibly ineffective and wasteful ways to leverage data . . . and also highly effective and efficient ways. For instance, using microtargeting to advertise to couples who appeared to be struggling in their marriage turned out to be wasteful if the invitation drove an individual immediately into a skills-based program, such as couple relationship education. The real successes lay in using the data to invite these couples into relationship with a church through strategic relational pathways. We realized that a church community was relationally "sticky"—and thus transformative—in a way a class in isolation could never be.

We went through a tremendous amount of trial and error, paying lots of dumb taxes along the way. But, in the end, we also discovered some incredibly effective strategies. With help from the Leadership Network, we administered a two-year test that used big data along with a focus on relationship ministry and millennial church engagement to give us a clear picture of COFI's work in thirty-three different churches across all three cities. Those churches grew (and sustained) average Sunday attendance by 23 percent. Generosity among their congregations also increased by 28 percent. (I cite this data not because growth is an outcome in the realm of faith. It is merely used here as a proxy for success and should not be confused for success itself—which is a changed life of faith through Christ Jesus. And on this side of the eschaton, there is no objective way for third parties to definitively measure such transformation.)

The Culture of Freedom Initiative didn't just help churches grow stronger. It also proved that churches can shift marriage dynamics across an entire city. Jacksonville, Florida, had historically been one of the worst cities for marriage in America due to its high divorce rate. The city had never been below the state average divorce rate since the advent of no-fault divorce. Our coalition worked with ninety-three different churches in Jacksonville—Baptist, Catholic, and community Bible churches—to move 58,912 people through four-hour or longer skills-based programs. Our data team used digital impressions to microtarget people across the county, driving engagement and participation in the relationship health ministry these churches put on.

The results were astounding. The divorce rate in Jacksonville fell 24 percent over the three-year project. Our work drew interest from leading academics in the field, as scholars at the University of Virginia and Florida State did their own evaluations. Dr. W. Brad Wilcox (one of the nation's leading sociologists on marriage) and Dr. Spencer James published an independent evaluation that found no demographic explanation could explain the decline in divorce other than COFI's intervention in the county. We were invited to

The divorce rate in Jacksonville fell 24 percent over the three-year project.

speak along with Dr. Wilcox at the American Enterprise Institute on these findings and the lessons learned from the initiative. During that presentation, I had the chance to thank some of our most important partners in this success. Richard Albertson, the founder and president of Live the Life Ministries, and Dennis Stoica, the organization's board chairman, both helped substantially on strategy, content, and execution.

* * *

During and after the Culture of Freedom Initiative officially concluded in December of 2018, we took stock of failures and successes. While still at The Philanthropy Roundtable, we had incorporated the Culture of Freedom Initiative into its own 501(c)(3) organization. I was the volunteer president of COFI while serving as the Roundtable's executive vice president. As the initiative came to a close, it was clear that the work needed to grow as a distinct nonprofit entity. Two of our founding donors—Sean Fieler, the founder and president of Equinox Partners, and Toby Neugebauer—stepped forward to lead the board as we began the work of scaling and replication. We distilled the most effective elements from the three-year test and folded them into our organization.

In February of 2019, the Culture of Freedom Initiative was rebranded as Communio, a nonprofit that consults with churches to bring integrated ministry strategies and technologies to foster relationship health for singles, marrieds, those engaged, and those in crisis. We've recently launched four new city-wide initiatives to strengthen marriage and grow churches—in Billings, Montana; the Permian Basin in Texas; Denver, Colorado; and Fort Worth, Texas.

I'm writing this book because I believe that the Church holds the key for addressing the collapse of marriage—and that addressing the collapse of marriage is also the key for rebuilding the Church in America. But that project will only take flight if we treat it with every ounce of focus, discipline, and strategic insight we can muster. In writing this book, I am excited to be able to partner with my friend Dr. John Van Epp. Few content creators grasp the centrality of relationship health to the future of the Church like John. For the Gospel to spread in the 21st century, it is critical that the Church focuses on fostering marital health and relationship health. But John can speak for himself.

Lessons Learned from Government Programs

It is amazing how two completely different paths of life can converge for people who share the same vision. I (John) was conducting trainings at a conference when a colleague approached me and said, "I recently took a position with a nonprofit run by JP De Gance and I think that you and he should meet."

Two weeks later, JP and I were introduced and almost immediately agreed to co-author this book. I've been dragging it around in skeletal outline for ten years, collecting and organizing research and anecdotes. Now I've found the second voice it needs.

I write as a therapist and relationship expert, but the seed of this book began germinating years before. Shortly after graduating and marrying my wife, Shirley, in 1979, I took a position with my home church to launch a mission church with seven families to establish in northern Ohio. It was an exciting adventure as the church grew quickly; within five years, we purchased a seven-acre property right in the heart of our city with a large building for our gatherings, offices, and even a house on the frontage of the lot.

Sometimes a vision of what God has put on your heart can go dormant, only to be resurrected years later. At the time, I had decided to conduct Saturday seminars on relationship topics that were included in the coursework I was taking in my seminary master's programs. I dreamt of establishing a family center as a ministry of the church, in which seminars and resources integrating research findings with biblical principles could be offered to the church and the local community.

But before I was able to accomplish these goals, I came to believe that God was leading me into full-time counseling. As I completed my Ph.D. program, I left the pastoral ministry to establish a counseling practice that continued for the next twenty-five years. I also taught marriage and family coursework as an adjunct professor in a nearby seminary, still carrying the spark of a dream that churches could become the epicenter of relationship education for their congregations and surrounding communities.

Something that became apparent very soon into my counseling was that many of the relationship problems that brought people to therapy were completely avoidable. Crisis could have been averted if the couple had just done some things differently earlier in their relationships. What was needed was a ministry that addressed the basic underlying problems—not just the later consequences.

So, in the mid-nineties, around the tenth year of my practice, I established my company, Love Thinks, LLC, and developed evidence-based relationship courses that I trained others to teach. For another ten years, I continued to balance working in my private practice and training others in these courses on dating, marriage, and family relationships. In 2009, I retired from my practice in order to work fulltime as the president of Love Thinks, and to focus on two major movements committed to taking relationship education into their communities. The successes—and failures—of these two movements directly inform the approach we lay out in the following pages.

* * *

The first movement I became involved with was the Community Healthy Marriage Initiative, which funded nonprofits with state and federal grants. Many working in this field were faith-based individuals who had created or become involved with parachurch organizations to impact the relationship health of their communities. But while some churches supported these nonprofits, next to none were doing this kind of community outreach: offering classes outside of their church campus, in community settings, simply to improve the relationship health of those who live in their community (e.g., improving dating practices; increasing satisfaction in marriage relationships; lowering divorce rates).

The initial efforts of these nonprofits produced some limited benefits, according to published research on the meta-analysis of their work. The efficacy of these services greatly increased, however, when they continued for ten or more years and reached larger percentages of individuals and couples in their community. In fact, one tri-county nonprofit in Indiana that used two of my Love Thinks relationship courses throughout their region found that the divorce rates dropped by more than 20 percent over a ten-year period.

For all its promise, however, the Community Healthy Marriage Initiative was fundamentally limited by the source of its funding: government. When politics controls the money, it determines the scope, numbers, and conditions of what will be allowed. *He who controls the purse strings, makes the rules.*

For instance, federal guidelines required that the populations served be greatly restricted, focusing primarily on low-income individuals and couples. As important and needed as this focus is, the narrow scope and temporary funding severely limited the likelihood of any significant, lasting changes in the health of couples and families throughout the larger spectrum of their communities.

In the case of that nonprofit in Indiana I just mentioned, for example, it had expanded its reach beyond working only with low-income populations—and as a result, had actually impacted the landscape of marital health with clear evidence of lowered divorce rates in the entire region. However, after ten years of success, it was not selected to receive a new federal grant—in spite of its clear successes—and was unable to continue providing services. Without its consistent and extensive efforts, the relationship health of the community slowly deteriorated.

The second major movement in skills-based relationship education I became involved with was in the Army chaplaincy. In 1999, after CH (MG) Gaylord Gunhus was appointed as the Army Chief of Chaplains, he was briefed by the commander at Schofield Barracks, Hawaii, about a group of chaplains who were taking relationship courses out of the Chapel and providing training to married couples along with a free night at the Waikiki Hale Koa Resort, a hotel frequently used by the Army. He brought the concept back to the Pentagon, expanded it to include singles and families, and initiated a program that has continued for over twenty years.

My entrance into providing instructor certification trainings in my programs with the Army Chaplaincy began in 2000 with my relationship course for singles, *How to Avoid Falling in Love with A Jerk or Jerkette®* (also titled, PICK a Partner®). Many chuckle at the title of my program, but it offers a rich integration of research with practical activities, making it an ideal evidence-based approach for strengthening the partner-selection skills of single soldiers.

I was then asked to train chaplain candidates during their Chaplain Basic Officer Leadership Course at Fort Jackson. Over the next eleven years,

I trained and certified all graduating chaplains in my courses based on my Relationship Attachment Model® (RAM®) for singles, couples, and families—along with additional courses in relationship counseling and spiritual readiness.

These efforts, combined with six annual chaplain certification trainings that I provided throughout the world, have resulted in over 15,000 chaplains and religious affairs specialists providing my Love Thinks evidence-based relationship courses to over a million service members and their families.

Over these last twenty years, the Strong Bonds initiative of the Army Chaplaincy has continued to include my Love Thinks courses and other evidence-based relationship programs centered on three major relationships: unmarried individuals and their relationship health, especially within their dating practices; married couples; and families. The impact that chaplains have on soldiers and their relationships became so convincing that the budget for this program doubled every year for the first ten years. The Army collected data for most of those years and confirmed a measurable and extensive impact on the health of marriages and families, and the reduction of divorce. It became one of the most valued programs for building resiliency in marriages and families in the entire Army. Still today, I continue to be blessed with the honor of serving Army chaplains, along with the Air Force and Navy Chaplaincy and mental health organizations within all branches of the service.

* * *

Two widespread efforts to strengthen marriage—one in civilian communities, and the other in military communities. What both efforts share is that they did not ask people to come to them. Rather, they went into their respective communities to where their people lived to offer relevant, evidence-based classes on relationships. Although these courses did not contain specific faith content, they were consistent with faith values and cultivated the improvement of relationship skills along with an increase in meaningful relationship virtues.

Both movements found consistent demand for and growth in their community outreach, and generally lacked sufficient money or resources to meet the numbers of those requesting their services. And because both are government funded efforts, they are always vulnerable to shifts in leadership and the winds of politics—shifts that often alter their mission or restrict their effectiveness.

Strengthening marriages and families is not only an opportunity but also a primary responsibility of all churches.

The story of that Indiana nonprofit is the story of all those funded by federal or state government. It's why government initiatives will never effectively or consistently improve the overall health of marriages and families throughout society, nor do I believe that it is it the government's sole responsibility to do so. However, when it comes to the mission of the Church, this book seeks to convince you that strengthening marriages and families is not only an *opportunity* but also a primary *responsibility* of all churches.

An Opportunity and a Responsibility for the Church

As a Christian, therapist, seminary professor, and former church planter, I have wrestled for the past twenty years of providing relationship health resources with what, to me, is the elephant in the room: *Where are the churches in these efforts?*

I searched the country and consulted with leadership in national organizations and could not find one church, on its own, doing this type of relationship education work in its community. Yes, there are a small number of churches that support local nonprofits providing community-based relationship programs. But overall, the vast majority of churches don't even realize this community healthy marriage and relationship movement exists. And most times, when churches did become aware of the needs of these nonprofits, they were unwilling to provide any financial support.

Let me give you one real-life story that is basically the norm in most areas across the country. Randy, a.k.a., Mr. Randy to his students, is a former twenty-year Youth for Christ regional director. He pastors a home church in a mid-sized city in central California where he has lived his entire life. He has devoted his career to building strong faith and character in youth and helping them in their relationship struggles. A few years back, he received funding from a state grant to teach my evidence-based course *How to Avoid Falling in Love with a*

Jerk or Jerkette to students in public high schools.

In four short years, Randy had taught this eight-hour course with workbooks to over 20,000 students in public school classrooms. As part of the grant requirements, he collected data on the impact of this course, validating the positive impact it was having on dating practices. In addition, he accrued thousands of pages of written feedback on what students learned and how they were engaging in safer and more discerning relationships.

Randy has a huge heart for the youth, and he went over and above his grant requirements. He provided every class with his personal cell so that students could text him anonymously with any relationship questions they had. Over 8,000 youth texted him (that is not 8,000 *texts*; that is 8,000 *students*). He helped build up healthy relationships and break up unhealthy ones. He worked with school administrators and social workers to intervene and support students who were abused and had never shared their plight.

Randy typically introduced this program to a school by presenting a thirty-minute overview to students and faculty in a school assembly. The need was so great that every school where he conducted this assembly asked him to offer the full eight-hour course. And after each year that he provided the "no-jerk" class, the school administrators would ask him to double and triple his efforts to reach more students. In some of these high schools, by the end of four years, he had taught every student in the school. He told me he could walk down a hallway and know every face that passed him. He was meeting a need that no one else was addressing.

However, at the beginning of his fifth year, his funding dried up. So Randy approached pastors and churches in his community, many of whom he knew personally because of his long-standing work with Youth for Christ. But after speaking with over twenty-five pastors and church boards, Randy could not find one church who was willing to support his nonprofit's work with students. Not one. He was directly impacting the lives and strengthening the relationships of literally *thousands* of teens, and not a single church would help him.

Randy's experience is more of the norm than the exception. Churches seem to believe that providing classes in community settings is not part of the work of the church but should be left up to social agencies, counseling centers, and parachurch organizations.

What's more, this pattern of neglect is mirrored in the dearth of church involvement in the relationship health of their own congregations. In the coming pages we will provide extensive research in support of this claim, but suffice it to say that at this point three out of four churches do not provide any substantive relationship classes or resources for their married couples, and more than 90 percent of churches do not have an adult singles ministry. This means that singles—who now make up almost 50 percent of the heads of households in the United States—are facing their massive relationship challenges alone.

This long-standing situation prompts a crucial question: *To what extent should churches in America take the opportunity to improve the relationship health of their own people and of those within their communities?*

And a second, even more important question must also be answered: *To what extent are churches in America responsible for the relationship health of their own people and of those within their communities?*

Opportunity and Responsibility . . . these are the two pillars that form the missional foundation of churches.

Opportunity: The decline of relationship health has reached epidemic proportions the in United States and throughout the Western world. And yet, we will show that most churches are not investing in their married couples, their engaged couples, or their dating singles in any substantial ways. Nor are they responding to the relationship crises in their communities by stepping up and offering resources that can improve these same relationships.

Responsibility: The good news is that there is a growing sense of responsibility among churches to become more involved in promoting relationship health among their congregations and within their communities. Over the last five years, JP and I have spoken to thousands of pastors and church leaders and shared with them a vision for *how* they can build relationship ministries for their people and a relationship mission to their community. The response from these churches has been overwhelmingly positive.

"But you will receive power when the Holy Spirit comes on you; and you will be my witnesses in Jerusalem, and in all Judea and Samaria, and to the ends of the earth." (Acts 1:8)—the relationship health of marriages, families, and

individuals in the communities that surround local churches has now become the new Jerusalem for the mission of the Church.

Now please hear us clearly: We are **not** saying that relationship health replaces the Gospel. Our claim is that by helping those in our communities with their most meaningful relationships in practical and concrete ways, we will meet some of the deepest and most relevant needs—and will ultimately build bridges of trust and respect that lead souls towards Christ.

* * *

The message of this book is simply this: ***Churches in America have the opportunity and responsibility to build relationship ministries and outreaches into their congregations and communities—congruent with their faith—that speak to the needs of singles, couples, and families, and, as a result, will grow their churches and transform their communities.***

Historically, missionary evangelism has grown out of an effort to meet the most dire and essential needs of a community or society—such as famine, inadequate shelter, medical and educational deficiencies, etc. Addressing the urgent need then becomes a platform for building a relationship and sharing the Gospel of Christ. Our belief is that here in the United States and throughout Western culture, that urgent need is the lack of relational health in dating, marriages, and families.

> *Missionary evangelism has grown out of an effort to meet the most dire and essential needs.*

The first section of this book describes the present crisis in relationship health and how over the last sixty years this crisis has been the most significant factor in disrupting faith in Jesus. The data we will review shows that nearly the entire decline of Christianity in America since 1960 can be explained by the collapse in marital and relationship health. In this section, we will also lay out what churches are doing (and failing to do) to address this relationship health crisis.

The second section explores the rationale for the centrality of relationships, the anatomy of what makes a relationship healthy, and the essential content for promoting relationship health.

The last section of this book proposes a model for how churches can establish a transformative ministry of relationship health for their congregations and mission of relationship health to their communities. This approach elevates marriage and relationship ministry from its current status as side ministry for a few within a church to its proper place as the Church's preeminent ministry in the 21st century.

Each chapter of this book has a primary author—either John or JP—although we contribute to each other's perspective throughout. And when either of us shares something personal, we will indicate who is speaking by putting our name in a parenthesis. As you now know, John is a committed Evangelical Christian, and brings to this book his experiences as a former therapist, educator, and pastor along with his current work of developing and training relationship programs and resources. JP is a committed Catholic, brother of a Catholic priest, and a father of eight who brings to the table his extensive experience in management, strategy, public policy, and ministry. We have sought to make this book an authentically ecumenical project with deep relevance to all believers in Jesus—Evangelical, Protestant, Orthodox, and Catholic alike.

JP and John bring to this book many years of research on the core problems surrounding dating, marriage, and family relationships—both inside and outside of faith communities. Separately, we have surveyed existing research in the psychosocial sciences, in addition to conducting our own original research. Together, we have distilled these extensive bodies of research to present to you the most salient findings that clearly define the problem *and* the solution—a solution that is both Scriptural and practical. We share a Biblical worldview, a mission mindedness, and a love of history and the Early Church. We have worked to integrate all these fields into a cohesive understanding of the challenges that face our families and specifically our churches. We firmly believe that the Church is the only institution that holds the

> *We firmly believe that the church is the only institution that holds the potential to save the future of marriage and family in America.*

potential to save the future of marriage and family in America.

This book goes far beyond defining the problem and explaining how we got here. We are both practitioners who have developed relevant, workable solutions that have been used by thousands of churches and taught to millions of people internationally. As a result, two of the three sections of this book focus on sharing what we have found truly works. We provide robust recommendations for churches and church leaders that derive from our years of trial and error. When we tell you about our work and provide examples of how it has been used to transform lives, please understand that our enthusiasm comes from our passion to restore healthy relationships, prevent brokenness, and help churches more effectively solve the relationship crisis within their memberships and communities.

We have titled this book *Endgame* for two reasons. In games like chess, an endgame occurs when both sides are down to their last pieces. The stakes are clear. The margins for error are gone. Victory depends on the successful execution of a winning strategy. But, quite frankly, we also chose it to get your attention: "endgame" sounds ominous, because it recognizes the finality of *end*. There's no going back.

Make no mistake: In the fight for faith and family in America, we have reached the endgame. The Church has only a few pieces left to play, and must deploy them strategically. The time for decisive action is now.

Seventy percent of all Americans said they belonged to a religious body in the year 2000. However, earlier this year, Gallup published new research that shows this number has dropped to 47 percent, the lowest number in recorded American history! [2]

Make no mistake: In the fight for faith and family in America, we have reached the endgame.

You'll also read in this book that our nation has never had fewer people getting married each year. Now, there is an old adage that marriage civilizes men. If that is true, this means we have never in our nation's history had more uncivilized men in our communities.

*The content
of evangelism
remains the
Gospel. But the
platform for
evangelism is
relationships.*

No matter how you measure it, as we'll see in the following pages of this book, Christian faith within the United States has sunk to historic lows. Too few understand that the collapse of marriage and the cascading effects of this collapse on our broader relationship health lies at the center of the widespread retreat from Christian faith.

Let us be clear: The content of evangelism remains the Gospel. But the platform for evangelism is relationships.

The enemy has been hard at work at destroying relationships by pummeling marriage.

This book seeks to first diagnose the threat to relationships and then become a how-to-manual for building the Church's 21st century platform for evangelism. Only the People of God can defeat this threat to our families, churches, and nation.

* * *

A QUICK RECAP

- Healthy marriage relationships are the bricks that lay the foundation of both society and the Church.
- The Community Healthy Marriage Initiative and Military Chaplaincies have directed government funding toward improving dating, marriage, and family relationships. However, with all their accomplishments, government subsidized efforts have significant limitations.
- Churches across America have both the opportunity and the responsibility to invest heavily in the relationship health of their congregations and communities; and their potential for improving dating, marriage and family trends are practically limitless.

SECTION I:

The Crisis of Relationships and the Decline of Christianity

Chapters 2-7

In chapter 1, we shared our journeys that led us to become convinced that churches have both the *opportunity* and *responsibility* to prioritize marriage ministry and relationship outreach.

So, in Section I, we will review extensive research about the decline of marital and family health, and how the collapse of the family is the major driver of the decline of Christianity. We will trace the decoupling of marriage from sex, romantic partnerships, and parenting, and examine how these trends have turned hearts away from God and church. You will see that the majority of church leaders believe that they have effective marriage ministries. However, only roughly one in four has anything substantial. As a result, the destructive decoupling trends of mainstream culture are increasingly common in church settings, sending faith into free fall.

CHAPTER 2

Fighting the Smoke Instead of the Fire

Were you ever a single married person?

My wife, Christina, and I (JP) jokingly refer to those early days of our marriage when we recently graduated college and didn't have any kids yet as our "single, married days."

Those were the days when you could pick up and go and do things without arranging for a babysitter or thinking through the complicated logistics of diaper bags, strollers, and who knows how many other essentials while transporting a baby or a toddler along for an outing.

You'll have to forgive the lighthearted and paradoxical nature of how we refer to those first fifteen months or so of our marriage. Today, we have eight kids ages sixteen and under, and have helped raise another four. We wouldn't want it any other way.

But back then we were twenty-three and twenty-four years old. I (JP) had met Christina two years earlier at church while we were students at the SEC All-Sports powerhouse: the University of Florida. It was one day after the Florida–Florida State game that season (much of my life is chronologically segmented by various Gator sporting events). At the time, Christina and I considered ourselves the relatable and cool married people in our church and decided to spend some of that cool capital volunteering with the youth ministry. We had a blast. We worked with some great kids, most of whom were enrolled in local public schools.

When our first child was born, he became the youth group mascot. Kids—particularly the girls—took turns passing him around. The high schoolers got to see a young marriage lived out. We kept up volunteering until the little guy began to walk—about two and a half years into our marriage. Unfortunately, our church didn't have babysitting, so we had to pull away from so much volunteering.

What I remember most from that time (other than the seemingly endless pizza dinners) is how widely the needs of the kids within the group varied—and how frequently those differing needs reflected their experiences at home. Those kids who needed the most support and greatest diligence in discipleship were largely the ones who came from homes with the greatest problems. I remember one particular young lady—we'll call her Jennifer. She was in the high school group every single Sunday for the first year we volunteered. She rarely spoke to anyone. She often sat by herself giving off an uninterested vibe. Eventually, my wife and I, in different ways, began to look out for her. We'd sit nearby and try to pull her into conversation with other kids in the group.

Jennifer lived mostly with her dad. Her dad came to church every Sunday and ensured that she came to the Sunday evening high school youth group. But it was clear from our conversations that they weren't getting along very well. She was at church out of a forced compliance from her dad. Her parents had divorced just a couple of years earlier, and her dad retained custody for a majority of the year. Her dad hoped the youth group would have a positive effect on her.

Through our conversations, I learned that Jennifer was struggling with her faith. She had begun to question much of Christianity. We had conversations but never made much progress. Sadly, she stopped attending church and appeared to fall away.

Jennifer is not an outlier. Years later, many of the kids from that youth group still live in the area but are no longer active in church. The ones who kept the faith are the ones who came from two-parent families.

Every year it seems there is a new study setting off new set of alarm bells because youth are falling away. Studies of religious practice and affiliation cite real stumbling blocks such as the hypocrisy of church members or the perceived politics of the community.[3] And this problem attracts a huge ministry focus, as seen in church and in parachurch efforts to disciple, evangelize, and otherwise reach youth.

A survey JP's ministry, Communio, commissioned with the Barna Group in 2019 found that 99 percent of Evangelical churches, 90 percent of mainline churches, and 78 percent of Catholic parishes reported having ongoing youth and high school ministries.[4] Of those who reported having an ongoing youth ministry, 79 percent of Evangelical churches, 74 percent of mainline churches, and 69 percent of Catholic parishes reported paying someone to run it.[5]

How much is cumulatively spent by these churches on youth ministry? There is no database that tracks this spending. But, to reach a conservative estimate, let's begin by just looking at the largest churches in the country.

According to the Hartford Institute for Religion, there are 19,210 Protestant churches of greater than 500 people in weekly attendance.[6] We'll focus our estimate on this largest cohort of churches, likely to have the most resources to spend on ministry.

Given the above Barna survey numbers, we estimate that 13,687 Protestant churches are paying someone at least a part-time staff member to run their youth ministry. On the Catholic side in 2018, there were more than 17,000 parishes in the United States.[7] According to the Center for Applied Research in the Apostolate—a Catholic research organization located in Georgetown—58 percent of Catholic parishes (or 9,860) have congregations exceeding 550 people. Extrapolating from Communio's Barna survey, this would mean 5,306 Catholic parishes are paying someone at least part-time to run their youth ministry. Between staff time and all other youth-oriented expenses such as catechetical supplies or youth activities, we could conservatively estimate that the average large church spends $45,000 per year. That would mean nearly $855 million is invested annually in youth ministry by the largest churches alone.

Beyond direct individual church investment, large parachurch ministries exist to disciple and evangelize to youth: Awana, Cru's youth and campus-oriented activities, Young Life, the Fellowship of Christian Athletes, the Fellowship of Catholic University Students, Catholic Athletes for Christ, St Paul's Outreach, and others. Just these seven organizations report (in their annual reports or IRS Form 990s) spending $1.1 billion [8] annually on ministry to youth and young adults.

Now, there are many smaller churches in America who spend resources on youth ministry, and most large churches likely spend much more than $45,000 on it each year. There are also many parachurch organizations, such as large youth summer camps and other small and large youth-oriented ministries, not included in this very conservative estimate. However, we have easily identified nearly $2 billion in annual spending focused on youth evangelization and discipleship. When including all other parachurch investments, a less conservative estimate of large church spending and smaller church investments, the real annual figure for ministry to youth could easily be between $4 billion and $6 billion in the US annually.

> We have easily identified nearly $2 billion in annual spending focused on youth evangelization and discipleship.

Obviously, these resources and efforts have produced amazing individual victories for the Kingdom of God. Youth who would not otherwise believe do so today. Leaders are being built in some of the most influential institutions in the world. Young adults who have learned about mission are entering churches and helping to cause renewal, becoming pastors and priests. But this is a search and rescue mission.

Zooming out from individual successes, how has this massive investment in young people by the Church paid off over the last several decades?

When you look at the demographics of believers today and factor in the opportunity cost of these investments, you could say the Church is experiencing what investors call "negative leverage"—the "borrowed" funds far outpacing the return on investment.

For millennials, 34 percent of those born between 1981 and 1989 hold no religious affiliation; among younger millennials (born between 1990 and 1996), that number rises to 36 percent.[9] (In contrast, only 23 percent of Generation Xers and 17 percent of baby boomers are unaffiliated with any religion.) The number of young millennials without religious affiliation is as large as the number who self-identify as Evangelical Christians—and more than double the number who self-report as Catholic. While the oldest members of Generation Z were born in 1997, early research on this group shows this cohort having similar patterns to millennials on faith and religious affiliation.[10]

Those who report no religious affiliation are known colloquially as the "nones" because they mark "none" on survey questions about religion. According to the Pew Research Center, overall, the nones keep getting younger and younger relative to older Americans. In 2015, American Nones had an average age of 36, down from an average age of 38 in 2007.[11]

The median age of leaving their childhood faith being 13 years old.

Now, keep in mind that most surveys only begin to track nones for the first time in young adulthood, but there is very strong evidence that the decision to leave one's faith occurs while still a child.

One fascinating qualitative study of former Catholics found that 74 percent of their sample said they left their faith between the age of ten and twenty, with the median age of leaving their childhood faith being *13 years old.* It would seem the child who stops believing often still participates in church activities and youth group.[12] The study found that 35 percent of these former Catholics are currently among the nones.[13]

If youth are making a decision to stop believing while in childhood, they are doing so despite an unprecedented number of expenditures by the Church on youth ministry.

This is not meant to diminish this incredibly important work, as it has presumably helped reduce the falling away that would have otherwise occurred. But looking at the big picture, this vast effort—what I sometimes call the "Youth Industrial Complex" (or in Catholic circles the "Sacramental Industrial Complex")—appears to be a large scale, smoke fighting crew. The falling away of youth isn't the actual fire itself. The fire is somewhere else.

Now, youth ministry efforts mitigate the damage from this fire. During a fire, protecting yourself from the smoke is critical for survival—and removing smoke damage is a necessary part of any recovery effort. But smoke protection and smoke mitigation will not put out any fire.

To put out the fire, we need first to find the fire. And once we find it, we need to develop a strategy to fight it.

To that first task of finding the fire: What if I told you that the entire faith-decline of the last sixty years in America could largely be explained through the collapse of one key measure?

If you knew what that measure was, would you be interested in trying to address it?

We Didn't Start the Fire

In 2013, I (JP) met my friend Mark Regnerus, a professor of sociology at the University of Texas. This was during my time at The Philanthropy Round-table when I was starting my journey to understand how philanthropy could uncover and find effective strategies to strengthen families and faith practice.

To build a strong diagnostic and a plan of action, I raised a six-figure sum to help Mark dramatically expand his 2014 Relationships in America Survey. I came back to him again in 2018 through Communio and helped commission a large portion of the survey in November of 2018. This one was called the American Political and Social Behavior Survey. These surveys were large and had more than one hundred unique questions.

We got the data back in December of 2018, during those leftover-fueled days between Christmas and New Year's Day. Mark and I hopped on the phone to discuss the findings and something started to bubble up in my mind. Maybe it was the eggnog, but, having had many conversations with Mark dating back to our survey work in 2014, I asked him to create a new crosstab. (A crosstab is when you examine poll or survey responses against the identity of different respondents—grouping for gender or age, for example—in order to see what differences actually exist among certain demographic groups.)

What I wanted was for Mark to create a crosstab that would group the respondents by:

- their generation (millennial, Gen X, boomer), and
- their frequency of church attendance (more than weekly, weekly, twice a month, once a month, and less frequently).

And then break the above groups down by their family of origin:

- those whose parents were continuously married;
- those whose parents married until the death of a spouse;

- those whose parents divorced after 18;
- those whose parents divorced before 18;
- those whose parents never married.

Most sociologists label "regular church attendance" as twice monthly or more. So we sorted baby boomers, Gen Xers and millennials into two categories—those attending church twice-monthly or more, and those attending monthly or less—to see what differences existed within their age group based upon the type of family structure they were raised in.

We had a pretty big "Aha!" moment.

The Pew Research Center and nearly every other survey firm find big differences in religious affiliation based upon age. Some studies ask these individuals why they no longer believe. But those responses frequently hint at later "left brain" rationalizations and fail to uncover the deeper story or the emotional driver of the decision. What we found, by looking at the family of origin data, is that differences between age groups in church attendance *vanish* if you control for just one variable: parental marriage.

> *Differences between age groups in church attendance vanish if you control for just one variable: parental marriage.*

Baby boomers, Gen Xers, and millennials who grew up in continuously-married homes all went to church at nearly the same frequency. The surprising thing to me was that it didn't matter if your mom and dad divorced or were never married—your likelihood as an adult not to attend church was statistically the same. Those who are familiar with family of origin data know that in other areas, there are substantial behavioral and social outcome differences between children of divorced parents and children who grew up in never-married homes. But in the area of attending church, those groups were behaviorally identical.

What this suggests is that if the family structure of millennials looked like the family structure of baby boomers, then their church attendance behavior would look the same as well (See Figure 2.1).

Figure 2.1
Church Attendance
All generations attend church
regularly at nearly the **same rate**
if their parents are married.

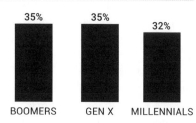

You see, 35 percent of all boomers, 35 percent of Gen Xers, and 32 percent of millennials in the 5,000+ nationally representative survey who grew up in continuously-married homes attended church at least twice a month or more.

The next time you are in church, look to your right and to your left. Realize that three-fourths of those in attendance under the age of 60 grew up in a continuously-married home.[14]

Millennials from continuously-married families are 78 percent more likely to attend church twice monthly or more frequently than millennials from divorced, never-married, or widowed homes. For white millennials, the relationship between stable marriages and church attendance is even stronger. A white millennial is 96 percent more likely to attend church if he or she came from a continuously-married family.[15]

Figure 2.2
Family Structure and the Rise of "the Nones"
Growth of religious Nones and children raised without
both parents follow the same trajectory.

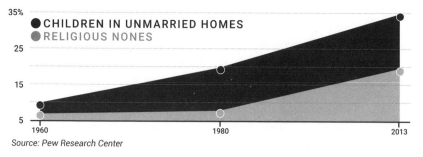

Source: Pew Research Center

For further confirmation beyond the Regnerus survey, let's take a look at a timeline of the growth of children being raised in unmarried households (either divorced or never-married). You can view the data in Figure 2.2.[16]

According to Pew, in 1960, 9 percent of children were raised in unmarried households. Religious non-affiliation was negligible at that time. Fast forward to 1980, when these kids become adults, and you see 7 percent of Americans report being among the nones. As the timeline roles forward, you see a nearly parallel relationship between children in unmarried homes and the rise of religious non-affiliation. This further validates the hypothesis that marital breakdown is driving the flight from faith. One would expect the number of the nones to grow so long as the share of unmarried families rises.

Now, what's great about family of origin data is that it helps resolve the debate between whether something is causal or corollary. No one can say that people choose to be in an intact family because they wanted to be a churchgoer. Family of origin is not something any of us control and it precedes in time the decision to attend church.

And what does this data demonstrate? It makes the case that, while church leaders have responded to the "smoke" of young people falling away with a focus on more effective youth formation and youth ministry, *the Church must instead fight the fire—the flight from healthy, Christian marriages.* Doing so would actually lead far more souls to Jesus Christ.

But we've got a long way to go. As we'll see when we review the results of the Barna Survey that Communio recently commissioned, churches currently allocate almost no capital or energy either to marriage ministry or to ministry for relationship health.

In fact, when you review survey data from a variety of sources, you discover that pastors tend to believe that they are doing much more than they are actually doing. They don't recognize how badly this need is unmet.

More importantly, the vast majority of all

> *Churches currently allocate almost no capital or energy either to marriage ministry or to ministry for relationship health.*

relationship ministry within the Church is focused on healing broken marriages or enriching existing marriages. Too few are getting at the problem that many single young adults no longer know how to form healthy relationships in the first place. Next to no one is systematically encouraging both the norms and the decision to marry.

The Crisis of the New Millennium is One of Relationship Health

The crisis facing the Church in the 21st century is therefore better understood as a crisis of marriage and marital health. But it flows out into a relationship health crisis in the family and beyond.

We now know that receptivity to the Gospel is heavily influenced by the health of the marriage we come from. This ought to make sense in many ways because Scripture begins and ends with a marriage—the one in the garden of Eden and the eschatological wedding between Christ and His Bride, the Church, in the Book of Revelation. Even God's relationship with His people is repeatedly referred to as a type of spousal love—we see this throughout the Old and New Testaments. In Isaiah, the prophet writes: "For your Maker is your husband, the LORD Almighty is his name—the Holy One of Israel is your Redeemer; he is called the God of all the earth" (Isaiah 54:5). The entire book of the Song of Solomon is an expression of marital love, and even the prophet Hosea's life is a graphic demonstration of how God views His people in the Old Testament as a spouse (in the ancient Israelites' case, it was a deeply-unfaithful spouse). The Apostle Paul tells us in Ephesians 5 that marriage is a living icon of Christ's relationship with the Church.

Let's unpack further some of the centrality of marriage to Scripture's story of salvation. In Genesis, when God pronounced that it was not good for Adam, the first man, to be alone, God affirmed the importance of having a spouse—someone who would share in a unified, intimate relationship.

So, with the creation of Eve—a counterpart who, like Adam, was created after the likeness and image of God—the marriage relationship was brought into existence. And from Genesis to Revelation, this marriage relationship is hailed as the preeminent human relationship, because it best describes the oneness between God and Israel, as well as between Christ and His bride, the Church.

In the Epistle to the Ephesians, for instance, the Apostle Paul intertwines the human and the heavenly marriages by linking the qualities that should emanate from a Christian marriage with the marriage relationship between Christ and his Church. He lays out his teaching on marriage by asking spouses to "submit to one another out of reverence for Christ" (Ephesians 5:21).

In the verses that follow, the Apostle Paul explains what this "submit to each other" looks like in marriage. The husband is to love his wife as Christ loved the Church. He must lay down his life for her, in all the small parts and large parts of marital life, each and every day of their marriage. We cannot fully appreciate today how radical this doctrine would be for the ancient mind. Indeed, this elevation of women plays a large part in Christianity's spread—as we'll see in Chapter 8. With this in mind, let's review what the Apostle wrote:

> Submit to one another out of reverence for Christ . . . Now as the church submits to Christ, so also wives should submit to their husbands in everything. Husbands, love your wives, just as Christ loved the church and gave himself up for her to make her holy, cleansing her by the washing with water through the word, and to present her to himself as a radiant church, without stain or wrinkle or any other blemish, but holy and blameless. In this same way, husbands ought to love their wives as their own bodies. He who loves his wife loves himself. After all, no one ever hated their own body, but they feed and care for their body, just as Christ does the church—for we are members of his body. For this reason a man will leave his father and mother and be united to his wife, and the two will become one flesh. This is a profound mystery—but I am talking about Christ and the Church. However, each one of you also must love his wife as he loves himself, and the wife must respect her husband (Ephesians 5:21, 24-33).

The Apostle Paul repeats this imagery of the Church as the bride of Christ when he calls out the Corinthian Christians who were slipping in their relationship to Jesus.

I am jealous for you with a godly jealousy. I promised you to one husband, to Christ, so that I might present you as a pure virgin to him. But I am afraid that just as Eve was deceived by the serpent's cunning, your minds may somehow be led astray from your sincere and pure devotion to Christ (1 Corinthians 11:2-3).

The centrality of the marital relationship in our relationship to God is not unique to Paul. As we noted earlier, powerful imagery of marriage is used throughout the Old Testament to depict God's love for His people, the Jews. For instance—the prophet Hosea was instructed by God to marry a woman, Gomer, who would be unfaithful to him. He was not to divorce her, but to persevere in his love, continuing to provide for her even after she deserted him for other lovers. When she reached rock bottom and was being sold into slavery, Hosea was to purchase her, take her back into his home, and, through love, gently lead her out of her shame and back to his heart.

Hosea's marriage was a living illustration of God's unalterable love for His people; God promised that He would never give up on Israel, even though Israel had been unfaithful to God. There was no relationship that could better personify God's intimate love and unwavering commitment to His bride, Israel, than the marriage relationship. Hosea poetically portrayed this marriage-message of hope to the Israelites as he spoke the words that their loving God would say:

"Therefore, I am now going to allure her;
    I will lead her into the wilderness
    and speak tenderly to her.
There I will give her back her vineyards,
    and will make the Valley of Achor (trouble) a door of hope.
There she will respond as in the days of her youth,
    as in the day she came up out of Egypt.
"In that day," declares the Lord,
    "you will call me 'my husband';
    you will no longer call me 'my master.'

I will remove the names of the Baals from her lips;
    no longer will their names be invoked.
In that day I will make a covenant for them
    with the beasts of the field, the birds in the sky
    and the creatures that move along the ground.
Bow and sword and battle
    I will abolish from the land,
    so that all may lie down in safety.
I will betroth you to me forever;
    I will betroth you in righteousness and justice,
    in love and compassion.
I will betroth you in faithfulness,
    and you will acknowledge the Lord" (Hosea 2:14-20).

This imagery of the marriage relationship capturing the love and oneness that God wants with His people culminates in the Book of Revelation, with John's vision of the magnificent celebration of the marriage feast that follows the marriage of Christ to His bride, the Church:

Then I heard what sounded like a great multitude, like the roar of rushing waters and like loud peals of thunder, shouting:

"Hallelujah!
    For our Lord God Almighty reigns.
Let us rejoice and be glad
    and give him glory!
For the wedding of the Lamb has come,
    and his bride has made herself ready.
Fine linen, bright and clean,
    was given her to wear."
(Fine linen stands for the righteous acts of God's holy people.)

Then the angel said to me, "Write this: Blessed are those who are invited to the wedding supper of the Lamb!" And he added, "These are the true words of God" (Revelation 19:6-9).

Following man's relationship with God, marriage was the primary relationship within human experience, according to the Genesis account. It was also the prototype relationship that most accurately portrayed the love God has for Israel, and Christ for the Church. In short, marriage on Earth is so essential because it points beyond itself and is the icon of our relationship with Christ for all eternity.

Growing Disagreement

Now, despite this wave of Biblical evidence, some in the Evangelical community have even claimed that too many Christians create an idol out of marriage[17] by placing undue emphasis on it or making it the focus of a happy life. More and more younger Christians are making this claim.[18] But this line of reasoning fundamentally misunderstands the story of salvation and the nature of God's love for us.

Obviously, not all are called to the married life. And that is good. There ought to be a diversity within the Church. Churches should help those who are single live in a way such that they know they also have a place and role. The Apostle Paul himself holds up the good of the perpetually single life as being even greater than the married state, because forgoing marriage on Earth points to the eschatological marriage of the Church with Christ (1 Corinthians 7:25).

All Christians need to know that when marriage and marital health breaks down, it has cascading effects on the Church that spill out across society.

But, with this understood, all Christians need to know that when marriage and marital health breaks down, it has cascading effects on the Church that spill out across society. Nor should we be surprised: this makes all the Biblical sense in the world.

In the next several chapters, we'll work to diagnose the current crisis within marital health. It's affecting far more than just marriage: It affects parenting, families, and the formation of our closest friendships. We'll review the epidemic of loneliness that public health experts have observed across the globe, which is shortening lifespans. Together, we'll explore the origins of this crisis in what we call the decoupling effect. Then, once we grasp how this crisis ripples across the world, we'll return to explore why this relationship crisis is so profoundly driving the decrease in Christian faith.

And once we grasp the true scope of this crisis, we'll begin to unpack some possible solutions to it. But the bottom line is this: We firmly believe that this marital and relationship health crisis is one that the Church alone is situated to resolve.

* * *

A QUICK RECAP

- We readily identified nearly $2 billion in annual spending focused on youth evangelization and discipleship in American churches. When one includes all other parachurch investments, a less conservative (and more realistic) estimate of the real annual figure for ministry to youth could easily be between $4 billion and $6 billion. United States youth ministry resources and focus have produced amazing individual victories for the Kingdom of God. But we must recognize that ministry to youth today is primarily a search and rescue mission.
- The decline of church affiliation in youth and young adults is the smoke— not the fire. That is, the decline is a consequence of the marriage crisis, the real fire behind religious disaffiliation. Until churches become serious about solving this crisis, they will continue to see fewer and fewer believers. At present, churches allocate almost no capital or energy to either marriage ministry or ministry for relationship health.
- Too few ministries address the problem that many single young adults do not know how to form healthy relationships. Next to no one is systematically encouraging the norms of marriage or the decision to marry.
- Marriage is central to Scripture's story of salvation, so the collapse of Christian faith in the wake of the collapse of marriage should surprise no

one. Christians must therefore understand that when marriage and marital health break down, it will have cascading effects on the Church that spill out across society.

CHAPTER 3

The Decoupling Effect

The Symptoms of an Epidemic of Deteriorated Relationships

Relationship health has deteriorated to an unprecedented degree, throughout America and most westernized countries. This deterioration is evident within parenting and families, marriages, romantic and dating practices—even among relationships in general.

Local churches must take seriously this deterioration of relationship health within their congregations and surrounding communities. They must embrace both the *opportunity* and the *responsibility* to translate their faith values into programs and practices that equip individuals to build and sustain safe, stable, and fulfilling relationships.

What does this deterioration of relationship health look like? Here is a broad sketch:

- More people than ever before confess feelings of chronic loneliness: nearly half of all Americans report sometimes or always feeling alone (47 percent) or left out (46 percent).[19]
- Two in five Americans (43 percent) sometimes or always feel that their relationships are not meaningful.
- One in five Americans reports that they rarely or never feel close to people (20 percent) or feel like there are no people that they can really talk to (18 percent).
- Only around half of Americans (53 percent) stated that they have meaningful in-person daily social interactions, such as having an extended conversation with a friend or spending quality time with family.
- Generational loneliness is worsening: Generation Z adults (born after 1997) report the highest rates of loneliness in history, followed by the

millennial generation (born between 1981 and 1996).

- Loneliness has reached such severe proportions in the UK that the nation appointed a cabinet member as "Minister of Loneliness," tasked with overseeing social programs to reduce feelings of isolation among Britons.[20]
- The rates of depression, anxiety, and suicide have increased in the past ten years for teens by 50 percent (ages 13-15 cohort) and 60 percent (ages 16-18 cohort).[21]
- Millennials report higher rates of depression and anxiety than any previous generation.
- Almost half of the adult American population is unmarried (45.5 percent) compared with just 28 percent in 1960.
- In the adult single population, 63 percent have never been married, 23 percent are divorced, and 13 percent are widowed. Of those living independently of their own accord, 53 percent of singles are women.
- For the first time in history, we have a generation (millennials) with more first-time mothers that are unmarried (55 percent) than married. This ratio is even higher (58 percent) among all first-time "Middle America" mothers since 2010.[22]
- The percentages of all unmarried births to native mothers in United States according to race are Non-Hispanic or Latina White (30 percent), African American (77 percent), Hispanic or Latina (56 percent).[23]
- A third of all kids will see two live-in partners in their home with mom by the time they turn fifteen years old. And 13 percent of all kids will see three or more live-in partners with their mom by that fifteenth birthday.

Some of you have lived long enough to witness the shifting norms of how people date, marry, and enter parenthood. You have watched the intact family deteriorate from being a stable and dominant building block of society to being an anomaly amid other family environments that are riskier and less secure for children and adults alike.

For many others, the world I just described is the world you have grown up in. These statistics are not that shocking for you because they have been the relationship climate that surrounded you every day.

But regardless of whether these statistics seem normal or shocking to you, one overarching question emerges from this badly frayed culture of relationships today: *How did this happen?*

How did we get to a point where more babies are born to unmarried moms than married? Where a third of all kids will see mom living with two or more unmarried partners by their mid-teen years? Where loneliness, depression, and anxiety have reached the highest numbers in the history of America?

Some propose that the weight of economic stresses has cracked the foundations of our relationships. And no doubt poverty and joblessness have played a part. But the real deconstruction of relationships has resulted from what we call the decoupling effect—seismic shifts separating three relationship practices that were once associated with marriage but that, over time, have become independent relationship practices: sex, romantic partnerships, and parenting. It is these shifts in marriage and family structure that have led to the severely weakened relationships we see today.

> *The real deconstruction of relationship health has resulted from the decoupling effect.*

In 1986, Pope John Paul II penned the famous words, "As the family goes, so goes the nation and so goes the whole world in which we live." Upon this premise we explain today's epidemic of personal anxiety, depression, and interpersonal aloneness. In other words, ***the deterioration of relationship health—among adolescents, in adult friendships, and throughout most interpersonal social networks—stems from the decoupling effect that has also largely caused the breakdown of stable and secure marriages and family environments.***

An Impending Storm

Around ten years ago, my wife and I (John) built a home on a barrier island in Florida. During construction, we quickly learned about hurricane ties: the metal straps that overlap two major structural sections of the house to hold them together. I remember counting around twenty-four screw holes in each side of these straps. It thus anchors, with forty-eight screws in a two-foot metal strap, pieces of wood from two different structural sections that would otherwise only be held together by nails. The hurricane tie embodies the basic principle of Ecclesiastes 4:12: "Though one may be overpowered, two can defend themselves." Through these hurricane ties, two sections become as one—and greatly increase their ability to withstand the winds of a storm.

In the construction of our home, the foundation and the ground floor were joined together with these hurricane ties. Then the floor was connected to each stud in the outer walls. And finally, the studs in the walls were tied together with the trusses by these metal straps. The three most important structures of a house (foundation, walls, and roof) were all conjoined to become one inseparable unit. Essentially, the only way for the roof or a wall to separate would be to take the entire structure with it.

So, let me ask you: When the storms come, in which house would you rather reside—the one cobbled together with nails, or the one with all three major structures joined as one by hundreds of hurricane straps?

And conversely, if someone wanted to *weaken* our house and increase the risk of it being destroyed in the next storm, they would have to decouple these three structures by removing all those hurricane straps. They would disconnect the roof from the walls, the walls from the floor, and the floor from the foundation.

This is exactly what has happened to the structure of marriage over the last fifty years.

The institution of marriage has crumbled because three major relationship structures that historically had been inseparable with marriage were *decoupled* from marriage. These are:

1. the decoupling of sex from marriage,
2. the decoupling of romantic partnerships from marriage, and
3. the decoupling of parenting from marriage.

Sex, romance, and parenting—these were the foundation, walls, and roof of stable relationships. Marriage was the durable bond, the hurricane ties holding the structure together. Our culture has systematically removed those ties, and we are all witnesses to the wreckage.

To be clear, there has always been sex outside of marriage . . . there have always been those who partnered without marrying . . . and there have always been those who were parents without partners. But for most of American history and across Western culture, those who decoupled these relationship practices from marriage were considered outside of the norm. In other words, the social consensus was that sex belonged in marriage, that those who wanted to live romantically together should marry first, and that children ought to be raised by two married parents.

Here is a sixty-year time-lapse photograph of how these relationship practices have become decoupled: In 1960, nearly 70 percent of American adults were married; now, less than half are. For those in their twenties, only a quarter are now married—compared with two-thirds in 1960. And when it comes to births, *eight times more* children are born to unmarried parents today than back in 1960.

> *When sex, partnering, and parenting became decoupled from marriage, then relational security, stability, and permanence spiraled downward.*

When sex, partnering, and parenting became decoupled from marriage, then relational security, stability, and permanence spiraled downward. Couples became sexually active quickly, cohabited impulsively, and became pregnant outside marriage in record numbers. Perhaps they thought they had a firm foundation for bringing a child into the world, but the high rate of breakups and the extremely low rate of making it to marriage had catastrophic results: a massive surge of single-parent households that tend to be extremely high-risk environments for the very children being raised in them.

These risks, as we will see in subsequent chapters, include increases in psychological and emotional disorders, and future relationship struggles. But the risks also extend to challenges within their experiences of faith. For as we showed in Chapter 2, the rise of the religious "Nones" seems to have increased proportionately with the increases in the number of children being raised without two married parents.

* * *

A QUICK RECAP

- The deterioration of relationship health has included historic increases in loneliness, depression, and anxiety, as well as a sharp decrease in meaningfully close friends or family.
- The United States also has hit historically high records of single heads of household, unmarried first-time mothers, and unmarried cohabitators. At the same time, the U.S. has reached historic lows in the percentage of couples becoming married.
- The overall deterioration of relationship health is due to the decoupling effect, as three major relationship structures have been decoupled from the marriage relationship:
  - o decoupling of sex from marriage,
  - o decoupling of romantic partnerships from marriage,
  - o decoupling of parenting from marriage.

CHAPTER 4

The Decoupling of Sex from Marriage

Stephanie Coontz, in *The Way We Never Were*, argued that much of what changed in the 1960s sexual revolution was simply that girls adopted "sexual behaviors that were pioneered much earlier by boys."[24] Coontz points out that every era throughout all millennia had unmarried sex, unmarried childbearing, and oppressive aspects to marriages and families. However, even though there are some obvious truths to her claim, this does not make every era identical, nor does it equalize the risks and benefits of all relationship practices.

When examining more current history over the last one hundred years, the decoupling effect can be traced back to two crucial time periods: the 1920s and the 1960s.

Sex in the Roarin' Twenties

The Roaring Twenties included a departure from the more carefully supervised and formally structured practice of courtship, ushering in "dating," a new approach to romantic relationships in which the automobile now could transport couples away from their parents' front porch and supervision. Even though this impacted the sexual activity of those who were unmarried, the social norm still considered sex as part of the marriage arrangement and not to be engaged in during courtship or dating.

Ernest Burgess and Paul Wallin, in their classic work, *Courtship, Engagement, and Marriage* (1952) reviewed several primary research studies of the early 1900 to 1950s that examined the frequency of sexual activity before and after marriage. In one of the earliest research studies published (1923), over 10,000 questionnaires covering topics related to education, employment, economic status, marital status, sexual activity before and after marriage, and parenting and children were mailed to women, guaranteeing their anonymity if they would fill them out and mail them back. The average age was thirty-eight years old, with over 50 percent being under the age of thirty-six. The results of this study found that only 7 percent of the married women reported having had sexual relations with anyone prior to marriage—in other words, 93 percent stated that they were virgins when they married.

The next major study, published in 1929, examined sexual histories from both men and women from the generation that followed those studied in the 1923 study just mentioned. Just one generation later, after the sexual revolution of the twenties, reports found a 300 percent increase in extramarital sexual activity, with close to a third of both men and women reporting that they had unmarried sex with the partner they subsequently married, and the majority of them (a total of 20 percent of all respondents) revealing that they also had intercourse with someone other than the person they married.

A third study conducted in 1938 of 777 married women found that two-thirds of those born after 1910 had sex before marriage, although the vast majority only had sex with the man they married.

What you see from these studies is that with each successive cohort, the numbers of those who were having sex prior to being married kept rising, until 89 percent of men and 63 percent of women who were born in the 1940s reported having sex outside of marriage.

This growing trend of sexual activity outside of marriage was eroding the American and Western cultural value that sexual involvement was only supposed to occur in a marriage relationship. However, despite an increasing number of people acting contrary to this standard, this value still continued to dominate the overall social view of sex and marriage—evidenced by fact that the vast majority of those who did have sex outside of marriage probably only had intercourse with their soon-to-be spouse. In other words, even though they engaged in sex prior to marriage, it appears they rationalized it to still be within the context of marriage, just a bit in advance of the actual wedding ceremony.

Sex in the Sixties and Today

Early in the sixties, there was a technological "shock wave" in the sexual world that was the final tipping point of decoupling sex from marriage: the advent of artificial hormonal contraception. Just about every scholar agrees that advances in contraceptives were the chief contributor that flipped the emphasis of what the masses considered to be the primary purpose of sex, from a procreative act to an act that pleasures.[25] In the generations prior to the sixties, the act of sex always carried with it the risk of pregnancy, which (outside of wedlock) would typically trigger a "shot-gun" wedding.

Prostitution, pornography, and sex outside of marriage have certainly existed in all generations. But these acts were contrary to social norms; they were frowned upon, and they were not the experience of the majority. Marriage legitimatized pregnancy and was considered the ideal context for raising children. As a result, the act of "sex implied commitment, because it risked pregnancy. Relationship security was often a value and a precursor to sex . . . in general, the average woman could and did count on seeing evidence of commitment before sex."[26]

This is why most sexual acts outside of marriage occurred in committed relationships that led to marriage. However, the advances in contraceptives cracked the weld that had kept sex in the bed of marriage. Sex finally became fully autonomous, set free from the long-standing association with marriage and baby-making, which ushered in a rebranding of sex as a pleasurable right and property of every individual.[27]

As a result, an even more dramatic acceleration of sexual freedoms swept our relationship culture. In the 1970s, 21 percent of women had no premarital sexual partners and 43 percent had just one premarital sexual partner. This means that about two-thirds of all women only had sex with their husbands, assuming that the one sexual partner they were with prior to marriage was the person they ended up marrying.

However, the number of women who were either virgins or who had only had sex with the man they married decreased to half of all brides in the 1980s (17 percent having had no sexual partners and 36 percent having had only one, presumably their future husband). By the 2010s, this dropped even further with only 5 percent of new brides being virgins, and more than 75 percent of those who married having engaged in intercourse with someone other than the person they married.[28]

The age of first sexual debut also changed over this timeframe, increasingly becoming younger. The chart below shows how the percentages of adolescents engaging in sexual intercourse has increased from the 1950s to the early 2000s. Although the percentage of high school seniors (ages eighteen to nineteen) has not changed dramatically from the 1980s to today (fluctuating between 55 and 59 percent), there has been a significant increase in the percentage of young teens (age fifteen) having sex (14 percent in 2003 to somewhere between 20 and 36 percent in 2017). This means that young people are engaging in sexual intercourse at earlier ages.

Figure 4.1

Premarital Sex by Age

Percentage of various groups who had premartial sex by specific ages, and median age at first premarital sex.

Group	Age in 2002–2003*	PERCENT WHO HAD PREMARITAL SEX BY EXACT AGE								Median Age at first premarital sex
		15	18	20	25	30	35	40	44	
NSFG 2002 RESPONDENTS:										
All	15–44	16	58	75	89	93	94	95	95	17.4
Women	15–44	13	54	74	88	93	94	94	94	17.2
Men	15–44	20	60	77	89	93	94	95	96	17.6
COHORTS TURNING 15 IN:										
1954–63	55–64	4	26	48	73	82	84	85	88	20.4
1964–73	45–54	6	39	65	86	91	93	93	94	18.6
1974–83	35–44	10	50	72	88	92	93	93	N/A	18.0
1984–93	25–34	13	59	76	89	94	N/A	N/A	N/A	17.3
1944–2003	15–24	14	54	74	N/A	N/A	N/A	N/A	N/A	17.6
THOSE WHO ABSTAINED UNTIL AT LEAST EXACT AGE:										
15	15–44	N/A	49	71	87	92	93	94	94	18.0
18	18–44	N/A	N/A	42	74	84	86	87	89	20.7
20	20–44	N/A	N/A	N/A	54	72	75	78	81	24.1

*Fourteen percent of NSFG 2002 respondents were actually interviewed in 2003.

Overall, the share of fifteen- to nineteen-year-olds who had had sexual intercourse has remained steady over the last twenty years. However, the proportion of young people who have had sexual intercourse increases rapidly as they age through adolescence, beginning with about one in five fifteen-year-olds but increasing to two-thirds of eighteen-year-olds reporting having had sex by the time they graduated high school.[29]

Cheap Sex

Twenty years ago, I (John) sat with my colleagues David Popenoe and Barbara Dafoe-Whitehead at a dinner in an international conference on marriage and family relationships. They had just completed an article that aptly captured the decoupling of sex and marriage, entitled "Sex Without Strings and Relationships Without Rings," that was published in 2000 in the annual report *The State of Our Unions: The Social Health of Marriage in America.*[30] Their data collection was part of a national study called *The Next Generation,*[31] which was studying mating and dating among not-yet-married heterosexual men and women.

Up to this point, most studies on these topics drew samples from college students. So—to add to the existing body of research, and to better understand the relationship aspirations, expectations, and practices of the majority of those in their twenties—David and Barbara convened ten focus groups of noncollege singles in five major metropolitan areas: northern New Jersey, Atlanta, Dallas, Chicago, and Los Angeles. Their findings have proven to be predictive of the most influential relationship trends of the last twenty years.

The first noticeable shift from previous decades was that the mating culture for twentysomethings was not oriented toward marriage, nor even dedicated to romantic love: "The men and women in these focus groups rarely volunteer the word 'love' or use the phrase 'falling in love.' Instead, they talk about 'sex' and 'relationships.' This double language reflects the two separate spheres of unwed coupling. Sex is for fun. It is one of the taken-for-granted freedoms and pleasures of being young and single . . . Both men and women also agree that casual sex is no-strings-attached sex. It requires no commitments beyond the sexual encounter itself, no ethical obligation beyond mutual consent."[32]

How ridiculously short was the amount of time noncollege singles deemed necessary to get to know someone.

As I (John) spoke with David and Barbara at dinner, they shared an even more striking revelation that emerged from their research interviews. Numerous singles had explained that if there was an interest in actually developing a relationship, then they postponed sex in order to focus on *getting to know* each other. What most struck me was how ridiculously short was the amount of time noncollege singles deemed necessary to get *to know* someone, suggesting that sex on the fourth "date" or after just a couple of weeks (versus an immediate hookup) is sufficient for more serious relationships. One participant represented this view of the majority with this comment: "If you wait too long, they think that you are not interested."[33]

Their study was not an outlier. JP noticed similar trends in reviewing research for Mark Regnerus's *Relationships in America* survey project, which interviewed 15,000 Americans between the ages of eighteen and sixty in 2014. The data from this extensive study was combined and organized together with four additional major national surveys and several data sets of in-person interviews by Regnerus and Jeremy Uecker, in their book, *Premarital Sex in America* (2011).

Regenerus further described key findings from this massive trove of data in *Cheap Sex* (2018), in which he provided an accurate landscape of sexual practices outside of marriage. Regnerus's conclusion is that "sex before a relationship begins is now the most common experience . . . Between 20-25 percent of men and women say they first had sex in their relationship 'after we met, but before we began to consider ourselves as being in a relationship.' It may be the case . . . that the introduction of sex 'is the thing that makes it become a relationship.'"[34]

According to Figure 4.2, 75 percent stated that they engaged in sex with their current or most recent partner within the first three months. But almost half (45 percent) said they first had sex by the time they had been together for two weeks. What all this shows is a dramatic shift over the last couple decades in the *acceleration* of sexual involvement as it was decoupled first from marriage, and now from any and all commitment.

Figure 4.2
Sexual Initiation with Current (or Last) Sexual Partner

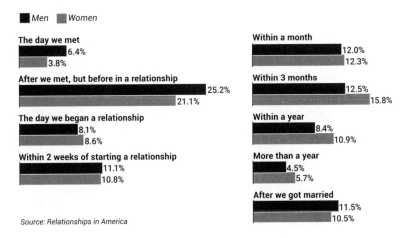

■ Men ■ Women

The day we met
6.4%
3.8%

After we met, but before in a relationship
25.2%
21.1%

The day we began a relationship
8.1%
8.6%

Within 2 weeks of starting a relationship
11.1%
10.8%

Within a month
12.0%
12.3%

Within 3 months
12.5%
15.8%

Within a year
8.4%
10.9%

More than a year
4.5%
5.7%

After we got married
11.5%
10.5%

Source: Relationships in America

Ambiguous and Undefined Relationships

The decoupling of sex from marriage, beginning in the 1960s, has now morphed into sex becoming decoupled from any level of relational commitment. As a result, undefined relationships have surged. After all, labels define relationships with some degree of commitment; the commitment embedded in a relationship label suggests unspoken but understood expectations and parameters. For example, when a couple tells you, "We are *engaged* to be married," this label clearly provides a definition of their relationship that includes a specific level of commitment: exclusivity, longevity, and seriousness. However, if another couple tells you that they are just *friends with benefits*, then again, this label indicates that although they lack any romantic commitment, they have some level of commitment for the respect and transparency that would be expected in a friendship.

If we remove all labels, we trend inevitably toward relationships without any definition of commitment. This creates an ambiguity in a relationship that gives a false sense of security.

To understand that connection, let's turn to a good friend and long-time colleague of mine named Scott Stanley. Scott's work focuses on the irreplaceable value of commitment in marriage and the assault on commitment from many of the relationship practices in current culture. He has published hundreds of research studies as one of the only investigators to delve into the confusion of undefined commitments. "One driver of ambiguity is that it offers emotional safety—perceived, *not real*, that is," he says. "If you are clearer to yourself and to others about what you really want most, it can hurt more when you do not get what you long for."[35]

Here is the logic: no definition, then no commitment. No commitment, then no obligations. No obligations, then no disappointments. No disappointments, then no hurt. No hurt, then no risks. There's just one problem, however: this logic is tremendously flawed.

The high divorce rates of the last fifty years, colliding with the uncoupling of sex from marriage and relational commitment, have created a relationship culture centered on highly sexual relationships that are free from obligations and potential disappointments. This has had a trickle-down effect that serves to eliminate even the labels for "dating" relationships, so that now most twenty- to thirty-year-olds would refer to any relationship that might resemble the "archaic" dating arrangement as "hanging out" or "just talking." There is an unconscious search for labels that have no defined commitments. Whatever the new label may be, it must clearly portray a "no strings attached" relationship.

> Undefined and ambiguous commitments have spawned a mass social confusion about what is happening in relationships.

Undefined and ambiguous commitments have spawned a mass social confusion about what is happening in relationships, with most individuals feeling too embarrassed or ashamed to ask—because even asking "*What is happening in our relationship?*" implies some level of commitment in the relationship.

In a 2013 *New York Times* article entitled "The End of Courtship?" Alex Williams interviewed twenty- and thirty-something singles about their romantic and sexual relationships. He reported back on his findings:

> "The word 'date' should almost be stricken from the dictionary," Ms. Silver said. "Dating culture has evolved to a cycle of text messages, each one requiring the code-breaking skills of a cold war spy to interpret."
>
> "It's one step below a date, and one step above a high-five," she added.
>
> Dinner at a romantic new bistro? Forget it. Women in their 20s these days are lucky to get a last-minute text to tag along. Raised in the age of so-called "hookup culture," millennials—who are reaching an age where they are starting to think about settling down—are subverting the rules of courtship.
>
> Instead of dinner-and-a-movie, which seems as obsolete as a rotary phone, they rendezvous over texts, Facebook posts, instant messages, and other "non-dates" that are leaving a generation confused about how to land a boyfriend or girlfriend . . .
>
> "I've seen men put more effort into finding a movie to watch on Netflix than composing a coherent message to ask a woman out" . . . A typical, annoying query is the last-minute: "Is anything fun going on tonight?" More annoying still are the men who simply text, "Hey," or "'sup."[36]

This trend to form sexually involved relationships with no defined commitments has been further exploited by online dating sites and apps. Dan Slater, in his cultural commentary *Love in the Time of Algorithms: What Technology Does to Meeting and Dating*, explained, "Once again, aspects of modern life—remoteness, access to all manner of relationships through social networks and online-dating sites—have elevated efficiency and convenience but also deepened the confusion when it comes to romance, especially for the first generation of people to have been born and raised in the post privacy (and perhaps postdating) era of the Internet."

Slater interviewed senior executives from most of the major dating sites and found that all but one concluded that there is an inverse correlation between commitment and the efficiency of technology. At the time of Slater's writing, Dr. Gian Gonzaga was the Senior Director of Research and Development at eHarmony, one of the most conservative sites when it comes to promoting commitment in relationships. But even he affirmed that you can "easily see a world in which online dating leads to people leaving relationships the moment they're not working, [and thus] an overall weakening of commitment."[37]

A few years ago, I (John) boarded a flight headed to Denver to conduct a certification training in several of my relationship programs. I often refer to flying as my mobile office, and so I was delighted to see that the seat next to me was empty. I had just organized my four-foot-wide workspace and settled into my seat, when a woman hurried down the aisle and cut my workspace in half. She watched as I removed my paraphernalia from her seat. I happened to be reviewing my training notes, and she must have seen the title of my book, *How to Avoid Falling in Love with a Jerk*. She laughed out loud and said, "I have to interrupt you and ask, what is that book all about?"

As we talked, I learned that my seat neighbor, Jasmine, was just about to celebrate her thirty-fourth birthday. And she was frustrated because she wanted a stable, committed relationship, but couldn't find a man who was interested. In fact, she said it's hard even to find a man committed enough to show up on a date!

The reason she was the last one to board the plane was that she's a flight attendant and had to wait to find out if there was an empty seat for her to commute to the Denver hub. She said that she had become somewhat dependent on dating apps whenever she had an overnight in a city and hoped to "go out on a date."

When I asked what she meant by her comment that too many guys just don't show up, she explained that she was discouraged because of the number of times she had been stood up on a date. I initially imagined she meant three or four times, but when I inquired, she told me it had happened more than twenty times! I was shocked.

Here was an attractive, financially stable career woman who was attempting to begin a relationship that had the potential of becoming serious, but who was contending with a dating culture averse to any signs of obligation or commitment. I looked at her online profile, wondering if there were some red flags or turnoffs in her descriptions or pictures. Everything looked great. The only thing we could find to explain this pattern was the comment in her profile that she was looking for a relationship.

You might think that interest in a relationship would be taken as a positive quality. But for her pool of prospective partners, "commitment" was a warning signal. Her theory was that most of the men who never showed had set several meetups, then gauged which one had the most promise of a hook-up and chose that one. Because she indicated that she was looking for something more, she was the first to be dropped.

The mores surrounding dating and sex have utterly changed. Mainstream culture has normalized accelerated sexual involvements, and in so doing, normalized high-risk relationships. No one can deny that the risks of STDs and pregnancy increase exponentially in a highly sexualized culture of dating where sex has been decoupled from marriage. Sex is likewise robbed of meaning when it is taken out of the context of a loving and committed relationship. And as we will see in the next two chapters, the decoupling of romantic partnerships and parenting from marriage are the natural consequences of redefining sex as an activity solely for the purpose of individual pleasure.

> *Sex is likewise robbed of meaning when it is taken out of the context of a loving and committed relationship.*

Unmarried Sexual Practices of Christians

Are the sexual practices of churchgoers any different than those of the mainstream culture? The answer to this question is the same as what we will find concerning the frequency of unmarried cohabitation and unmarried childbearing (our next two chapters). Essentially, the trends in major denomination-

The trends in major denominational categories of Christianity parallel those in mainstream culture, albeit with slightly lower percentages.

al categories of Christianity parallel those in mainstream culture, albeit with slightly lower percentages.

Conservative Evangelicals (also referred to as "Fundamentalists" in some research studies) tend to adhere to a clear Biblical prohibition to sex outside of marriage. And yet, "in the General Social Survey (GSS), in 2014 through 2018 combined, only 37% of fundamentalist adults said sex outside of marriage was 'always wrong,' while 41% said it was 'not wrong at all.'"[38]

I (John) spoke with David Ayers, author, researcher, and Professor of Sociology at Grove City College, Pennsylvania and Fellow for Marriage and Family with the Institute for Faith and Freedom about these trends, and he explained, "Most Christian young people are sexually active by the time they are young adults, with roughly two-thirds of the most conservative Christians (Evangelical Protestants) having engaged in sexual intercourse by their twenty-second birthday." You can see in Figure 4.3 that this increases to around 75-80 percent in other denominational categories.

Dr. Ayers continued: "The GSS shows that among never-married fundamentalist adults between 2008 and 2018, 86% of females and 82% of males had at least one opposite-sex sexual partner since age 18, while 57% and 65%, respectively, had three or more. These percentages were even higher for those under 30."[39]

Earlier in this chapter, we identified the mainstream trend that has shifted from unmarried individuals only having "premarital" sex with the partner they eventually marry, to having sex with most dating partners. Christians seem to be following a similar trend. Dr. Ayers summarized the data by pointing out that around a third of fifteen- to seventeen-year-old Evangelicals have had four or more sexual partners, but by age twenty-two, that has increased to 43 percent of females and just over half of males.

Figure 4.3
Percent of Never-Married Young People Who Had Sex, by Age, Gender, and Religious Affiliation

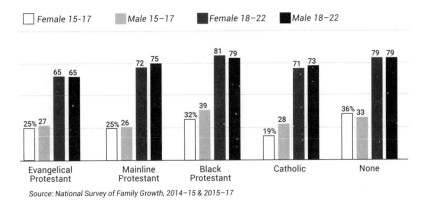

☐ *Female 15-17*   ▨ *Male 15–17*   ■ *Female 18–22*   ■ *Male 18–22*

	Evangelical Protestant	Mainline Protestant	Black Protestant	Catholic	None

Evangelical Protestant: 25%, 27, 65, 65
Mainline Protestant: 25%, 26, 72, 75
Black Protestant: 32%, 39, 81, 79
Catholic: 19%, 28, 71, 73
None: 36%, 33, 79, 79

Source: National Survey of Family Growth, 2014–15 & 2015–17

The good news is that frequency of attendance at church services does make a difference. In Figure 4.4, those who attend weekly are significantly more likely to not have had sex than those who only attend monthly or less. Not surprisingly, the percentages tracking *the importance of one's religion among Evangelicals* practically match these attendance numbers—with little more than half of eighteen- to twenty-two-year-olds who consider their faith as "very important" have had sex, while 75-80 percent of those who consider their faith as "somewhat important" have had sex (not shown in a graph).[40]

These lower percentages demonstrate the influence that the Church and its teaching can have on the relationship choices of singles. However, the fact that only a minority of the most conservative of Christian young people adhere to waiting until marriage suggests that the messages and ministries of churches have not presented compelling enough reasons for building romantic relationships differently than mainstream cultural trends. This is a lost opportunity within the Church and, unfortunately, it will be mirrored in the trends of cohabitation and unmarried childbearing among churchgoers, as we will see in the next two chapters.

Figure 4.4

Percent of Never-Married Evangelicals Who Had Sex by Levels of Religious Service Attendance, Age, and Gender

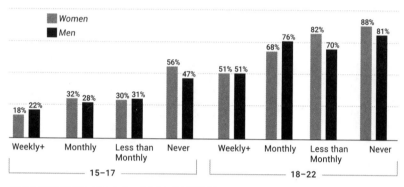

Source: National Survey of Family Growth, 2014–15 & 2015–17

* * *

A QUICK RECAP

- The 1920s were the first major period in American history in which sex before marriage started to become more common, although it was still not considered acceptable in mainstream society.

- There was a steady decrease of "virgin" marriages (around 93 percent) to only 11 percent of men and 37 percent of women by the end of the 1940s. However, most of these men and women only had premarital sexual relations with the partner they ended up marrying.

- The second major historical period of changes in sexual practices was the 1960s, a decade which initiated a social norm of sex *outside* of marriage (in contrast to just before a marriage).

- Three sexual trends occurred from the 1960s through the 2020s: increased number of sexual partners without any defined commitment; increased acceleration of sexual involvement with a new partner; and a younger age of first sexual debut.

- Over those decades from 1960 to 2020, romantic relationships continued to increase in accelerated sexual involvements but decrease in clearly defining commitment levels, which has led to more unstable relationships and cohabiting unions.
- Unmarried sexual trends in church settings mirror those of mainstream culture, although the importance of one's faith and frequent church attendance increases the likelihood of not having sex outside of marriage.

CHAPTER 5

The Decoupling of Romantic Partnerships from Marriage

As sex became decoupled from marriage, it made increasing sense for couples to live together outside of marriage. This trend began as a "next step" toward marriage in the 1970s but has evolved to be viewed as a "risk-free" step that can be taken at any point in a romantic relationship.

A woman named Mara[41] walked into my (John's) counseling office several years ago, expressing that she felt depressed. As I conducted a brief history of her moods, nothing stood out for a pattern of depression other than her three-year relationship with James, which had been a source of mixed emotions for her.

She and James met while working at a bank. James was a financial advisor and Mara was a teller. Although she always thought he was attractive, nothing had ever happened, just some subtle flirting. However, one afternoon they walked out of work together and ended up standing for hours in the parking lot, talking and laughing about coworkers and funny incidents with customers. They decided to grab something to eat and ended up at James' apartment to watch a show.

Mara did not go back to her own apartment that night. In fact, she spent very few weekends at her own apartment, and within a few months, it only made sense to drop her lease and move in with James.

"How is your relationship now with James?" I asked.

Mara sighed, "It's complicated."

"In what ways is it complicated?" I probed.

Mara went on to explain that she cut her hours at the bank when she began some classes in a nursing program, and eventually quit to go to school full-time. Living with James made that possible, but now it seemed that she and James were not really close and argued a lot.

"Well, I don't know if we argue," Mara said reflectively. "We just don't really have a lot between us. You know, like, we have sex, but he doesn't ask me about my classes, or the friends I now have from my program, and he goes out a lot when I am attending class and I don't really know what he is doing or who he is with. We are irritable with each other a lot . . . it is kind of like we don't like each other, but we are roommates."

"Have you considered breaking up?" I carefully asked.

"Yes, well, no—I don't know what I would do. Like I said, it is complicated."

"When you and James talk about your relationship, where does he want it to go?" I again probed.

"We don't really talk that much about where our relationship is going. I mean, there is a lot going on right now, and we sometimes argue, or complain about each other, but we don't have any deep conversations about how we are doing or where we are going. If it is meant to be, then it will happen, right?"

The Science of Cohabitation

James and Mara are typical of couples that have moved in together outside of marriage, although many other couples end up having more severely conflictual relationships. Even though they seemed to have few problems, James and Mara unknowingly paced their relationship in ways that increased their risks of failure and decreased the likelihood that they would address and resolve their issues.

Psychologists can inform the public that despite popular belief, premarital cohabitation is generally associated with negative outcomes.

Living together outside of marriage has been researched extensively for more than fifty years. For instance, there was a recent meta-study that collected and organized almost 1,000 published research studies about cohabitation in order to summarize the impact of cohabitation on relationship quality and longevity. Many of these studies followed individuals into their subsequent marriages and examined the connection between cohabitation with one or more partners prior to marriage with outcomes in marital closeness, sexual satisfaction, intimacy, and even divorce rates (referred to as "marital stability"). This meta-study concluded with a quote that is reminiscent of the Surgeon General's warning on a pack of cigarettes: "The major practical implication of this review is [that] psychologists can inform the public that despite popular belief, premarital cohabitation is generally associated with *negative outcomes*, both in terms of marital quality and marital stability in the United States."[42]

Just to back up for a minute: I previously said that cohabitation was originally viewed as the "next step" of commitment in a dating relationship. It typically occurred during engagement or as a step toward engagement. However, as moving in together outside of marriage became more common, the connection between cohabitation and commitment became *decoupled*, with more and more couples choosing to live together without any defined, mutual commitment. A primary driver of this decoupling was the growing belief that cohabitation has no risks—that it is just convenient, economical, and a way to fully get to know someone. If everything works out, great. If not, then at least there was no marriage, which means no divorce.

However, when you examine this large body of published research as that meta-study did, an opposing conclusion raises its ominous head: Cohabitation is **not** risk-free. In fact, it is replete with risks. But what is it that makes cohabitation outside of marriage so risky?

James and Mara's story illustrates many of the same risks that research has revealed. First, the arrangement of moving in together often happens with little to no planning. On the surface, you may think, "So what?" But as it does in most major decisions in life, a lack of planning in cohabitation leads to unforeseen complications and hardships. This explains why cohabitation arrangements break up around five times more frequently than marriages. And why unplanned pregnancies occur three times more often with cohabiting couples than married couples.

> *The arrangement of moving in together often happens with little to no planning.*

When Mara was asked how it came about that she and James decided to move in together, her answer was one of the answers most commonly given in research studies. She looked puzzled and then mumbled, "It just kind of happened. I mean, I was always over there and after several months, James said that I might as well move in—so I did."

Preparing for marriage almost always prompts future planning.

In contrast, preparing for marriage almost always prompts future planning. In fact, couples who remain in their own residences and follow a progression of dating, becoming engaged, planning for their marriage, and then marrying are mutually involved in considering and discussing their future together during each decision point along their relationship journey. I am not saying that this progression always works out, but I am pointing out that one sequence is consciously planned while the other is not.

A second, related risk is the absence of meaningful conversations about levels of commitment. As I pointed out in the previous section, all forms of DTR (defining the relationship) have become awkward and avoided in most relationships—resulting in undefined and ambiguous commitments, often with two partners having differing levels of commitment. This puts couples at a huge risk for unmet expectations, coasting for years in a mediocre relationship, and, ultimately, painful breaches of trust.

A third risk is that the cohabiting arrangement lessens personal independence and increases the risk of becoming entangled and trapped in a joint life together without the foundation of commitment or proven compatibility.

When Mara moved in with James, she never considered what aspects of her freedom and independence she was forfeiting. If she had stayed in her own apartment, she might have still made the decision to enroll in a nursing program, but her financial plan would have been much different. She also would have been able to evaluate her relationship with James more objectively, looking closely at how they supported each other and stayed close during stressful times without having to worry that identifying a deficiency in their relationship would threaten the security of her residence, education, or career choices.

Instead, now that she lives with James, she has many overlapping responsibilities that have created an interdependency that colors her consideration of her relationship and life decisions. This is exactly what much of the published research has been concluding about the cohabitation trend. Couples frequently step into this arrangement without discussing their commitment or their future together, resulting in frequent mismatches of expectations and commitment levels. Once living together, couples find their lives become more and more entangled with sharing the utilities, rent, or mortgage, and joint purchases of pets, furniture, household items, vehicles, vacations, trips, and educational pursuits.

This is why many couples coast from cohabitation to marriage, only to then realize that they are not that happy together. The "risk-free" decision to move in together actually reduced their independence, entangled them in mutual responsibilities and dependencies, and decreased the likelihood that they would actively address their issues prior to marriage. Instead, they take the path of least resistance. Confronting their issues and possibly breaking up is complicated, just like Mara described in her relationship with James. Much of her depression was related to living in an unhappy relationship in which she now felt trapped. You can easily imagine how, after so long, the momentum of a shared life together would tilt James and Mara toward marriage, with one or both of them secretly hoping that getting married would somehow infuse their relationship with everything it was lacking.

This is one of the primary explanations for why couples who cohabit prior to marriage have lower satisfaction once married, and higher divorce rates than couples who have never cohabited.

A final risk—one which Mara was definitely feeling although she had not yet articulated it—is that the breakup effects of a cohabiting relationship are much more like the breakup effects of divorce than

> *The breakup effects of a cohabiting relationship are much more like the breakup effects of divorce than people ever imagine.*

people ever imagine.

We have known for a long time that second marriages have around a 15 percent higher risk of divorce than the average divorce rate of first marriages. In a landmark study on premarital sex, cohabitation, and divorce, Western Washington University scholar Jay Teachman found that both premarital sex and cohabitation greatly increase the likelihood of divorce compared with couples who did not engage sexually or cohabit prior to marriage. But one of his findings suggested that the breakup effects of a cohabiting relationship are more similar than previously believed to the breakup effects of divorce.[43]

Most of us can imagine reasons why those who were previously married are more likely to divorce their second spouse—unresolved emotional and relational issues, complications from an ex or the children of a previous partner, overlapping relationships (affairs), becoming desensitized to breaking up ("If I did it once I can do it again"), and a lowered tolerance to a partner's issues, to name a few.

Now here is the thing: Teachman's research concluded that those who cohabited with a partner, broke up, and then went on to meet and marry another partner ended up having similar divorce rates to those in second marriages, even though it was their first marriage. (They had around a 15 percent higher divorce rate than the average first marriage.) The implication is that many (if not all) of the factors that increase divorce rates for second marriages also apply to first marriages that follow a cohabiting breakup. When two cohabiting partners separate and begin to cut the many threads that have woven their lives together, they are often left with the same painful losses and broken hearts that result when a marriage is dissolved.

It is ironic that in our mainstream culture, marriage tends to be portrayed in such negative ways—e.g., marriage takes more than it gives, and creates too much risk because it can lead to divorce—while moving in with a partner without a clearly defined commitment is portrayed in such positive ways, as if cohabitation has unlimited gains with little to no risks. And yet, as I have shown, the preponderance of published psychosocial research strongly supports just the opposite.

Christians and Cohabitation Outside of Marriage

One of the lines we have heard repeated countless times since the SARS-CoV-2 assaulted our world is, "You must listen to the science." When it comes to the science of cohabitation, however, it seems few listen. And you would think that when science validates Scripture, then those with a Christian faith would *definitely* listen. However, that does not seem to be happening either. The majority of Christians (including Evangelicals) who are under forty-five years old have cohabited, plan to do so in the future, or are open to that possibility. And among Evangelicals who have ever cohabited, only 49 percent of first cohabitations culminated in marriage.[44] This is heartbreaking when one considers the similarity of cohabitation breakups and divorce discussed in the previous section.

When the views of younger Christian singles are examined, the trend to cohabit is even more pronounced. In Figure 5.1, you see that only around 25 percent of the most conservative Christian young people say that they will definitely not cohabit, with that number dropping to under 20 percent of mainline Protestants, and under 15 percent of Catholics.[45] In contrast, almost half of Evangelicals and around 60 percent of Catholics and mainline Protestants state that they will probably or definitely cohabit. As explained in Chapter 4, beliefs predict behaviors, so it is very likely that within another generation there will be little difference between mainline culture and Christian culture in this area of cohabitation.

In Evangelical circles, it is sometimes argued that Evangelical cohabitation is different from "worldly" cohabitation because it is overwhelmingly tied to impending marriage. But the facts suggest otherwise. Among female Evangelicals who have ever cohabited, only 18 percent were formally engaged when they moved in with their first cohabiting partner, and another 18 percent had definite plans to marry; thus, only 36 percent in total had serious marital intent.[46]

These percentages are fairly similar to those of African American Protestants and Catholics. This means that two-thirds of cohabiting Christian singles would not describe their cohabiting relationship as clearly heading toward marriage. As mentioned in a previous section of this chapter, the greatest risks for cohabiting couples occur when their commitment is low or undefined. Unfortunately, this describes close to 65 percent of cohabiting Christian singles.[47]

Figure 5.1

Views of Young Adults, Ages 15-22, on Their Chances of Cohabitating

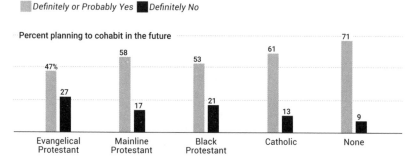

Source: NSFG 2017–19. respondents ages 15 through 22 who have never married or cohabitated

Figure 5.2

Cohabitation Plans and Practices by Importance of Religious Faith to Daily Life and Age

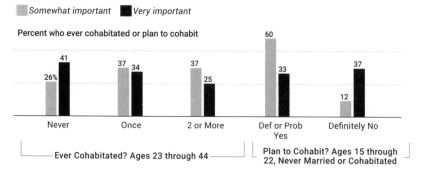

Source: NSFG 2017–19 combined. Both figures 3.2 and 3.3 include Evangelical Protestants only.

Figures 5.2 and 5.3 provide a big picture of what is happening in the cohabitation plans and intentions of Evangelical teens through their early twenties, and the cohabitation practices of those in their early twenties through early forties.

On the one hand, we find that those most serious about their faith are more likely to have plans and practices that are consistent with Scriptural teachings. This affirms that both Christian beliefs and church attendance make a difference. On the other hand, "even among these 'ideal' Evangelicals, most respondents ages 15 to 22 are not determined to forego living together until marriage, and most respondents ages 23 to 44 have cohabited. In fact, roughly one-quarter of those who attend church regularly have cohabited two or more times, and most have done so at least once."[48]

Figure 5.3
Cohabitation Plans and Practices by Level of Church Attendance and Age

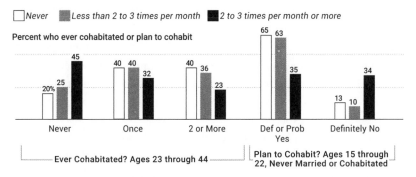

Source: NSFG 2017–19 combined. Both figures 3.2 and 3.3 include Evangelical Protestants only.

The trends of sex, cohabitation, and unmarried parenting (Chapter 6) within all denominations of Christianity match the trends of mainstream culture—they simply trail by a few years. This seems to be an indictment on the lack of effective ministry approaches within churches to inculcate in their youth and single adults relationship-related beliefs and practices that emulate Scriptural principles. This paradigm shift in priorities and approaches must begin in the pulpits of churches and extend throughout all ministries and outreaches. Churches must go upstream relationally—by helping not just youth but also their parents, equipping them to instill Scriptural values in their children and confront the cultural norms that are sabotaging their future marriages and families.

* * *

A QUICK RECAP

- Rates of cohabitation (living together outside of marriage) increased as mainstream American culture began to view sexual involvement and marriage as unrelated.
- There are more than 1,000 published research studies on the topic of cohabitation. This massive body of research has clearly identified risks of cohabitation:
  - o The first risk is that most cohabiting relationships often involve little planning, which has contributed to a breakup rate five times higher than marriage, and an unplanned pregnancy rate three times higher than among married couples.
  - o The second risk of cohabitation is that these relationships often preclude meaningful conversations about commitment, which ends up masking different levels of commitment between partners. This can lead to a mediocre relationship that coasts for years, peppered with painful unmet expectations.
  - o The third risk of cohabitation is the loss of personal independence, as an interdependent arrangement is formed that is often highly bonding without matching levels of commitment or even compatibility.
  - o A fourth and final risk of cohabitation is the effects of breakup: The socio-emotional fallout when a cohabiting relationship ends is much more similar to that of divorce than to the breakup effects of a non-cohabiting relationship.
- Rates of cohabitation across Christian denominations largely track those of mainstream culture.
- Churches must go upstream relationally—by helping not just youth but also

their parents, equipping them to instill Scriptural values in their children and confront the cultural norms that are sabotaging their future marriages and families.

CHAPTER 6

The Decoupling of Parenting from Marriage

Earlier this year, I (John) walked on stage with five colleagues at an international fatherhood conference—a New York Times best-selling author, a pediatrician, and several directors of state and federal departments of Health and Human Services. We were the plenary panel of experts expected to discuss major concerns for fathers and their children, at a time when approximately 20 to 25 million children are living without a father in the home. This is 25 to 40 percent of all children, according to various censuses in the last ten years. Statistics about fatherless children are staggering—with 90 percent of homeless and runaway children, 71 percent of pregnant teens, 63 percent of youth suicides, 71 percent of high school dropouts, and 85 percent of youths in prison all coming from fatherless homes.

When it came to my turn to explain what I believed was a major cause of fatherlessness in America, I started with this statement:

"The primary problem of fathers today is not their parenting . . . it is their *partnering*.

"Let me explain. Columbia and Princeton Universities joined forces to conduct a national and longitudinal study on families titled Fragile Families.[49] Researchers conducted assessments of 5,000 firstborn children along with interviews of their mothers and fathers from twenty mid-sized cities across the country. They then conducted follow-up interviews and assessments at the end of years one, three, five, and nine. This study provided a robust ten-year understanding of the different trajectories of couples and families resulting from how they had formed their relationships at the birth of their first child.

The primary problem of fathers today is not their parenting . . . it is their partnering.

"In this study, approximately 40 percent of the mothers and fathers were unmarried at the time of their first baby's birth and 60 percent were married. By the way, these percentages are representative of the national averages in United States, although the percentage of unwed mothers in sub-populations can rise as high as 80 percent. And in this survey, most of the 40 percent of unmarried mothers were romantically involved with the father of their child, with more than half of them living together.

"When the mothers were asked, *'Do you plan on marrying the father of your child?'* Seventy percent said, 'Yes!'

"So, let me ask all of you in the audience this question—when they asked the fathers, *'Do you plan on marrying the mother of your child?'*—what percentage of fathers said, 'Yes' . . . was it higher or lower than the percentage of mothers?"

The audience was packed full of professionals who have worked in the field of fatherhood for decades. Almost unanimously, the crowd shouted, "Lower, much lower!" Some shouted 35 percent, 25 percent, and there were those who exclaimed, "Ten percent!"

When the crowd quieted, I (John) lightheartedly reprimanded them, "You lack faith in the very population you serve! The percentage was actually *12 percent HIGHER than the mothers . . . 82 percent of fathers said they planned on marrying the mother of their baby!*"

I let that defense of men settle in before concluding with the most important finding of this study.

> When your relationship begins with marriage before you have a child, you have a much greater likelihood of being together at the end of the fifth year.

"But here is the thing," I continued. "On the five-year follow-up, only 16 percent had actually married, and over 65 percent had already broken up. Think about what this means—65 percent of the children who were born to unmarried parents became fatherless by the fifth year of their life."

And then I compared the breakup rates of those who were unmarried at the time of their baby's birth to the 60 percent of couples who were married prior to conceiving their first child.

"When compared to those couples who were married before they had their first child, these unmarried couples were ***three times*** more likely to call it quits and move on to a new partner. In other words, when your relationship begins with marriage before you have a child, you have a ***much*** greater likelihood of being together at the end of the fifth year than those who had their first child outside of being married.

"This is why I say that that the biggest problem fathers face is not their parenting, but their partnering; because as goes the partnering, so goes the parenting. You can see that unmarried parenting is a major feeder system to fatherless homes, and the statistics about children who grow up in these fatherless homes are absolutely appalling."

Warren Farrell sat next to me on that conference stage, and when I glanced over, he had written on his pad of paper, "So true!" When our keynote was complete, we had some time to talk together, especially about his work on fatherlessness. He explained that after publishing his 2001 book, *Father and Child Reunion*, he received numerous requests for a list of the benefits of father involvement and the damages of dad deprivation. He put an appendix in his 2018 book, *The Boy Crisis*, of a list of fifty-five areas incorporating more than seventy specific outcomes in these two crucial areas. Here are just a few:

- Father involvement is *at least five times as important* in preventing drug use as overall closeness to parent, parental rules, parental trust, strictness, or a child's gender, ethnicity, or social class.
- A study of boys from similar backgrounds revealed that by the third grade, the boys who lived with fathers scored on average higher on every achievement test and received higher grades.
- A father's positive contact with children during the first two years resulted in fewer signs of unwanted and uncontrolled behavior in the children.
- Every 1 percent increase in fatherlessness in a region predicts a 3 percent increase in adolescent violence.[50]
- Children from fatherless homes are twice as likely to get divorced themselves.
- If separated parents find new partners, the children living in those homes

are ten to fifty times more likely to be sexually or physically abused than those who live with two biological, married parents.[51]

This last statistic is appalling, and has been replicated in studies since the 1980s. Of course, you can find dysfunction in every type of family structure, including married-parent homes. And an abusive married-parent home will almost always fall short when compared to some different family structure that is nevertheless loving and healthy.

Just to be clear: All family structures can provide love, security, and health within the fabric of a diverse society. But when examined in large numbers, married-parent homes raising their biological children are the standard for a society because they provide the most stable and secure environments for children to feel loved, be safe, and develop in every way. All other family structures must always be examined by how they measure up to the gold standard of married-parent homes with biological children.

In the National Survey of Children's Health conducted by the CDC in 2011, the numbers of Adverse Family Experiences (AFE—sometimes called Adverse Childhood Experiences) were examined in households with two married biological parents and in households with only one biological parent. Seventy percent of households had no AFEs. However, in contrast, around 80 percent of households with only one biological parent had at least one AFE, and almost 50 percent had two (see Figure 6.1). Those with AFEs are substantially more likely to die by suicide and suffer from depression as adults.[52]

> *When sex, romantic partnerships, and parenting are coupled together as a package deal in marriage, we then have the lowest divorce rates and the highest marriage satisfaction rates.*

Economic Upward Mobility and Relationship Choices

What we have seen thus far is that when sex, romantic partnerships, and parenting are coupled together as a package deal in marriage, we then have the lowest divorce

Figure 6.1
Adverse Family Experiences by Family Structure

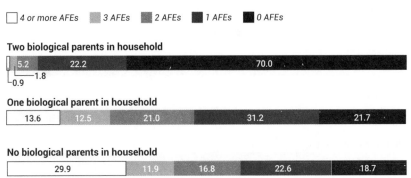

☐ *4 or more AFEs* ▨ *3 AFEs* ▨ *2 AFEs* ▇ *1 AFEs* ▇ *0 AFEs*

Two biological parents in household

| 5.2 | 22.2 | | 70.0 |
—1.8
└0.9

One biological parent in household

| 13.6 | 12.5 | 21.0 | 31.2 | 21.7 |

No biological parents in household

| 29.9 | 11.9 | 16.8 | 22.6 | 18.7 |

Note:Children living with step or adopted parents were excluded. AFE is adverse family experience.
Source: State and Local Area Integrated Telephone Survey, National Survey of Children's Health, 2011–2012

rates, the highest marriage satisfaction rates, the best mental, emotional, physical, and educational outcomes for children, and the lowest levels of abuse and Adverse Family Experiences. But when these three major relationship structures are decoupled, there follows an erosion of personal and relationship health, and (as we will see in our next chapter) an equal erosion of spiritual and religious health.

Reversing these trends is possible, and can dramatically alter the course of one's life. For starters, consider the economic implications. When examining adults (ages twenty-eight to thirty-four) who had a child, 50 percent of those who married prior to having children are in the higher-income bracket, whereas almost 50 percent of those who had a baby before marriage are in the lower-income bracket (47 percent - see Figure 6.2). This pattern holds true for racial and ethnic minorities (71 percent), as well as young adults from lower-income families. For instance, 76 percent of African American and 81 percent of Hispanic young adults who married first are in the middle or upper third of the income distribution, as are 87 percent of whites.

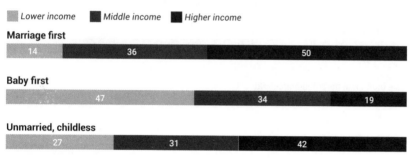

Figure 6.2

Percentage of Adults Ages 28-34 in Each Income Bracket

Lower income Middle income Higher income

Marriage first

| 14 | 36 | 50 |

Baby first

| 47 | 34 | 19 |

Unmarried, childless

| 27 | 31 | 42 |

Source: Home Economics Project, a research effort of the American Enterprise Institute and the Institute for Family Studies.

There are scholars who argue that the arrow points the other way—that socioeconomic status drives family structure rather than relationship choices having the power to alter economic mobility. However, there is strong evidence that one's economic future is greatly impacted by the relationship choices one makes, specifically in the areas of marriage and parenting. Compared with the path of having a baby first, marrying before children *more than doubles* young adults' odds of being in the middle- or top-income tier, even after adjusting for education, childhood family income, employment status, race/ethnicity, sex, and other factors. What this suggests is that the choice to marry before having your first child is a critical component in setting yourself up for upward economic mobility.

"Finally, 97% of millennials who follow what has been called the 'success sequence'—that is, who get at least a high school degree, work, and then marry before having any children, in that order—are not poor by the time they reach their prime young adult years (ages 28-34)."[53]

One of the most convincing statistics underscoring the economic impact of this sequence is found in the number of those who moved from a lower-income bracket to a higher bracket based on their relationship choices. ***For those who grew up in the lowest third economic bracket but made the choice to*** *marry before having their first baby, 71 percent moved to the middle or top third of the distribution in their young adulthood. This is almost three out of four young adults who moved out of poverty.*

Unmarried Childbearing Among Christians

Sociologist Brad Wilcox analyzed a large national data set a little over ten years ago. At that time, the overall percentage of children born to unmarried women was 33 percent, with 24 percent of evangelical Protestant mothers giving birth when they were unmarried. However, when Wilcox parsed out the Evangelicals who were regular churchgoers from those he called "nominal" Evangelicals, he found that only 12 percent of babies were born to unmarried women. In contrast, the "nominal" evangelical Protestant mothers matched the national average of 33 percent of births to unmarried women.[54]

Previous research that Wilcox and Nicholas Wolfinger conducted in 2007 also found that evangelical Protestant women who attended church regularly were 63 percent more likely than the average nonmarried woman to marry the father of their baby within a year of giving birth. And if the father also attended church regularly, this increased to 95 percent more likely to become married *prior* to the baby's birth.[55]

As we have seen in the previous two chapters, regular church attendance and holding one's faith as "very important" does make a difference in relationship decisions and trajectories. These studies support that same point, showing that evangelical women who attend church are less likely to have a child when unmarried, and more likely to get married to the father if they do become pregnant when unmarried.[56]

However, when it comes to the decoupling of marriage from sex, romantic partnerships, and parenting, there are too many similarities in the relationship

> For those who grew up in the lowest third economic bracket but marry before having their first baby, 71 percent moved to the middle or top economic bracket.

trends within churches and the trends within mainstream culture. Churches must greatly increase their compelling evidence for following Scripture in the formation of romantic relationships and the consideration of marriage.

We have identified many of the advantages to building a marriage relationship prior to bearing children—these benefits include the stability of the marriage, the health and wellbeing of the baby, and, as we described in the previous section of this chapter, the economic upward mobility of the family. And in the last three chapters, we have seen that faith practices definitely impact relationship choices.

Reversing the Decoupling Trend and Replenishing the Church

But is there evidence that relationship choices impact faith practices? Does improving relationship health in our dating practices, marriages, and families also improve our religious landscape?

It is commonly believed that the decline of Christianity and religious health in America has contributed to the deterioration of dating, marriage, and family health. Therefore, the thinking goes, if we just concentrate on improving religious worship and discipleship, improvements within our marriages and families will surely follow.

Mary Eberstadt acknowledged the vital impact that religion has upon family formation and functioning, and the seismic shifts that have occurred in the deterioration of marital and family health in America and throughout Western civilization (as we also showed in the last few chapters). However, in her book *How the West Really Lost God,* she defied the conventional cause-and-effect relationship that posits declining family health as a result of declining religious health.

The proposition of this book is that there was—and still is—a critical defect in the conventional secular story line about how and why Christianity has collapsed in parts of the West. The missing piece is what I will dub 'the Family Factor.' Simply stated, what the Family Factor means to signal is a new idea. It is that the causal relationship between family and religion—specifically, the religion of Christianity—is not just a one-way, but actually a two-way street. In other words, I will argue that family formation is not merely an *outcome* of religious belief, as secular sociology has regarded it. Rather, family formation can also be, and has been, a causal agent in its own right—one that also potentially affects any given human being's religious belief and practice . . . What has been missed is a fact so prosaic that it has seemed to go without saying—namely, that the family has been an important, indeed irreplaceable, transmission belt for religious belief in a number of different ways.[57]

Eberstadt builds an irrefutable case that there is not a linear, one-way relationship in which religious health directly affects family health. Instead, she proves that "family and faith are the invisible double helix of society—two spirals that when linked to one another can effectively reproduce, but whose strength and momentum depend on one another."

We agree! Churches in America (and around the world) *must seriously focus on the mission* of improving the dating, marriage, and family relationship health within their own congregations, and then, equally importantly, within their communities. We will clearly establish that when churches make this one of their top priorities in their ministries, staffing, and budgets, they can tremendously alter the divorce rates and increase the number of people entering healthy marriages within their congregations and even their communities. Infusing ministries and outreaches with relationship courses and programs will squarely position the church in America as a change-agent of relationship culture while *also* dramatically transforming the landscape of religious affiliation and attendance.

Our contention is this: The decoupling of marriage from sex, partnerships, and parenting has bankrupted the relationship health of society. But churches have both

> *Infusing ministries and outreaches with relationship courses and programs will squarely position the church in America as a change-agent.*

the *opportunity* and *responsibility* to seriously invest in this mission to strengthen healthy dating practices, marriages, and families within both their congregations and their communities.

The need is great . . . and the time is now. Churches *can* become the primary source of relationship health that individuals and couples within their communities desparately need and want. This is the new mission, the new outreach platform for the church in the 21st century.

* * *

A QUICK RECAP

- Once sex and romantic partnering were decoupled from marriage, the rate of unmarried childbearing increased astronomically. We described these statistics in Chapter 3: the national average of unmarried, first-time mothers is 40 percent although 55 percent of millennial first-time mothers are unmarried. The percentage of mothers having children out of wedlock according to race are:[58]
    - o White mothers (30%),
    - o Hispanic mothers (56%)
    - o African American mothers (77%)
- The decoupling of parenting from marriage has increased greatly because of increases of unmarried cohabitation.
- The decoupling of parenting from marriage has contributed to the epidemic of fatherlessness, which is associated with increases in drug use and violence as well as poorer scores on achievement tests and grades in school.
- The decoupling of parenting has also led to ten to fifteen times higher likelihood of Adverse Family Experiences (e.g., physical and sexual abuse) when the mother cohabits with or marries partners other than the biological father.
- Economic mobility is impacted by relationship choices. Three out of four individuals who are born in poverty but marry before having a baby experience economic upward mobility to the middle or upper third of income brackets.

- These decoupling trends have fueled the decline in church affiliation and attendance, with historically low rates of church attendance and a historically high number of people self-describing as having no religious affiliation today.
- Among regular churchgoers, the rates of births outside marriage are much lower, but the trends are ominous.
- "Family and faith are the invisible double helix of society—two spirals that when linked to one another can effectively reproduce, but whose strength and momentum depend on one another." - Mary Eberstadt

CHAPTER 7

The Flight from Marriage Produces Bad Fruit for the World and the Church

I (JP) want to introduce you to my friend Pat Fagan, who heads up the Marriage and Religion Research Institute (MARRI), formerly at the Family Research Council and now housed at the Catholic University of America. Born in Ireland, Pat is a father of eight who has spent his career as a clinical therapist and has commissioned dozens of original research projects in marriage, family, and child development and religious practice.[59] Without a pessimistic bone in his body, Pat has a personal winsomeness in how he approaches the challenge of relationship and marital health.

My favorite story with Pat involved going to lunch with him at a restaurant in D.C.'s Foggy Bottom. The waiter—overhearing our conversation about faith—leaned in and admitted he had grown up as a Christian. He said he didn't have any problem with his childhood faith, but he just wasn't part of any church anymore.

Seeing the ring on the waiter's finger, Pat says, "Do you want to know the secret to having a great sex life?"

The server listened intently.

Pat replied, "Go to church."

He then pointed out that the social science overwhelmingly shows that churchgoing Christians have sex more frequently and are happier in their sex life than those who don't attend.[60] Pat said all of this with his wry Irish smile.

Well, if you could see that server's face! He said he was going to make it a priority to get his wife out to church that very Sunday. Pat's was an unconventional approach to evangelization.

In his work, Pat has developed an exceptionally useful index called the Index of Family Belonging. It's a measure of the number of children between the age of fifteen and seventeen who are with a married set of biological parents. In his most recent published index, just 46 percent of kids in that age group had biological parents married to one another. As out-of-wedlock birth becomes more normative, this number is likely to grow. Some believe only a third of all kids born today will reach their fifteenth birthday with a married mom and dad.

Pat's researchers at MARRI have been able to drill down and apply his index to smaller geographic areas called Census Super-PUMAs,[61] which are regional areas of the population with at least 400,000 residents. And they've found that when the Index of Family Belonging is low within an individual Super-PUMA, it is the single most powerful factor in predicting an area's dependence on welfare programs that target organic poverty.[62] It has the "strongest attenuating influence on teenage out-of-wedlock birth." The Index of Family Belonging also has a greater influence on high school graduation rates than the fraction of adults with a college education in the same area.[63]

Pat and his research team have also reviewed the existing social science literature and shown that whether our parents remained continuously married actually affects our desire to get married, the perceived quality of our own marriages, and our interest in becoming parents:

• A larger fraction of those from intact families than non-intact families report being happy in their marriages.[64]
• If you are an adult who grew up in a continuously-married home, you are far more likely to say being married is very important.[65]
• This even impacts our desire to become parents, as daughters raised in "intact families are less likely to say they do not plan to have children than daughters living with divorced or remarried mothers."[66]

What this means is that as the share of adults from continuously-married homes declines, the number of individuals getting married will inevitably decrease. It becomes a self-replicating process. In 2018, the U.S. marriage rate reached its lowest point since 1867—the first year for which the federal government data on marriage is available.[67] In 2018, just 6.5 marriages occurred for every 1,000 people in the population. And it's safe to say that the impact of the pandemic on marriage rates, at least during 2020, is unlikely to boost marriages.

The average age for marriage among millennials is now thirty for men and twenty-eight for women.[68] Out of all births in the United States today, 40 percent are outside of marriage. As we note in Chapter 2, almost half of the entire American population (45.5 percent) is unmarried today, compared with just 28 percent in 1960. In the adult single population, 63 percent have never been married, 23 percent are divorced, and 13 percent are widowed. Of those living independently of their own accord, 53 percent of singles are women.

As the share of adults from continuously-married homes declines, the number of individuals getting married will inevitably decrease.

If this is the state of marriage, what can the Church do about it?

Beyond Chaos and Fairytales

In the early stages of building the Culture of Freedom Initiative's successful three-year test to measurably strengthen marriage on a citywide level, my team wanted to bring the best elements of business practice into the service of ministry. So we hired a leading market research firm called The Right Brain People, which is made up of believers in Christ who are also behavioral psychologists with deep experience in consumer research. We were looking for their expertise to better understand the emotional drivers of why young people choose to get married, stay married, cohabit, or get divorced. For research purposes, we agreed to think of marriage as a "product" in order to apply their analysis. Our hope was to bring these insights to the Church and thereby improve ministry strategies.

It was an unusual research project, to say the least.

The firm had previously been hired to use their emotion-based market research techniques for twenty-two of the forty largest advertisers in America. They had done work for McDonald's, Walmart, Jared's, and General Motors, among others. Their research in the '80s helped McDonald's create the value meal and allowed General Motors to save the Corvette when it was on the chopping block. They had also been hired by the Vitae Foundation in the mid-1990s to help the pro-life movement rethink how to talk about abortion. It was their research that gave rise to messages like "Abortion hurts women" and "Women deserve more than abortion" because they found in their research that the effect of abortion on women, rather than on the unborn child, was most emotionally persuasive. The founder of the firm, Charlie Kenney, was aligned with our work and wanted to help.

We thought that if Charlie and his team could help make headway on a seemingly intractable social issue like abortion, then surely he could help us rethink how to help churches talk about marriage and relationships.

His research was conducted in two parts, a qualitative phase that sought to uncover, through longform ninety-minute interviews, the underlying emotional drivers of relationship behavior. The second part was quantitative, which sought to measure the relative strength of those emotional factors that arose in the interviews. Because millennials with a college degree and higher-income millennials in general marry at higher rates than those millennials without a college degree, we asked the research project to focus on those young adults who did not have a four-year college degree and didn't have a household income over $65,000.

Family trauma and domestic chaos are far more the norm than the exception among young people. Church leaders must begin with this understanding.

After gathering the data from the interview phase of the research, Charlie named the qualitative report *Beyond Chaos and Fairytales.* Communio has since created a series of training modules to help walk pastors through its key findings and develop ways to apply these findings to their preaching, teaching, and messaging. We leveraged his findings in the test phase of our outreach from 2016 to 2018 to help churches successfully lower the divorce rate countywide in Jacksonville by 24 percent.

What the research found is that family trauma and domestic chaos are far more the norm than the exception among these young people. Church leaders must begin with this understanding if they are going to find any effective ways to reach young people with the Gospel and reinforce the lifelong commitment of Christian marriage.

This task is made more difficult by the fact that positive views of marriage are frequently shaped by movies and the media. It was surprising for interviewers to hear respondents say, unprompted and on many occasions, that their positive expectations for marriage were shaped by the happy endings of weddings as told within Disney animated movies.

The researchers found that the juxtaposition of family trauma in childhood with expectations of a "happily-ever-after" has created both high expectations around "the brand" of marriage (the fairytale) along with a set of life experiences where they lack the practical ability to live up to those expectations (the chaos). Those who cohabited at one time but who eventually married reported during the interviews that living together before being married allowed them to carefully test the relationship and avoid creating the family trauma that arose in their own background.

For many, this means that their prolonged singleness and cohabitation often emerges out of deep wounds within their family of origin.

Even among the most staunchly pro-marriage millennials in this study, the researchers found that 73 percent believed that cohabitation should be viewed as either usually moral or always moral. This obviously presents major challenges to the Church as cohabitation is associated with a higher incidence of divorce. We explored much of the science around cohabitation in Chapter 5. It's important to note that women in cohabiting relationships are also among the most vulnerable to domestic violence. 40 percent of the relationships of unmarried parents end by the child's first birthday—and 60 percent are no longer romantically involved with each other by the time the child reaches the age of five.[69] Because unmarried dads are so rarely involved dads, this means the overwhelming number of children conceived in a cohabiting relationship find themselves without an active dad early in their childhood.

Tell Me About Your Father

As we have seen in the survey data, family trauma doesn't only affect the way young adults view marriage, it also shapes their faith practice and willingness to attend church. To understand this better, I also asked Right Brain People to conduct a series of qualitative interviews with millennials around the emotional drivers of church attendance behavior.

What they found is that those millennials who were the least emotionally interested in attending church were also the least likely to report having a positive relationship with their parents:

- In fact, the study found that 57 percent of the most emotionally uninterested in church participation reported having something less than an excellent or very good relationship with their father.
- Only 18 percent of this group reported having an excellent relationship with their dad.

Conversely, those the Right Brain researchers found to be the most emotionally positive about attending church regularly also were the most likely to report having an excellent relationship with their parents, and particularly with their father.

Now, we can see in the psychological market research conducted by Right Brain People that the lack of a healthy father relationship has an impact on whether or not someone attends church, how they view church, and whether or not the person has any faith at all.

The father relationship may be the secret ingredient.

We know from other social science research that unmarried dads are uninvolved dads: "Without marriage, fathers are less likely to be living with, spending time with, and providing financially for their children. Based on the percentage of children who are not living with or regularly visiting their fathers, the precariousness of the connection between fathers and their families is greater now than at any point in our history."[70]

This may explain why kids from divorced homes, widowed homes, and never-married homes often approach faith in such a similar way. The father relationship may be the secret ingredient that explains why millennials from continuously-married homes are nearly twice as likely to attend church compared to their counterparts from divorced, never-married, or widowed homes. A much-cited study from Switzerland found that both the father's presence and his practice of faith was the most powerful determinant in a child's likelihood to practice the faith as an adult.[71]

But exactly why is this the case? I believe it is wrapped up in the Trinitarian mystery and God's revelation as Father. To flesh this idea out further, I (JP) reached out to my friend Dr. Paul Vitz, a former atheist and professor of psychology at New York University. After years of being an atheist, Paul became a believing Christian and has published his own peer-reviewed work on the psychological drivers of atheism. I got to know Paul because he founded the Institute for Psychological Sciences (IPS) in Northern Virginia, which later became Divine Mercy University.

When my sister's four kids moved in with us (as I discussed in Chapter 1), we weren't situated to pay the full freight of having them receive counseling and therapy. Friends in the area told us about IPS, so we decided to seek out counseling and therapy for my nephews and nieces through the IPS extern program, which allowed graduating counselors to provide counseling under the tutelage and active engagement of a professor. Getting to know Paul's work through this experience, I later invited him to speak to members of The Philanthropy Roundtable on the central thesis of his book *Faith of the Fatherless: A Psychoanalysis of Atheism*.

The arguments of that book are so important for pastors to understand if they are going to understand the psychological drivers of why healthy marital relationships make such a huge impact on the faith of Christians and the rise of the nones. (Again, recall that unmarried fathers, statistically speaking, are either less-involved or uninvolved fathers.) The connection between fatherlessness and faithlessness only reinforces how important it is for churches to encourage and support the formation of healthy marriages.

During one of our early conversations on this topic, Paul leaned in and told me, "You know, JP," pausing for dramatic effect, "It is hard to know the Father's love, if you do not first know a father's love."

It is hard to know the Father's love if you do not first know a father's love.

His central claim is that the inability to have a healthy attachment with your father is a key predictor of whether or not you become either an atheist or practice a pantheist or naturalist theology. His argument does not mean all fatherless people become atheists or agnostics. It is that fatherlessness, the inability to have a healthy attachment to one's father, and the lack of any effective substitute father, collectively, that is a leading factor driving the rise of agnosticism or atheism.

"One main physiological reason is that if your father is seen as rejecting, or abandoning, or in some sense abusive, it psychologically serves as a barrier to understanding God as Father," Paul told me during a recent phone call. "So that's the big physiological barrier. If your own father was totally unsatisfactory, you can't approach God as Father. I mean that from a psychological sense."

Figure 7.1

Family Structure and the Rise of "the Nones"
Growth of religious nones and children raised without both parents follow the same trajectory.

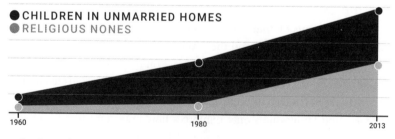

Source: Pew Research Center

As a nation, we only begin to observe a significant number of children without a dad in the home around 1960, when that number reaches about 9 percent and rapidly grows.[72] The effect of fatherlessness doesn't show up in religious behavior until those kids begin to become adults, when nearly the same number in 1980 report having no religion. You can see in Figure 7.1 that the growth in religious non-affiliation seems to chase the number of kids who lack married parents as those kids without married parents become adults.[73] We reviewed this phenomenon in Chapter 2.

In *Faith of the Fatherless*, Paul analyzes the father relationships of the world's thirty or so best-known atheists. What he finds, almost without exception, is that a defective relationship with a father is present in all of them.

Many had fathers who died during their youth, such as Friedrich Nietzsche, David Hume, Albert Camus, or Jean-Paul Sartre. Others had abusive or weak fathers, such as Thomas Hobbes, Voltaire, Sigmund Freud, or H.G. Wells. In his book, Paul writes about the famous contemporary atheist, Madalyn Murray O'Hair, who had a troubled relationship with her father. Her son wrote in his memoir that as a child, "We rarely did anything together as a family, the hatred between my grandfather and mother barred such wholesome scenes."[74] O'Hair's son recounts, as Paul describes in his book, that his atheist mother attempted to kill her own father with a butcher knife, screaming, "I'll see you dead. I'll get you yet. I'll walk on your grave."[75]

This theme of fatherlessness resurfaces in a number of the New Atheists. Daniel Dennett lost his father at the age of five due to a plane crash. Christopher Hitchens described a distant relationship with his father.[76]

"Now, I want to mention some other evidence—this I haven't written up yet," Paul told me. "When I published my book in 2013, there was one of the New Atheists for whom I had no evidence of a negative father—and that was Sam Harris . . . Since then, a long interview with him has come out in which he talked about how his father abandoned his family when he was two—and his mother raised him. I think he was raised in California and his father went off to New York. In the interview, he makes some kind of comment like, 'What kind of man could possibly abandon his two-year-old child and his wife?' I have a student here who's now found the same kind of father trauma in two, maybe even three major media people who are atheists that he is investigating."

The collapse of relationship and marital health is fueling the collapse in fatherhood. Efforts to drive an increase in fatherhood without any focus on the father's marital relationship will have only middling results. Ultimately, the Church, because of the power of the Gospel of Jesus Christ, is the answer to our relationship health crisis.

The Domino Effect

Let's take a minute to look at where we are heading if U.S. and Western culture continue on this same trajectory without the Church altering its course. There is a domino effect, and it goes like this:

Domino 1: We have clear evidence that if the Church continues not to positively impact the quality of dating, marriage, and parenting relationships the three areas of decoupling) in mainstream culture, then . . .

Domino 2: There will be a continued increase of broken marriages, fractured families, unstable romantic unions, and fatherless parenting. These in turn are major drivers of . . .

Domino 3: Hearts hardened to the Gospel, with continued decreases in active faith and church participation. An inevitable outcome will be . . .

Domino 4: Greater secularization of society—scientism replacing theism with an increase in moral relativism. Historically, this shift has always led to two social outcomes . . .

Domino 5: Dehumanizing practices carried out through totalitarian enforcement, which ultimately leads to . . .

Domino 6: Persecution of believers because Christianity is viewed as an obstacle to the "social agenda."

The Church can remove the lynchpin from this unholy chain of events.

The Church can remove the lynchpin from this unholy chain of events simply by consistently reaching out to a darkened world of relationships to improve the health of marriages and families. It is our faith in Jesus Christ and our relationship with Him that allow and inspire us to foster healthy,

God-affirming relationships. Looking at the cultural nihilism that has taken hold of human relationships, Christians can powerfully show a contrast to the world. We can demonstrate by our lives that it is Christ who lives in us (Galatians 2:20), who lives in our relationships, and who lives in our marriages.

In the next chapter, we will show you that when churches impact their surrounding community with relationship outreach and skills-based relationship ministries, there follows a groundswell of receptivity to the Gospel, and churches grow. However, we will also show that the vast majority of churches are doing very little to bolster marriage and relationship health in their own congregations—with essentially no churches conducting outreach to their community with relationship ministries.

Let us be perfectly clear: The content of evangelism will always be the Gospel. But the platform for evangelization in the 21st century is relationships. The collapse of relationship health has closed many hearts to the Gospel message. We are now at our endgame and the Church must make the strategic move to serve this essential need of relationship health with those who are dating and those who are married. It is only then that we will watch hearts open back up.

* * *

A QUICK RECAP

- When the Index of Family Belonging (the share of children raised in intact marriages) is low within a geographic area, it is the single most powerful factor in predicting an area's dependence on welfare programs that target organic poverty.
- The Index of Family Belonging has the "strongest attenuating influence on teenage out-of-wedlock birth." It's also incredibly influential on high school graduation rates, with a "greater influence on high school graduation rates than the fraction of adults with a college education in the same area."
- Whether or not one's parents remain continuously married affects even the child's desire to get married in the future. It impacts the perceived quality of our own marriages, and our interest in becoming parents.
- The research found that family trauma and domestic chaos are far more the norm than the exception among young people from decoupled homes.

Church leaders must begin with this understanding in their ministry.

- The juxtaposition of family trauma in childhood with expectations of a "happily-ever-after" has created both high expectations around "the fairytale brand" of marriage and a set of life experiences which leave people without the practical ability to live up to those expectations.
- The father relationship may be the secret ingredient. "It is hard to know the Father's love, if you do not first know a father's love."— Dr. Paul Vitz
- The Church can remove the lynchpin from this unholy chain of events by bolstering marriage and relationship health ministry.

The Qualities of Healthy Relationships and the Growth of Christianity

Chapters 8-12

In Section I of this book, we surveyed how the decoupling of marriage from sex, romantic partnerships, and parenting has had catastrophic consequences for society at large and the Church in particular. But the good news, we insisted, is that the Church has not yet realized the responsibility or even the opportunity it holds in ministering to this problem.

In Section II, we begin by showing that the Church's strategy to spread the Gospel in the 21st century must be restoring relationship health. We will then look more closely at the bedrock requirements of healthy relationships, which—with a strategic investment in marriage and relationship ministry—church leaders can help cultivate in their churches and in the surrounding community.

CHAPTER 8

The Church's 21st Century Mission: Relationship Health to Evangelize the World

How the Early Church Spread the Gospel: Healthy Relationships

Christians need to look back and reclaim their own history: It was the example of Christian marriage and healthy relationships in the early Church that substantially converted the pagan world.

In the ancient Greco-Roman world, relationship health was the rarity and not the rule. Rodney Stark has chronicled this in his book *The Triumph of Christianity.* He has definitively shown through his scholarship that Christianity largely conquered ancient Rome before Constantine's Edict. A forgotten part of the Gospel's draw was the way Christian relationships were lived out. In particular, our marriages were different.

> *It was the example of Christian marriage and healthy relationships in the early Church that substantially converted the pagan world.*

Men and women possessed an equality in Christianity that was non-existent elsewhere. Stark writes of these vast differences:

Hellenic women lived in semi-seclusion, the upper classes more than others, but all Hellenic women had a very circumscribed existence; in privileged families the women were denied access to the front rooms of the house. Roman women were not secluded, but in many other ways they were no less subordinated to male control. Neither Hellenic nor Roman women had any significant say in who they married, or when. Typically, they were married very young—often before puberty—to a far older man. Their husbands could divorce them with impunity, but a wife could only gain a divorce if a male relative sought it on her behalf. However, a Hellenic wife's father or brother could obtain her divorce against her wishes! Both Roman and Hellenic husbands held the absolute power to put an unwanted infant to death or to force a wife to abort, but Roman husbands were not allowed to kill their wives.[77]

Marriage in the pagan world far more often included child brides. These marriages were not just ceremonial. They were frequently "consummated at once, even when the girl had not yet reached puberty . . . There are reports of the defloration of wives as young as seven! This practice caused Plutarch to condemn Roman marriage customs as cruel, reporting 'the hatred and fear of girls forced contrary to nature.'"[78]

Stark confirms that infanticide of female offspring was widely practiced, and it likely fueled the need for child marriage.[79] Because of the sex-ratio imbalance, men made sure to secure a virgin bride as soon as possible. The best estimates were 131 men to every 100 women in the ancient Roman world.[80]

The Apostle Paul, after the Holy Spirit prevented him from bringing the Gospel to Asia (Acts 16:6), went west into this Greco-Roman world on mission. Given the state of the culture and relationship norms, the attraction of Christ's message to many men and women must have been magnetic. In radical contrast to pagan marriage and the pagan view of the sexes, Christian marriage held out an equality between the sexes. In Chapter 2, we reviewed the Apostle Paul's Letter to the Ephesians, where he lays out his principle of mutual submission for Christian spouses: "Submit to one another out of reverence for Christ" (Ephesians 5:21).

The Apostle Paul goes on to describe marriage as an icon of Christ's love for the Church and the Church's love for Christ. For Paul, being "subject to one another" meant that, while wives were to be subject to their husbands, men had a parallel obligation to love them in imitation of Christ in His love for the Church. Paul also provided women an equivalency in the idea of their conjugal rights (1 Corinthians 7:3). Even Paul's mutual prohibition on divorce in the same chapter (1 Corinthians 7:10-11) elevated the wife in dignity and prevented her from being abandoned. Our modern ears miss how revolutionary these teachings were. Christ's sacrificial death and role as the suffering servant must have taken on a powerful meaning to men and women in the ancient world. It was absolutely radical—and remains radical today.

> *Christ's sacrificial death and role as the suffering servant must have taken on a powerful meaning in the ancient world. It was absolutely radical—and remains radical today.*

Because of this Christian perspective on sex and marriage, Stark writes, very few Christian girls suffered similar fates of child marriage. "Most married when they were physically and emotionally mature; most had a say in whom they married and enjoyed a far more secure marriage."[81] The earliest catechetical instruction outside of Scripture—the Didache or the Teaching, which most scholars believe was written during the first century of Christianity and might predate or at least be written contemporaneously with some of the works of the New Testament—explicitly forbids the killing of a child after birth or through abortion.[82] This meant girls were not being exposed or killed off in infancy. There were no Christian women dying horrible deaths due to a husband-forced abortion in the ancient world. As a consequence of this, there were no sex-ratio differences within Christian communities.

This openness to life, this upholding of the equality of the sexes and the great good of marriage, sharply contrasted to the pagan Romans:

> The primary reason for low Roman fertility was that men did not want the burden of families and acted accordingly: many avoided fertility by having sex with prostitutes rather than with their wives or by engaging in anal intercourse. Many had their wives employ various means of contraception which were far more effective than had been thought until recently; and they had many infants exposed. Pagan husbands also often forced their wives to have abortions—which also added to female mortality and often resulted in subsequent infertility.[83]

Contrary to modern stereotypes, sex in early Christianity was held up as a great good and celebrated within marriage. The willingness to have and accept children—both baby boys and baby girls—was revolutionary. Stark recounts that ancient Christian tombs just as frequently bear memorials and tributes to the women laid in them as to the men, a practice that was a complete anomaly in the Greco-Roman world. In fact, the few ancient examples of works written by women are almost exclusively from Christian women of that era. *The Passions of Saints Perpetua and Felicity* is one such example. This text comes from a journal kept by Perpetua and recounts her imprisonment and persecution in North Africa during the early 200s A.D. For centuries, her diary was read during liturgies.[84] It is impossible to imagine the work of women being so upheld elsewhere in the world at that time.

This equal dignity that the Gospel gave women can be seen later in the early Church. St. Augustine of Hippo, most likely arguing against the still smoldering Gnostic heresy that denied that Christ came in the flesh, argued that God's incarnation through Mary, a woman, ought to destroy the pagan world's view of women: "That dispensation did honor to both sexes, male and female, and showed that both had a part in God's care; not only that which he assumed but that also through which he assumed it, being a man born of a woman."[85]

These substantial relational advantages of Christianity over the pagan world-views, Stark believes, contributed to the Christian conversion of the Roman world. Truly, women flocked to Christianity. So, in essence, we have a leading secular scholar concluding through his research that it was the dignity with which women were held, the relationship health of the early Christians, and the health of their marriages that provided the fuel for the conversion of ancient Rome.

This triumph of Christian marriage largely lasted until the twentieth century. This is not to say that Christian marriages always lived up to the high ideals of the Gospel. This is also not to say that men and women did not suffer at times in bad marriages and relationships. We know that on this side of eternity, humans will experience suffering, and, oftentimes, our own sin can be the cause of the sufferings of others.

However, while the world between the 4th century and the 20th was far from perfect, this shouldn't obscure the fact that the 20th century experienced a decoupling of sex from marriage that had not been seen since ancient times. Western culture, and the Church, has been living through the fallout ever since. Our failure to grasp and adequately minister to this new social reality is disrupting the spread of the Gospel.

How Churches Today Can Spread the Gospel: Healthy Relationships

To renew the Church and spread the Gospel in the 21st century, the Church today should take encouragement from the example of the early Christians. By systematically focusing on improving relationship health both within our memberships and within our surrounding communities, we can produce a great revival in the life of the Church and our nation.

Now, many may believe that the Church is already engaged in this arena. We cannot emphasize enough that this perception is one of the primary barriers to producing change. Many believe marriage ministry is the norm in churches today.

As John and JP began to look at this issue more deeply, we were struck by how few pastors believe there is a gap here in their church's ministry. LifeWay Research conducted a survey in 2015 that found most Protestant pastors believe they are already doing a good job within ministry to marriages:

- 75 percent agree their church provides enough help for married couples;
- 65 percent agree their church provides enough help for people who have divorced;
- 89 percent agree their church invests in the health of marriages.[86]

Great news if true. But is it accurate?

To drill down and answer this question more substantively, my (JP's) organization, Communio, reached out to the Barna Group in 2019 to commission a new survey of pastors—statistically representative of Evangelical, mainline, and Catholic churches—to better understand how the Church overall is investing in different ministries. Where does the focus on marriage stack up?

In the survey, 63 percent of Evangelical pastors reported having an ongoing marriage ministry. Just 35 percent of mainline and 39 percent of Catholic pastors said the same thing. But once you scratched under the surface, you started to see that what these churches believed was an ongoing marriage ministry was in many ways ephemeral.

Now, we saw in Chapter 2 that 99 percent of Evangelical churches, 90 percent of mainline, and 78 percent of Catholic churches reported having an ongoing youth ministry. In fact, 73 percent of all churches reported paying someone to run the youth ministry. As we saw there, the investment of staff time and dollars in youth remains substantial, running into the billions on an annual basis.

But answers to our follow-up questions for pastors—on what they consider to be marriage ministry, what staffing they allocate to it, and what resources they spend on it—made painfully clear that churches' overall perceptions on marriage ministry does not align with reality.

Just 28 percent of Protestant churches and 24 percent of Catholic parishes had a substantive marriage ministry. In all, 85 percent of all churches reported spending *nothing*, zero percent of their annual budget, on marriage. There was very little difference between Evangelical and Catholic churches in this regard. Just 24 percent of churches allocated any portion of a staff member's time to running a marriage ministry—and almost none allocated a full-time staff member to marriage ministry.

In the survey, Barna laid out a list of eleven potential activities that churches could engage in within the realm of encouraging or strengthening marriages. Six of those activities were deemed less substantive. These were things that required little effort or that every church could and should be doing (such as preaching on marriage, reactively offering pastoral counseling when a couple asks for it, referring couples to professionals, or having marriage books on hand). The other five were substantive marriage ministry activities:

• Hosting marriage retreats;

• Hosting marriage workshops or seminars;
• Hosting date nights;
• Having couples' groups;
• Training and equipping mentors for married couples.

Of these activities, only 14 percent of mainline Protestant pastors, 24 percent of Catholic pastors, and 33 percent of Evangelical pastors said they did more than two on an annual basis. And, to emphasize the facts once more: 94 percent of mainline churches, 82 percent of Catholic parishes, and 80 percent of Evangelical churches indicated that they spent zero percent of their annual budget on marriage ministry or relationship ministry.

The neglect goes even deeper. Because relationship health is important for everyone, we wanted to see what churches were doing for singles, who must navigate the dating landscape we walked through in some detail in Section I. In our age of smartphones, Tinder, social media, and ubiquitous pornography, many young adults simply no longer know how to date. The culture is now destroying marriages before they can even form.

So, are churches leaning into this crisis in any practical way?

In a word, no.

Just 1 percent of mainline pastors, 8 percent of Catholic pastors, and 10 percent of Evangelical pastors reported having any sort of ministry for singles.

Clearly, there is a huge ministry gap on all fronts regarding relationship ministry. But if it is filled effectively and strategically, the Church can renew the world.

To me, this is a reason for tremendous hope.

If marital and relationship health was this bad, and the Church was already allocating tremendous resources and attention to this area, this book would have a fairly abrupt ending. I'd pivot toward advice on where you and I might consider building a bunker to ride out the inevitable societal collapse that would follow.

Since, thankfully, this is not the case, the fact of the matter is that there are vast opportunities for the Church to invest in singles and couples. Think about it: What if the Church allocated the type of time and attention to marriage that it

The Church must recognize that this is the great battle of this new millennium.

applies today to youth ministry?

Perhaps some in the Church fear such a shift in emphasis, because it might hit too close to home or tread on what feels like very personal ground. Whatever the reason for the collective inaction here, the Church must recognize that *this is the great battle of this new millennium.*

In a very real sense, the battle has been underway and intensifying for the past sixty years—and the Church has chosen not to enter the fray in any practical pastoral way. This fact shouldn't discourage us, however. Across Christian history, we see that the Church typically responds to a challenge after the threat arises. And, because of the gifts of the Holy Spirit, when the Church gets engaged, change happens:

- When many challenged the divinity of Jesus Christ and the co-equal and co-eternal nature of the divine persons of the Trinity, the early Church called councils to successfully address the challenge.[87]
- When plagues devastated the ancient and medieval world, Christians created hospitals. The modern hospital is quite literally a Christian invention.
- When civilization in the West collapsed under the force of Barbarian invasions, it was the Church that preserved the Holy Scriptures as well as the learnings and wisdom of the ancient world through the formation of monasteries and our earliest universities.

In America, the second Great Awakening addressed the greatest social challenges in our history:

- Slavery: Evangelical Christians largely combated the challenge of slavery by creating the abolition movement.[88]
- Illiteracy: Most Americans were illiterate in the early 19th century, and only half of all American children received formal education. Without any widespread public education and almost exclusively through the

proliferation of Protestant Sunday schools, America became the most literate nation on earth in the second half of the 1800s.[89]

- Widespread alcoholism: In the early 1800s, the average American consumed the equivalent of a bottle and a half of standard 80-proof liquor every single week. One historian said of the period that "Americans drank from the crack of dawn to the crack of dawn." The Church met this challenge as largely Evangelical Christians organized the temperance movement, which brought alcohol consumption down 81 percent by the later 1800s.[90]

Perhaps the single biggest threat today to the Church is the wrongheaded belief of too many in the Church that the Gospel no longer has power. The decline of marriage and relationship health is a massive threat. But clearly, the Church has solved seemingly impossible issues in the past.

In fact, the Church has already demonstrated it can move the needle in this area as well.

> Perhaps the single biggest threat today to the Church is the wrongheaded belief of too many in the Church that the Gospel no longer has power.

The Jacksonville Transformation

Jacksonville, Florida, is not a small town. The city and county merged governments and it now claims nearly a million residents. What most people don't know is that the city has been historically bad for marriage. It has had the highest divorce rate among all large Florida counties (with populations of 300,000 and above) for forty of the prior forty-four years. Since the advent of no-fault divorce in Florida, Jacksonville had *never* had an annual divorce rate lower than the statewide divorce rate. This ignominy earned it the distinction of being declared the sixth-worst city in America for marriage in 2014, according to *Men's Health* magazine. If there's a place that stands in need of robust marriage ministry, it's Jacksonville, Florida.

Having left the political world in January of 2013 to focus on working as the chief operating officer and later the executive vice president at The Philanthropy Roundtable, I really wanted to understand how we could improve society-wide measures of faith practice and family stability. In working with serious business leaders and philanthropists, I saw how frequently they want to put their dollars where they can make the most difference. So I created a bold test project that would run major philanthropic experiments to measurably increase the number of kids living with both married parents and the number of people regularly attending church.

Starting in 2013, we spent the entire year studying the sector of relationship and marital health to understand what gaps existed. Our team, motivated by our faith, wanted to bring the best techniques from the realms of business and politics to baptize and sanctify them and leverage them for the Kingdom. And so, from 2014 to 2015, we commissioned the Right Brain People studies, funded Mark Regnerus's research, and even developed the world's first predictive data models for ministry. We asked modeling companies to create models that would help us understand which couples were most at-risk for divorce in the county, and who among the unchurched was most amenable to invitations to attend church. I brought on a former pastor who had a background in using predictive analytics in college admissions and asked him to help oversee the development of this capability.

We called this project the Culture of Freedom Initiative because we wanted to make the case that the future of a healthy and free society was actually wrapped up in the virtues of strong marriages, families, and churches. In all, we raised more than $20 million in risk capital for a three-year experiment to find out what did and did not work for strengthening marriages and increasing church engagement on a citywide level. We worked in Dayton, Ohio; Jacksonville, Florida; and Phoenix, Arizona. Our core strategic assumption was that authentic life change only comes about through personal relationship—and there is no more life-changing relationship than the one with Jesus Christ. And so, our goal was to scale the number of life-changing relationships that could exist within a given city around the context of marital health.

The initiative approached each city very differently and tested different strategies. We also blended Church, parachurch, and nonchurch partners.

In all, we formed fifteen different grant partnerships with organizations we internally called "City Champions" but who were largely content authors and generators.

I can tell you with confidence, we have learned that there are many things that do not work . . . at all.

We approached the process as one of trial and error. We knew we would make mistakes. But we wanted to fail fast and continue to iterate. Some of the biggest mistakes involved helping churches move people into relationship ministries far too quickly. We tried using digital advertising with microtargeting to encourage a large scale of high-risk folks to run directly into skills-based programs.

When I put it down on paper with the benefit of hindsight, I expect it's obvious to anyone reading this why that didn't work.

Well, we definitely weren't as smart as you.

You couldn't leverage a cutting-edge marketing tool on behalf of a church to invite someone who had no relationship with a person at the church to sign up and attend what was essentially an eight-hour class. There was far too much spinach in that offer for a first-time interaction. In our first year of operation, we learned that lesson the hard way.

Another mistake we made involved content. Good content was important, of course, but we learned that content generators were largely ineffective at moving their resources efficiently with a geographic focus. Every content partner—except one, Alpha—missed its targets.

But, thanks be to God, we did find strategies that did work. And Jacksonville is where the project hit pay dirt.

First, we had two phenomenal in-state strategists, Dennis Stoica and Richard Albertson of Live the Life. In all, the Culture of Freedom Initiative worked with ninety-three churches in Jacksonville County. It was representative of the entire Christian Church—we had Baptist churches, Catholic parishes, community Bible churches, and mainline church partners. We also worked with a number of secular nonprofits and local faith-based nonprofits in the county.

In all, the initiative moved 58,912 people through four-hour or longer classes across the county from January 2016 through December 2018. We did not dictate which skills-based relationship health classes were utilized. When we reviewed the academic literature for evidence-based curricula, we realized that a number of effective tools already existed. This included facilitator-led tools like Live the Life's Adventures in Marriage class or Richard Marks's marriage intensives. It also included some great plug-and-play content like the Marriage Course by Alpha or Oxygen for Your Relationship. So instead of dictating content, we served churches in helping them make loads of digital impressions in the community, drawing folks to different date night events to build up the marriage ministries they chose.[91]

Researchers conducted their own independent evaluations and concluded that there was no demographic explanation for the decline other than our initiative's intervention.

During that three-year period, the divorce rate plummeted 24 percent. For the first time since the advent of no-fault divorce in Florida, Jacksonville's divorce rate fell below the state average. In fact, over that timespan it became the county with the *lowest* divorce rate among all large counties in Florida.

Dr. Brad Wilcox, the academy's leading expert on marriage, and several other researchers conducted their own independent evaluations of our work and concluded that there was no demographic explanation for the decline other than our initiative's intervention.[92]

The Thirty-three Church Experiment

Measurably shifting family dynamics was great, but our board was convinced that we needed this work to become rapidly scalable. So we sought to understand how this work actually impacted churches. To that end, we funded a partnership with the Leadership Network, in which they helped us pull together a group of churches and oversaw a test in which we helped churches make use of data insights for outreach with a focus on relationship ministry and millennial engagement. The group of thirty-three churches included

Evangelical, mainline, and majority-black churches.

I grant you that, in ministry, the most important results are not ones anyone on this earth can count or measure. True conversion in Jesus Christ is not something that can be weighed or independently evaluated. As a consequence, you are left with tracking crude proxies to try to understand whether the Church is gaining ground or retreating. Recognizing this, we settled on indicators that were quick and measurable related to attendance and generosity. We knew these numbers were proxies, limited in what they could tell us. But at least they were objective and easily verifiable.

The coalition of churches in the test grew in sustained average Sunday attendance over the two-year project by 10,019 people. This was a 22.9 percent increase in the average attendance across the thirty-three churches. Their average weekly giving increased by $381,379, or 28 percent.[93]

Identifying this growth was critically important to the scalability of the initiative. For while philanthropy may have helped us identify and kick-start the initiative, we provided pastors with a powerful incentive to continue it by showing that developing a data-informed relationship ministry focus could allow them to reach more souls for Jesus Christ and grow their churches. Voluntary church adoption could then become the mechanism to replicate and scale the ministry.

Going to Scale

Our team had validated a new strategic approach to strengthening marriage at a city-wide and church-wide scale. We now wanted to spark a national renewal of the family through the Gospel, and this required making a big shift. The initiative could no longer be a project of The Philanthropy Roundtable.

With the support of the Roundtable, our staff and donors decided it was time to spin off completely. We had formed a separate 501(c)(3) organization in 2017 to help execute the experiment, so now we changed the name of our initiative to Communio. It had recently become common for technology companies to have an -io ending and the internet domain for technology companies is .io. The name, of course, is Latin for community, and there are no two pillars of community more important than strong families and strong faith.

We called our strategic framework the Data-Informed, Full-Circle Relationship Ministry®. By "Data-Informed" we mean using data to diagnose relationship health challenges in a church's membership and in the surrounding community. We also mean using the best data to drive participation from the unchurched in your new ministry. By "Full-Circle" we mean applying ministry outreach, engagement, and skills-based strategies at every stage of relationship life to maximize the number of people who could live a healthy life. Right out of the blocks, this would include a deliberate focus on single life—those never married and those who were single again. It had become clear to us that this was a critical gap in current ministry: Almost the entire marriage movement has focused on the currently-married or the engaged.

Communio's work with churches to develop ministry strategies around single life brought us into a great partnership with my co-author, John Van Epp. His singles and marriage courses had been taught to over a million people, with published research validating the positive improvements they make in dating practices and marriage relationships. And John had combined these programs into a relationship series that would involve the entire church. This series, like all his courses, was built around his Relationship Attachment Model (RAM), a tool that we immediately recognized as having tremendous utility for all of our client churches.

His six-week churchwide RAM Series provides curricula to children and youth ministry right up to and through adult ministries, including Sunday messages. It is a full church resource, and we pulled it into our consulting relationship with our largest church partner—LCBC in Lancaster, Pennsylvania.

LCBC is the largest Evangelical church in the Quaker State, with 17,000 average weekly attendees across fifteen different campuses. Their vibrant and growing church needed a resource that was not just for the married people who attended. We helped them select the RAM Series and design a Ministry Engagement Ladder® for their church that would allow LCBC to not only transform the relationships in their membership, but to reach out into their surrounding communities to transform central and southwest Pennsylvania. Near Valentine's Day, 2020, just a few weeks before the pandemic started, our team assisted LCBC in holding its largest ever date night to kick off their new focus on healthy relationships. More than 6,200 attended—38 percent of whom were first-time ever guests.

In addition to our work with individual churches, Communio has also begun four new city-wide initiatives in small and large size cities: Billings, Montana; Midland and Odessa, Texas; Fort Worth, Texas; and Denver, Colorado. These initiatives encompass work with Catholic, Evangelical, and mainline churches interested in strengthening marriages and relationships. Client churches today span all four US time zones, with interest increasing internationally from Singapore, Canada, Europe, and Australia.

The fields are white for the harvest (see John 4:35).

* * *

A QUICK RECAP

- Christians need to look back and reclaim their own history to understand that it was the example of Christian marriage and healthy relationships in the early Church that substantially converted the pagan world.

- By systematically focusing on improving relationship health both within our memberships and within our surrounding communities, we can produce a great revival in the life of the Church and our nation.

- Just 28 percent of Protestant churches and 24 percent of Catholic parishes had a substantive marriage ministry. In all, 85 percent of all churches reported spending zero percent of their annual budget on marriage. Just 24 percent allocated any portion of a staff member's time to running a marriage ministry—and almost none allocated a full-time staff member to marriage ministry.

- Just 1 percent of mainline pastors, 8 percent of Catholic pastors, and 10 percent of Evangelical pastors reported having any sort of ministry for singles.

- Clearly, there is a huge ministry gap on all fronts regarding relationship ministry. If it is filled effectively and strategically, the Church can renew the world.

- This is a reason for tremendous hope. What if the Church allocated the type of time and attention to marriage that it applies today to youth ministry?

- The Church has been at its best when faced with great challenges. The

Church has handled Trinitarian heresies and ancient plagues. More recently, it led the abolitionist movement, reduced widespread alcoholism in the 19th century, and made America the most literate nation on earth.

- An ecumenical group of Baptist, Catholic, and other Evangelical churches worked with Communio to lower the divorce rate by 24 percent in just three years in Jacksonville, Florida.
- Churches focusing on marriage and relationship ministry isn't just good for the community—it's good for spreading the Gospel. These churches grew substantially!
- The fields are white for the harvest (see John 4:35).

CHAPTER 9

Healthy Relationships Require Intentional Management

I (John) was at a marriage and healthy relationship conference about fifteen years ago. I was eating dinner with many of the keynote speakers and conference leaders. These were well-known authors, university and seminary professors, and researchers in the field of relationships. There was a question that had been rolling around in my head for quite some time about relationships, and so I asked it aloud: "Could you say, in one sentence, what exactly is a *healthy relationship?*"

This term had been referenced in every presentation. It was the perennial gold standard by which programs and relationships, especially marriage relationships, were measured. But what had been bugging me was that no one ever seemed to define what exactly a healthy relationship is.

It was interesting to watch everyone toss their opinions into the ring as my question set off more of a brainstorming session rather than a single-sentence definition. They all had good input, but when the discussion was done, we were left with a laundry list of characteristics rather than a consensus on a succinct meaning of the term.

Was this merely an intellectual exercise? Hardly. If we do not understand something, then it is hard to deal with it effectively. This problem is common in therapy, where clients are often confused about what they are feeling and why. During my twenty-five years of counseling, I would sometimes see this and explain, *without clear definition there can be no transformation.*

Let me give you an example. One of my clients, let's call him Geoff, kept saying he was depressed. But it seemed to me that he was struggling more with feeling angry and powerless at work because of a supervisor who had been holding him back from being promoted for years. When I reframed his depression as a feeling of powerless rage, the light bulb came on for him. Almost immediately, his depressed feelings of being stuck were replaced with a sense of empowerment.

"Now I get it!" Geoff exclaimed. "I am not so much depressed . . . I am torqued because for years I have been overlooked and I have been just stuffing it, pretending everything is fine. But now, I am going to do something about it." After discussing it more, he continued, "Here are my choices: I can stay in my job and make my peace with my position; I can confront my boss and tell him why I deserve a promotion; or I can look for another job. But what I *cannot* do is say that I don't understand why I feel so unmotivated."

A healthy relationship is a relationship bond that is intentionally managed with genuine relationship virtues and proficient relationship skills.

Only when Geoff could define his experience could he design his choices. As long as he was clueless, he was powerless. Definition empowers transformation.

So, I must tackle my own question: In just one sentence, what exactly is a healthy relationship? *A healthy relationship is a relationship bond that is intentionally managed with genuine relationship virtues and proficient relationship skills.*

Imbedded in this definition are four major ingredients of healthy relationships that church teachings and ministries must consistently strengthen:

1. Healthy relationships require intentional management;
2. Healthy relationships consist of strong bonds;
3. Healthy relationships express genuine virtues;
4. Healthy relationships exercise proficient skills.

It is important to note that all four ingredients are included in every type of relationship. A *relationship type* is a status of a relationship like marriage, dating, parent-child, family, friend, acquaintance, or business.

Churches primarily pay attention to relationship types. It is common for a sermon series, Bible studies, or even some ministries to focus on only one

You would devise the best plays for a strategic offense and defense, require your athletes to learn your playbook, and drill them on the skills needed to perform at their best.

As with office managing, coaching would require you to personally know each player, their strengths and weaknesses, and exactly how to bring out the best in them. You would instill attitudes of trust and respect, cooperation, and commitment. You would establish regular team meetings to help them through conflicts, hear what they need, and build strong bonds.

Imbalances Are Normal in Healthy Relationships

If the first reality of relationships is that they do not run themselves, then the second reality is that relationships do not fix themselves.

All relationships slowly deflate in strength and regularly need adjusting. They are thriving one minute and then waning the next. It is as though relationships have appetites—it is normal for them to feel full and satisfied when essential needs are fed, but then they get hungry again as new needs arise.

Let's say you are promoted to a new position that requires travel. With the blessings of advancement and increased income comes the curse of time away from your spouse and children. Next thing you know, one of your teenage kids walks by you, heading off to their room, and it hits you: *"I feel like I don't even know them anymore!"*

My (John's) wife, Shirley, told me one day how much she loves and misses me. But not exactly in those words. It was when the UPS driver came to the door and I jumped up and said, "Oh, don't let him leave—I need to talk with him." Shirley mumbled under her breath, "Isn't he lucky to get a minute of your time."

Now some of you may think that an off-handed remark like that is a criticism. But I know that it came from a heart of love that was just struggling with the insanity of a hectic schedule that had squeezed out all our time to be together, talking, planning, thinking out loud . . . and simply catching up with what had been happening in each of our lives. Let me explain.

We were anticipating this stress because I had just revised seven workbooks used in two of my relationship courses, and so now I needed to update the 350 pages of lesson plans and all the PowerPoints and redo the twenty-some hours of filming to match the new changes. All of this needed to be done yesterday to have a smooth transition from the previous edition to the new, and we were all geared up to meet the challenge. But then a couple of unforeseen events took our stress to an entirely new level.

First, our youngest daughter (23 years old at the time) was diagnosed with three pulmonary emboli and hospitalized for two weeks (thank God, she has healed beautifully since then). Then eight days later my stepmom passed away unexpectedly in her sleep. Eight out of the nine siblings and their families converged within a week to mourn this loss. We hosted several of our out-of-town family members and then provided a memorial dinner for forty in our home. Needless to say, it was a very exhausting and emotional month for all of us with little time for Shirley and me to just be alone together.

Since this challenging time, which occurred several years ago, I frequently think of the tagline "Life comes at you fast." I find myself echoing those words as life speeds up, turns a corner, and new challenges emerge. And I have become convinced that the "balanced relationship" is an illusion.

There is no couple that "arrives" at some perfect balance that allows them to sit back and coast for the next fifty years. Just about the time they feel that they have a routine that is working for their relationship . . . *life comes at them fast.*

Identify the small leaks before they lead to big blowouts.

Couples who have been able to maintain a strong and close relationship over the rocky terrain of life did not accomplish it by achieving some higher-order, balanced state that immunized them against the ills of the world. Instead, they stayed in charge of running their relationships, identifying the small leaks before they led to big blowouts.

Too many times, relationships are presented in one of two categories: healthy or unhealthy, functional or dysfunctional, good or bad. And the implication is that if your relationship is *healthy*, then it will have no deficits or imbalances!

This misrepresentation of the "healthy relationship" is a myth that conjures up insecurity, guilt, and unrealistic expectations. We must hammer home this reality: Normal, healthy, functional, and good relationships regularly go out of balance.

I can say, with confidence, that *no relationship (or marriage) is truly balanced.* I would not be surprised if many of you have just breathed a sigh of relief at the thought that it is normal to become imbalanced. I must admit, I too found relief in accepting that all relationships—and especially my marriage—are destined for times of imbalance.

I prefer to use the word *balancing* rather than balanced. Healthy relationships are balancing relationships. It is counterproductive to suggest that there is a state of relationship health that a marriage can attain that then requires no more effort . . . "We have arrived; we are balanced; we have a healthy relationship."

It was *normal* that Shirley and I had three unrelated but overwhelmingly emotional and stressful situations happen at the same time. (It is so common that there is an old saying that "bad things come in threes.")

It would have been impossible to stay "balanced" in key areas of our relationship over those months, in our time together, our communication, our romance, and most every other area. We became imbalanced because of unavoidable priorities outside of our relationship that life naturally brought. This is normal. It is not bad.

In other words, it is just a matter of time before you experience some disruptions in your relationship routine—a birth of a child, a job change, a new stage of parenting, a disability or illness, the loss of a loved one, the holiday crazies . . . the causes are endless.

This is what happens in all relationships—with spouses, children, friendships, even our relationship with God. This is why we are warned to guard our hearts (Proverbs 4:23), stand firm in our faith (1 Corinthians 16:13), and renew our first love for Christ whenever it slips (Revelation 2:4-5).

This is why you must "intentionally manage" your relationship with God. You do this when you prioritize consistent reading of Scripture and other devotional literature, engage regularly in prayer and worship, and share with others within the body of Christ. These are some of the actions that maintain the

There is no relationship that runs itself, including our relationship with Christ.

strength of your relationship with God.

But if we are honest, all of us have had times when our "intentional management" is crowded out by other commitments, obligations, sins, and the busyness of life. We then realize we have drifted, neglected our spiritual practices, and consequently, need to take steps to renew our walk with God. There is no relationship that runs itself, including our relationship with Christ.

Relationships Are Empowered by God, but Run by Us

The Apostle Paul's Epistle to the Philippians contains the most profound description of Christ's humility. He explained that Jesus had existed from all eternity with all the rights and privileges of Deity. However, Jesus did not consider equality with God something to hold in His grasp, but instead, He chose to give it up to take on our humanity so that He could secure our salvation through the most humiliating of deaths, death on a cross (Philippians 2:5-8).

Theologians have aptly called this Christological gem the single greatest description of the incarnation; the condescension of the Second Person of the Trinity into human nature. When these verses are examined in the original Greek text, they appear in the form of a hymn and were likely sung by the early Church.

But aside from the unfathomable depth of this depiction of Christ's loving humility, this passage from Philippians is most immediately about our *human* relationships with each other. These are the words that precede it: *"In your relationships with one another, have the same mindset as Christ Jesus."* And that exhortation is preceded in turn by four verses encouraging humble, selfless attitudes and actions in your relationships with others.

This context explains the point Paul was making: If *God Himself* was willing to humble Himself, putting aside all His divine rights and privileges, and, purely out of love, to die for undeserving people . . . then *how much more should you* practice humility and selfless love in your relationships with others!

It culminates with a powerful conclusion about *how* you can attain this quality of relationships with others:

> Therefore, my dear friends, as you have always obeyed—not only in my presence, but now much more in my absence—continue to **work out** your salvation with fear and trembling, for it is God who **works in you** to will and to act in order to fulfill his good purpose (Philippians 2:12-13).

When I was in seminary, it was common to hear a professor say, "Whenever in Scripture you see the word, 'therefore,' you need to know what it is 'there for.'" In this passage, the word, "therefore" is used to highlight the logical conclusion of *how to* bring about the *ought to* that just preceded it.

In this conclusion, Paul emphasized that internalizing a Christlike attitude of humility and selfless love in your relationships must ultimately be a joint effort between you and God. It doesn't "just happen" without intentionality and hard work. And even though you fully trust and rely on God, it will never happen unless you do your part.

We need to conduct a quick Greek word study and compare the two translations of the word "work," so that we can better understand the balance between God's work and the effort we humans put into our spiritual growth in general and our relationships specifically.

When we read, "for it is God who *works* in you," the Greek word is *energeo*—from which we get the word "energy." God promises to energize you; according to this verse, God is infusing energy into your willpower and ability to act so that you can fulfill His good purposes of agape love in your relationships, which is clearly the contextual emphasis.

You might conclude that you have no responsibility in this process beyond relying on God's power, except that promise is preceded by a related command: "Continue to *work out* your salvation with fear and trembling."

This is a different Greek word for "work"—it is *katergazomai*, which means "to perform or execute a task, to accomplish or achieve something, to labor and bring about results."[94] God may be energizing you, but you need to be putting forth the effort to make it happen.

Let's now put our understanding of these two Greek words in context with the entire flow of this passage. The Apostle Paul is clearly instructing Christians in how to create and maintain relationships, emphasizing that they can only be successfully managed with a balance between God's resources and our responsibilities.

The entire discourse in Philippians 2 begins with a quick Pauline overview of God's resources for healthy and godly relationships—*"Therefore if you have any encouragement from being united with Christ, if any comfort from His love, if any common sharing in the Spirit, if any tenderness and compassion . . ."*—and then immediately shifts to the human responsibility of putting in the work to make relationships Christlike: *"Then make my joy complete by being like-minded, having the same love, being one in spirit and of one mind. Do nothing out of selfish ambition or vain conceit. Rather, in humility value others above yourselves, not looking to your own interests but each of you to the interests of the others."* [95]

> You need to take responsibility to mine out all that God has deposited in you from your salvation experience, the practical skills and virtues needed to run your relationships.

A classic "if . . . then" logic structures the passage. The Apostle Paul introduces the subject of relationships by pointing out that God has done His part, so now we must do ours. Then, in the verses that follow (verses 5-11), Paul conducts the hymn that we previously mentioned of Christ's humility and sacrificial love, the ultimate illustration of what we need to do in our relationships.

Finally, in his dramatic conclusion in verse 12, Paul hammers home his point that God has provided us with the energizing resources for transformative relationships, but it is our responsibility to put in the work to intentionally manage those relationships so that they fulfill God's design.

William Barclay explained that the Greek word used for "working out" our salvation was cited in the ancient writing of Strabo, a Roman scholar, around sixty years prior to Christ. He was writing about Roman soldiers who were laboring in the mines in Spain, and he used this word to refer to their work of "digging and extracting" silver from the depths of the earth.[96]

I like that imagery. Essentially, then, Paul is saying, "You need to take responsibility to *mine out* all that God has deposited in you from your salvation experience, the practical skills and virtues needed to run your relationships in loving and Christlike ways."

A relationship does not run itself, nor does God run your relationships without your active participation. It may sound super-spiritual to say, "God does it all and all I do is yield to Him," but the Biblical reality is that God has called you to dig in, mine out, and make quality relationships happen.

* * *

A QUICK RECAP

- Healthy relationships do not run themselves, nor do they fix themselves. They must be intentionally managed.
- There is a myth that, if a relationship is "good enough," then it will not require any effort to maintain.
- The closeness in even the best of healthy relationships naturally "deflates" over time, leading inevitably to imbalances that need to be recognized and corrected.
- For Christians, relationships are run in a joint effort between personal responsibility and effort along with Divine resources and empowerment.

CHAPTER 10

Healthy Relationships Consist of Strong Bonds

If we are to intentionally manage our relationships, then we need to have a clear understanding of what it is that we are managing. As we already said, without definition, there cannot be implementation! It is like having a job without a job description. So, what exactly *is* a relationship?

You might think this would be easy to define. However, most people fumble the definition of a relationship, giving answers that miss the mark and land in one of two categories. The first category is *relationship activities* like talking, listening, arguing, having fun, loving, or supporting . . . activities that you do in relationships. The second category is *relationship types* like marriage, friendship, acquaintances, associates, or some other type of relationship.

When you look up the word in the dictionary, you find that a relationship is defined as "a *connection* that occurs between two or more people."[97] But that is vague. Is there any way to identify the specific connections that comprise relationships? We believe there is.

Relationship Bonds

I (John) have devoted almost all my career to the development and application of a theoretical model of the universal connections or (as I prefer to call them) *relationship bonds* that comprise all relationships. Let me trace a bit of my history of trying to create this working model of a relationship.

During my graduate studies back in the mid-1980s, I found that there were large bodies of research and theory on major connections or bonds that occur in relationships. For instance, "trust" was evaluated and used in the titles of over 5,000 published research studies in scientific journals during the last century. It was included in every major psychological, sociological, and relationship theory, and had been a topic in countless books and articles.

Trust is one major element of human connection. In close relationships, it is absolutely vital for developing and maintaining feelings of security, intimacy, and safety. But trust was not the only connection I found. In fact, I found four other major types of connection that have generated similar amounts of research, theory, and practical self-help books. I will describe in detail all five later in this chapter, but for now, they are "know," "trust," "rely," "commit," and "touch."

I labeled these five major connections the *relationship bonds*, because they are found in all relationships and uniquely *contribute to the feeling of a bond* or closeness with another person. In some cases, each bond was presented in publications as synonymous with intimacy, or emotional closeness, or even love. But in all cases, each of these major connections was clearly shown to be a major source of bonding between two or more people.

A second common feature is that they all *exist in ranges*. Trust, for instance, is not an either/or experience in relationships, but rather it exists across a large range of differing levels, from extremely low to extremely high.

Finally, these connections *all interact with each other.* If one increases or decreases in strength, then it tends to impact the levels of the others. And whenever one or more is significantly out of balance with the others, then conflicting and confusing feelings occur in the relationship.

I wanted a model to visualize these five major relationship bonds and also capture the ways they interact and fluctuate. I designed this model to be true to this large body of theory and research, consistent with Scripture, and interactive and easy-to-understand.

The major bonds of relationships can be compared to a mixing board with five sliders, with each one having a similar range. The degree of strength of each relationship bond is represented by how far the slider is moved up.

Relationships can be compared to a mixing board with five sliders, with each one having a similar range.

I called my model the Relationship Attachment Model, or RAM for short (see Figure 10.1). Together, these five sliders provided an interactive portrayal of the five invisible bonds that comprise all relationships. And because it is interactive, it is possible to profile your relationship to depict the specific strengths as well as the areas of deficit.

Over the past three decades, the RAM has been empirically validated in both qualitative and quantitative peer-reviewed published studies. It has been the framework for all my relationship programs, with over a million participants having learned the RAM by taking my relationship courses in social agencies, churches, faith communities, and educational settings like high schools, undergraduate and graduate programs, counseling centers, and all branches of the military.

Figure 10.1

R.A.M.
**Relationship
Attachment Model**

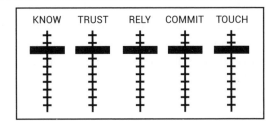

The Churchwide RAM Series

Needless to say, I think my Relationship Attachment Model is a highly valuable tool for use in church ministries. There is a catch, however: The RAM is *not* permitted to be taught or used without a license from Love Thinks (www.RAMseries.com).

Several years ago, I gave a presentation to the student body at the Naval Academy on the RAM as a tool that they can use in their dating relationships. My material was based on my *How to Avoid Falling for a Jerk (or Jerkette)* book and my relationship program by the same title. Little did I know, but the Admiral and her staff were sitting in the back, their attention riveted by my model.

As I was leaving the lecture hall, the Admiral asked if I would meet in the conference room with her and her staff. Once at the table, I was asked to briefly explain my theory behind the RAM and the practical value that it holds for all relationships.

I was not quite finished when the Admiral interrupted and, looking at her staff, said, "This is the perfect model to include in our leadership philosophy course!" Excited chatter immediately ensued. I was thrilled and petrified at the same time.

After swallowing hard, I respectfully explained that I would be honored to discuss ways that they can license the RAM to be used in their coursework, but that it is the copyrighted and trademarked bread and butter of my relationship programs, not public domain. Fortunately, they were quick to validate my concern, and very interested in talking further about how they could license my model.

The good news, though, is that churches can *also get a license* to use the RAM in their sermons and ministries (again at www.RAMseries.com). We have packaged the RAM in a six-week, churchwide series that includes sample sermon manuscripts, elementary and youth video-based curricula, and video-based small-group studies for couples and singles.

Churches have been using the RAM to bring together their entire church, from ages 5 to 105, in learning the same language for understanding and talking through their relationships with each other and even with God.[98]

In Chapter 8, we began to share the story of one church that worked with Communio to evaluate and set aggressive goals for improving the relationship health of their congregation and engaging in relationship outreach to their community. They licensed the RAM Series to kick off these goals and were able to engage more than 70 percent of their people (10,000+) with eight hours of relationship content. We'll revisit this church and its experience in our conclusion.

Relationships are complicated, and it is no wonder that people do not give much thought to what it means to manage their relationship.

Truth be told, relationships are complicated, and it is no wonder that people do not give much thought to what it means to manage their relationship. That is why people find a model that portrays the invisible and dynamic bonds of their relationships so helpful and empowering.

As I mentioned before, you can visualize these dynamic bonds as five channels on a mixing board, with each one contributing its own unique tone. Put them all together, and the different levels mix into a single sound. In a similar way, the blend of the levels of the five relationship bonds will produce the "sound" of your relationship.

These five bonds exist in all relationships, including our relationship with God. Let me briefly explain each of them, and then offer a plan for intentionally managing your relationships.

Relationship Bond #1: Know

The first bonding connection is the degree to which you know someone. When you think of what it means to know someone, it certainly begins with knowing things *about* that person. But this surface knowledge is only part of what it means to fully know a person.

A Scriptural word study reveals two major aspects to the concept of *knowing*: factual awareness and emotional encounter. Factual awareness is the extent that you know the facts about someone's life, their experiences, feelings, and thoughts. But this can be a cold, distant, and uncaring awareness.

The second aspect, an emotional encounter, means that you are touched by what you intellectually understand. Your emotions and will are activated. What you "know" may make you feel happy or sad, relieved or agitated, assured or anxious. You have an encounter with the one you know. Another way to say this is that you *take to heart* what you learn about your someone.[99]

In Psalm 139, verses 1-4, we read:

You have searched me, Lord,
    and you know me.
You know when I sit and when I rise;
    you perceive my thoughts from afar.
You discern my going out and my lying down;
    you are familiar with all my ways.
Before a word is on my tongue
    you, Lord, know it completely.

Does this sound like objective, factual knowledge? No, it clearly is personal. God is interested in your motives, your actions, your thoughts, your words. He knows you because He has "encountered" you in all your ways, beginning with "knitting you together in the womb" (verse 13).

In verse 5, the Psalmist continues, "You hem me in behind and before, and you lay your hand upon me"—an image used to convey deep love and security. A small child will often become afraid in a public place when separated from a parent. But when the parent pulls the child into their blanketing arms, completely submerging the child in enveloping love, then fear melts into confidence. This is the imagery that is cast by the words, God has hemmed me in . . . and laid His hand upon me.

> God knows you because He has "encountered" you in all your ways.

I coined a term, the *Know-Quo* (short for quotient) that helps to simplify the equation for growing and staying in the know: Talk + Togetherness + Time. These 3Ts capture both the process of getting to know someone, and the necessary relational ingredients for staying in the know.

Obviously, *talking* is a prerequisite for getting and staying in the know. But great conversations need to be matched with quality *time* spent *together* in a variety of experiences, moods, and circumstances. In marriage, when you engage in all three, you move past just *knowing about* your spouse to bonding together in deep intimacy.

Tim Keller captured the heart of truly knowing a spouse when he wrote: "To be loved but not known is comforting but superficial. To be known and not loved is our greatest fear. But to be fully known and truly loved is, well, a lot like being loved by God. It is what we need more than anything." It takes all Ts to continue to "grow in the know" in healthy marriage relationships.

So, what about dating—how should a couple engage in the 3Ts there? I believe talking, togetherness, and time are especially important for singles to understand in their attempts to "get to know" a partner.

In the singles video-based small-group study included in the RAM Series, my daughter Dr. Morgan Cutlip and I talk about the ninety-day probation period. In the first couple of months of a new relationship, you often meet a dating partner's *representative*. Not until around the third month does the *real* person begin to show up. This is because the 3Ts are absolutely necessary for discovering the patterns and habits of a person. Talking needs to be backed up by togetherness in a diversity of situations and moods over a period of time long enough for patterns to slowly emerge.

Relationship Bond #2: Trust

The second relationship bond represented in the RAM is trust. Every relationship has some level of trust, and like with the other four bonds, trust is *not* an all-or-nothing experience. It ranges from extreme mistrust to extreme confidence.

Trust produces feeling of security, confidence, and safety. Trust says, "You can be open and vulnerable with this person; you can be yourself; you will not get hurt."

> *Trust is that feeling of confidence and security that flows from what you think of someone.*

But trust is more than just a *feeling*, it is a belief in another. Therefore, trust is that feeling of confidence and security that flows from what you *think* of someone. Your belief or opinion of someone is ultimately the generator of your feelings toward that person.

Let me give you two examples of how trust works, one from dating and another from marriage.

The trust-belief in another is like a mental profile of that person. In a new dating relationship, this profile is sketched quickly, and often inaccurately. In a new relationship, you take the few pieces of what you know about the other person and begin to construct a mental profile of who you believe them to be and how much you can trust them. Your mind determines the trustworthiness of that person in a manner similar to the work of a criminal profiler.

A profiler approaches a crime scene with an established set of standards to compare the evidence concerning the present crime with previously documented crime patterns. I am not suggesting that you are looking for a criminal, but your mind automatically *fills in the gaps* of what you do *not* know about this person with associations from previous people that you have known—e.g., "previously documented crime patterns." If this "hit" triggers positive associations, then you may sketch a glowing trust profile of them, when actually you do not know them at all! We will refer to this mental profile or representation of a person as your "trust-picture."

The point is this: Your initial trust-picture may end up being a complete misrepresentation of the real person. In my book *How to Avoid Falling In Love with a Jerk*, I go into great detail about how to construct an accurate trust-picture of a dating partner by exploring key areas of that partner while pacing all five relationship bonds in the RAM in safe ways (as I'll also explain, in slightly less detail, in the next section). Benjamin Franklin aptly described differences in how we should maintain trust in dating versus marriage when he wrote, "Before marriage, keep your eyes wide open; but afterwards, half shut."

You see, profiling your partner doesn't stop just because you are married. You continue to profile your spouse by taking what you know and organizing it in a mental portrait with some things about your partner in the foreground and others in the background. This mental representation or trust-picture is more like a caricature of your partner.

A caricature is a profile that exaggerates certain characteristics. For instance, caricatures have frequently been drawn of presidents over the years—Clinton's big nose, Obama's big ears, and Trump's "yuge" hair. These features are always out of proportion to the rest of the picture, because they bring to the forefront of our mind what some artist sees as the defining characteristic of that person.

In a similar way, every married person focuses on specific qualities of their spouse while minimizing others, creating a trust-picture that selectively magnifies certain qualities. This trust-picture then acts as the lens by which you sharpen the focus of your attitude toward the positive or negative.

Obviously, like all five of the relationship bonds, trust is a two-way street. But understanding how your feelings of confidence in someone are generated from what you focus on will empower you to be more intentional about how you build and maintain trust within your relationships.

Trust is a relationship bond that is woven in all relationships, including our relationship with God. We need to develop and maintain a trust-picture of God that accurately represents the God who has been revealed to us in the Bible. However, it is possible to have a distorted "God-image." This happens when your trust-picture of God has focused on only a few attributes of God, to the neglect of others. True spiritual growth should deepen an accurate knowledge of God and a correspondingly accurate trust-picture of God (see 1 John 2:12-14).

Within marriage, it is vital to maintain a secure trust. This means that you must give trust to a spouse, keeping a positive attitude toward them, focusing on their strengths, minimizing their weaknesses, forgiving their faults, and rebuilding your belief in them when it has been damaged.

> *It is possible to have a distorted "God-image."*

But trust also requires trustworthiness. Trust is *earned* when someone is there for you, stepping up to meet your needs, and doing what they promised. This is where the next relationship bond of reliance comes to play: Reliability is the proving ground of trust.

Relationship Bond #3: Rely

Trust is about the feelings of confidence that come from the way we think about someone, but "rely" is about the feelings of fulfillment that come from the way that needs are met—the ways that you depend on someone to meet your needs and wants, and that they depend on you.

When my daughters were growing up, they took their grades seriously. One of the things they both despised in school was those group projects in which their class grade would be determined by the work of the entire group. One afternoon, my youngest, Jessica, walked through the door after school with a scowl on her face.

"What's wrong?" I asked.

"I was assigned to work in a group with Sammie. And she never does her part. And our grade will be a group grade. So I am going to get a B or C, all because of Sammie. It is NOT fair!"

Jessica knew Sammie well enough to know that she could not be trusted to pull her weight. Her know-level of Sammie was high, her trust-level was low, but—here is the rub—Jessica's rely-level was super high—she had no choice but to rely on a group member that she did not trust. And that drove her crazy. You see, Jessica's trust was more about what she thought of Sammie, whereas her reliance was more about how she had to interact and depend on Sammie. In your relationships, maintaining a trust-belief in each other is vital, but it needs to be reinforced with the actions of reliance.

When you scan the online shelves for a good book on marriage, most of the best-sellers will be about this specific relationship bond: understanding and meeting the unique needs of your spouse. You will find books about the differences between men and women,[100] the key roles of a husband and wife in marriage,[101] and numerous templates for organizing the personal needs that should be met in a relationship.[102] The reason why there are so many books about this subject is that the relationship bond of reliance is one of the most powerful ways we feel loved and connected.

Every relationship has the relationship bond of reliance woven through its fabric. But when reliance is reciprocated, then the *mutual* meeting of needs will increase the equity and security experienced in your relationship.

Relationship Bond #4: Commit

Commitment is the relationship bond of investment, priority, dedication, obligation, and promise. Essentially, commitment is an act of your will on behalf of another. This means that your commitment can be measured by the ways that you consciously choose to do something for someone. Commitment says, "Show love even when you do not feel like it." It is driven by the value you place on a person and your willpower to manifest that value in concrete actions. Commitment, then is a major intersection between the five relationship bonds and relationship virtues, a topic we will discuss in the next chapter.

Commitment is an invaluable relationship bond within our marriages, families, friendships, work relationships, and faith communities. Commitment is woven throughout our relationships at work and at play—just check out how committed you are to your favorite sports teams! If you are like JP, then you have a special room in your house dedicated to the Florida Gators. Every relationship can be measured on the commitment scale, from only a little investment with low priority, to someone you would give your life to save.

The driving force of sacrificial commitment is at the heart of agape love. Jesus wrapped love and commitment together when He told His disciples, "My command is this: Love each other as I have loved you. Greater love has no one than this: to lay down one's life for one's friends" (John 15:12-13).

Second only to our commitment to Christ is the commitment we forge in marriage. This commitment is captured in the traditional marriage vows, "For better, for worse; for richer, for poorer; in sickness and in health; until death separates us."

We find profound evidence of the truth of this commitment beyond just the words of the marriage vows. A team of prominent social science researchers interviewed 645 spouses who rated their marriages as *unhappy* from data in the National Survey of Families and Households. Five years later, these same adults were interviewed, so that the researchers could compare the outcomes of the different paths that were taken by these unhappy spouses.[103]

Marital conflict and strife take a toll on psychological well-being. So you might well think that those individuals who were able to exit their unhappy marriages would be more likely to become happy in their own lives.

Instead, researchers found surprising outcomes that contradicted conventional wisdom, and supported the power of commitment in marriage. First, a majority of those who divorced were still unhappy five years later. But more than 65 percent of couples who were unhappy but remained married, reported that they had become happy just five years later.

What changed? Did anything really change, or was it just their perspective that changed? The researchers were unable to make absolute conclusions, but the odds were in favor of unhappy marriages becoming happy marriages in just five years. Even more convincing was the fact that "the *most unhappy* marriages reported the *most dramatic turnarounds.* Among those who rated their marriages as very unhappy, almost eight out of ten spouses who avoided divorce described themselves as happily married five years later."[104]

In your marriage—and, really, in all relationships—commitment enables perseverance, and perseverance allows for relational healing and redemptive shifts in perspectives, behaviors, and priorities.

Relationship Bond #5: Touch

On March 25, 2010, Kate and David Ogg rushed to the hospital. Kate knew her twins were in danger, as she was giving birth just twenty-seven weeks into her pregnancy. Their daughter, Emily, survived the premature birth, but her twin brother, Jamie, languished—and after twenty minutes of trying to get him to breathe, the doctors pronounced him dead.

After Kate was told Jamie did not make it, the nurses placed the newborn on Kate's bare chest, so Kate and David could say their goodbyes. Kate immediately instructed David to strip off his shirt and lie down in her bed to cocoon little Jamie between their bare bodies.

"I wanted to meet him and to hold him and for him to know us," Kate explained. "If he was on his way out of the world, we wanted for him to know who his parents were and to know that we loved him before he died."

Kate and David snuggled Jamie tightly between their chests, whispering soothing words over his tiny, two-pounds-and-three-ounces frame. But after about five minutes, something unexpected happened—Jamie moved, and after two hours of skin-to-skin contact, Jaime opened his eyes.

Kate and her husband sent for their doctor multiple times, who delayed attending because he thought they were holding on to false hopes that their baby was still alive. But when he finally arrived, he was shocked at the miraculous recovery.

Jamie is now eleven years old, and he and his twin sister are developmentally on track. The practice that Kate believes saved his life is called kangaroo care, or the skin-to-skin method, and it has been credited with dropping preemie mortality rates from 70 percent to 30 percent in the Australian town where it was first practiced.[105]

Loving touch has the power to heal and give life. Physical expressions of love create bonds from the moment we enter this world to the moment we depart. Through touch, we express love and affection to our families, affinity and support to our friends, loyalty and respect to our co-workers, encouragement and triumph to our teammates . . . the list is endless. It is through touch that we say hello and goodbye, that we encourage and discipline, that we celebrate and grieve; it is through touch that we soothe and heal emotions, loneliness, hurts, fears, and, in the case of Jamie, the threat of death.

Touch is the fifth universal relationship bond and one that has generated mountains of research in the sciences of psychology, sociology, and biology. Kory Floyd, a professor of communication at the University of Arizona, after studying the effects of what he called *skin hunger*, concluded that those who experienced insufficient amounts of affection were more lonely, depressed, had less social support, experienced more mood and anxiety disorders, and had a decreased ability to interpret and express emotions.

Touch also includes the entire arena of sexual attraction and interaction and, like affection, sexual touch is a major source of intimacy and bonding. As the Scriptures repeatedly and plainly explain, "The two shall become one flesh" (Genesis 2:24; Matthew 19:5).

This bonding power of sexual activity has been validated over and over in the field of neuroscience, with a plethora of studies conducted on the dramatic increase of oxytocin, just one of several brain chemicals that promote bonding during sex. This hormone floods the brains of both men and women (especially women) during the sexual act, greatly enhancing a bond that creates feelings of connection with a partner, longing for that partner when apart, and a sense of belonging with that partner.

The RAM and Our Relationship Bonds with God

These five relationship bonds are just as active in your relationship with God as they are in your relationship with other people. Stepping into a saving relationship with Christ requires some knowledge—you have to *get to know Christ* and then, to grow in that relationship, you must consider "everything a loss because of the surpassing worth of *knowing* Christ Jesus my Lord" (Philippians 3:8).

The God of eternity entered into the world of human touch through the Incarnation, and then took human touch back into eternity through the Resurrection.

But what you know cannot remain simply intellectual assent. It must lead to a deep trust—a belief.

And your belief must be one that prompts active steps of reliance, for as the Apostle James wrote, *"Faith by itself, if it is not accompanied by action, is dead."* (James 2:17).

Then there is the Lordship of Christ. Your commitment must rise to the heights of making Jesus the Lord of your life. And finally, touch—but how does touch fit into my relationship with God, you ask?

Simply stated, through incarnation and resurrection.

The God of all eternity chose to enter the human experience by incarnation. But then, after securing our salvation on the cross, He was resurrected.

They were startled and frightened, thinking they saw a ghost. He said to them, "Why are you troubled, and why do doubts rise in your minds? Look at my hands and my feet. It is I myself! Touch me and see; a ghost does not have flesh and bones, as you see I have."

When he had said this, he showed them his hands and feet. And while they still did not believe it because of joy and amazement, he asked them, "Do you have anything here to eat?" They gave him a piece of broiled fish, and he took it and ate it in their presence (Luke 24:37-43).

Take a moment to really think about this: The God of eternity entered into the world of human touch through the Incarnation, and then took human touch back into eternity through the Resurrection. This makes physical touch part of heaven!

We are promised to also be resurrected in a similar form (1 Corinthians 15:12-50). Just think of it, after your resurrection, you will be able to both physically kneel before the Lord Jesus and be welcomed into Paradise with an embrace.

Running Your Relationship with the RAM

The RAM has provided an interactive representation of what is happening in your relationship with others and with God in the five major relationship bonds that generate your feelings of closeness. It is like your relationship GPS—it can help you identify where you are, then map out where you need to go. Let me give two examples, one in dating and the other in marriage, of how the RAM can be used as a tool for managing relationships.

A major aspect of dating is the way two people go about building their relationship, often referred to as relationship formation. How quickly does a couple form trust, or commitment, or engage in sexual activity? The pacing of dating relationships has been shown in research to be highly predictive of future aspects of one's marriage. However, most singles have no way of understanding or evaluating this pacing process. But this is where the RAM is really empowering.

For those in dating relationships, a simple RAM guideline keeps their relationship growing in safe ways: *Do not allow the level of one relationship bond to exceed any to its left on the RAM chart.* I call this the "safe zone." It goes like this.

Do not trust someone more than you know them; do not rely on them more than what you know and trust; do not commit to them more than what you know, trust, and rely; and do not go farther in your touch than your commitment, reliance, trust, or what you know. This sequence becomes a *logic model* for the Biblical principles on healthy premarital relationships and sexual purity. I will explain this further when I give examples of building relationship skills within the RAM Singles Study® in Chapter 12. But let me move on to my second example.

The RAM can also help couples navigate their marriage relationships. When it comes to managing a long-term relationship, sequence is not nearly as important as identifying the areas that have slipped. As we said earlier, it is normal to fall out of balance. But with the RAM, couples have an interactive tool to identify their imbalances and, in a common language, talk through where they are, where they want to go, and how to get there.

Relationships are connections, and when we clearly define the specific relationship bonds that exist in our relationships, we can manage those relationship bonds with the same intentionality that we have in the other major areas of life.

Although the identification and organization of these five universal relationship bonds are exclusive to my RAM, it is important to provide people with some plan for intentionally managing their relationships, especially within dating, marriage, and family. A relationship will not run itself, nor will it fix itself. Therefore, effective relationship ministry must involve equipping individuals and couples with practical tools to successfully run their relationships.

* * *

A QUICK RECAP

- There are relationship types (e.g., marriage, friendship, co-worker, etc.) and relationship activities (e.g., talks, recreation, romance, etc.).
- John coined the term *relationship bonds*, which refers to the major connections that exist within relationships. He developed a theoretical and interactive model (RAM) of five universal relationship bonds that are included in all relationships: know, trust, rely, commit, and touch.
- The RAM can be licensed by churches to engage their people in a six-week total churchwide healthy relationship series with sermons, video-based curricula for elementary and youth, and video-based small-group studies for couples and singles, all built around the RAM.
- Relationship bonds exist in ranges and interact with each other. Also, they are reciprocal, meaning that each person within a relationship engages in each of these bonds of connection to some extent.
  - o *Know* involves the facts you know about someone, and the experiences of togetherness you have shared over time with a person. This is captured in the 3Ts: Talking + Togetherness + Time.
  - o *Trust* involves the opinion you have about what you know about a person. It is a feeling of security and confidence that comes from how you have arranged what you know into a mental profile of that person, with specific qualities in the foreground and others in the background.
  - o *Rely* involves the ways that you depend on someone to meet needs, desires, or obligations. It prompts feelings of fulfillment.

- o ***Commit*** involves the priority, dedication, obligation, and promise invested in a relationship.
- o ***Touch*** involves any type of physical presence and interactions: affection, friendly and supportive touch, sexual chemistry, and sexual interactions.
- The five relationship bonds pictured in the RAM describe a relationship with another person and also a relationship with Jesus Christ.
- The five relationship bonds pictured in the RAM also describe the five major areas of a relationship that need to be intentionally managed. Therefore, it can be utilized as a tool to identify and talk about strengths and needed areas of adjustment within relationships.
- The RAM also provides a logical sequence for building a new relationship, called the safe zone: Do not allow any of the relationship bonds to significantly increase beyond the levels of those to its left on the RAM chart.

CHAPTER 11

Healthy Relationships Express the Virtues of Agape Love

It was Wednesday, the last day that Jesus ever taught in the Temple, and his Jewish opponents had formed what would become their last question, a question that they hoped would completely confound Jesus. A scholar of the law stepped up and posed this query: "What is the most important commandment?"

Now, before we quote Jesus's answer, understand that after He answered this question, "no man dared to ask him any more questions" (Mark 12:34). They were "muzzled or gagged" by His profound wisdom (this is the meaning of the Greek word commonly translated as "silenced" in Matthew 22:34). Toward the end of Jesus's life, we have no additional questions presented to Him by any Jewish leadership. His answer was the culmination of everything He had ever taught and represented, and it figuratively strapped a muzzle over the mouths of his opponents.

So, what did Jesus select as the most important commandment among the over four hundred laws recorded in the Jewish Scriptures?

"The most important one," answered Jesus, "is this: 'Hear, O Israel: The Lord our God, the Lord is one. Love the Lord your God with all your heart and with all your soul and with all your mind and with all your strength.' The second is this: 'Love your neighbor as yourself.' There is no commandment greater than these . . ." And from then on, no man dared ask him any more questions (Mark 12:29-31, 34).

Everything that God had spoken through his prophets and had written in His laws could be summed up in this one word: love. He essentially said, "Love God . . . and love others." Love is the greatest overarching virtue that is to permeate all our relationships, with God and with people.

Love Versus Relationship

Think about love versus relationships. No one will deny that relationships can exist *without love*. For instance, you can have relationships that are hateful, vengeful, unforgiving, and unloving. You can have unhealthy and self-serving relationships. By definition, a "relationship" does not imply anything positive or negative; it requires a modifier to determine its quality.

While it is possible to have relationships without love, it is not possible to have love without relationships.

And that is why love is used to describe our relationship with God and others. Agape love is the modifier that defines what God requires in our relationships. It is the ideal virtue that should be infused in all the ways we relate to others.

So while it is possible to have relationships without love, it is *not* possible to have love without relationships. To love God or others means that you must have a relationship. Love is the mandate, but relationships are the prerequisite. Relationships are the vehicle to express the virtue of love.

The "love chapter" in 1 Corinthians is one of the most frequently quoted passages of Scripture, particularly in weddings. It raised agape love to the hallmark virtue within all relationships.

If I speak in the tongues of men or of angels, but do not have love, I am only a resounding gong or a clanging cymbal. If I have the gift of prophecy and can fathom all mysteries and all knowledge, and if I have a faith that can move mountains, but do not have love, I am nothing. If I give all I possess to the poor and give over my body to hardship that I may boast, but do not have love, I gain nothing.

Love is patient, love is kind. It does not envy, it does not boast, it is not proud. It does not dishonor others, it is not self-seeking, it is not easily angered, it keeps no record of wrongs. Love does not delight in evil but rejoices with the truth. It always protects, always trusts, always hopes, always perseveres. Love never fails (1 Corinthians 13:1-8).

C. S. Lewis, in his book, *The Four Loves*, explains the four Greek words translated "love" in the Scriptures. *Eros* referred to romantic or sexual love, *Storge* to affectionate love shared by family members, *Philia* to friendship and companionship love, and *Agape* to the highest quality of love—the love that is the essence of God, the love that willingly puts another's interests above one's own, the unselfish and sacrificial love that God demonstrated toward us, that "while we were still sinners, Christ died for us" (Romans 5:8).

Relationships are the vehicle to express the virtue of love.

Personal Virtues Versus Relational Virtues

Jesus established an inseparable connection between personal virtues and relationship virtues. Agape love is the thread that weaves together *two* commandments into *one*. No Jewish writer or scholar prior to Jesus had combined these two Scriptures into a summary of the entire law and prophets. Essentially, Jesus proclaimed that these two commandments are of equal importance, and that what is often referred to as our vertical relationship with God is inseparably intertwined with our horizontal relationships with people.

Therefore, these two commandments are two sides of one concept, and together they establish that true spirituality is characterized by the development of personal virtues from loving God that are expressed in the virtues of agape love toward others. It is exactly what the Apostle John reiterated in his first epistle when he wrote, "Whoever claims to love God yet hates a brother or sister is a liar. For whoever does not love their brother and sister, whom they have seen, cannot love God, whom they have not seen" (1 John 4:20).

Love is the framework upon which the entire law of God hangs. As the famed pastor John MacArthur puts it,

Christianity isn't that complicated, neither is Judaism. It just says: love God, love men. If you love God, you'll do what He says. If you love men, you'll do what they need, that's all. That's life for us. That's the whole thing. Because verse forty sums it up. "On these two commandments"—like two nails, two pegs—"hang all the law and the prophets." Everything else God said in the Old Testament hangs on those two things. If you just love God with all your being and love everybody as you love yourself, you don't need any more rules. That's it. You just don't need any more—everything else is just a definition of that. Everything else is just an explanation of that.[106]

I like that last line: *Everything else is just an explanation of that.* This is exactly the point that the Apostle Paul elaborated in his epistle to the Romans:

> *True spirituality is characterized by the development of personal virtues from loving God that are expressed in agape love toward others.*

Whoever loves others has fulfilled the law. The commandments, "You shall not commit adultery," "You shall not murder," "You shall not steal," "You shall not covet," and whatever other command there may be, are summed up in this one command: "Love your neighbor as yourself." Love does no harm to a neighbor. Therefore, love is the fulfillment of the law (Romans 13:8b-10).

God wants to reshape personal character to function on a different wavelength, one of agape love and empowerment in the Spirit. Because when agape love is planted in your relationships, it will germinate a flourishing of other virtues. Here is a short list of virtues that flow from agape love that have both personal and relational aspects to them:

- **Humility:** "All of you, clothe yourselves with humility toward one another, because, God opposes the proud but shows favor to the humble" (1 Peter 5:5). "In humility, value others above yourselves" (Philippians 2:3).
- **Sacrifice:** "Walk in the way of love, just as Christ loved us and gave Himself up for us as a fragrant offering and sacrifice to God" (Ephesians 5:2).
- **Compassion:** "Therefore, as God's chosen people, holy and dearly loved, clothe yourselves with compassion, kindness, humility, gentleness and patience" (Colossians 3:12).

- **Forgiveness:** "Bear with each other and forgive one another if any of you has a grievance against someone. Forgive as the Lord forgave you" (Colossians 3:13).
- **Purity:** "But the wisdom that comes from heaven is first of all pure; then peace-loving, considerate, submissive, full of mercy and good fruit, impartial and sincere" (James 3:17).

God Is Love

Why is love the ultimate virtue for relationships? It is vital to acknowledge that love is more than the standard Christians live by; it is the divine virtue that has eternally existed within the relationship of our triune God.

Dear friends, let us love one another, for love comes from God. Everyone who loves has been born of God and knows God. Whoever does not love does not know God, because **God is love** (1 John 4:7-8).

Love is more than the standard Christians live by; it is the divine virtue that has eternally existed within the relationship of our triune God.

Relationships and love have been in existence for all eternity. Before creation ever existed, when there was *only* God, this *one* God consisted of three Persons in a *relationship*, and these Persons have always existed in perfect agreement and oneness—eternally communicating in relation with each other in agape love. Hence the Apostle John concludes that God *actually is* love. Here is a contemporary distillation of this profound theological mystery that we find quite helpful:

All three Persons of the Trinity comprise the one, perfectly unified God. They share the same nature and essence, and they are all the same God, although each individual Person of the Trinity is distinct and unique. The fact that God exists in three Persons is important for several reasons. For one, God is love (1 John 4:8). But, in eternity past, before God created any other being, could He have truly been love? That is, can love exist where there is no one to *be* loved? Because God exists in three co-equal, co-eternal Persons, love exists, too. Eternal love has been expressed eternally among the Persons of the Godhead. The Father, Son, and Spirit have always loved each other, and so love is eternal.[107]

Love is inherent to the very nature of God and is the starting point for any Biblical theology of relationships. That love finds expression in the creation of mankind—for of all the created beings, humans were the only ones created in the image of God and hence designed to showcase the "divine DNA" of love through relationships.

Pope John Paul II captured this truth in his *Theology of the Body* when he expanded on the concept in Genesis 1 of being made in the "image and likeness" of God:

> The function of the image is to reflect the one who is the model, to reproduce its own prototype. Man becomes the image of God not so much in the moment of solitude as in the moment of communion. Right "from the beginning," he is not only an image in which the solitude of a person who rules the world is reflected, but also, and essentially, an image of an inscrutable divine communion of persons.[108]

The Biblical description of the origin of the human race centers on the distinguishing mark of humans fashioned in the image and likeness of God:

> Then God said, "Let us make mankind in our image, in our likeness, so that they may rule over the fish in the sea and the birds in the sky, over the livestock and all the wild animals, and over all the creatures that move along the ground." So God created mankind in his own image, in the image of God he created them; male and female he created them (Genesis 1:26-27).

In *Our Triune God*, theologians Philip Ryken and Michael LeFebvre emphasize the deep relationality of the Genesis account:

> From all eternity, the three Persons have enjoyed perfect love within the
> Godhead. When it pleased God to make mankind in His own image, He
> created us as social beings. We were created for relationship with God and
> to reflect his likeness not merely as individuals but in relationship with one
> another. This may be why the author of Genesis dared to use plural
> pronouns to describe God at that point in the creation account where he
> tells of God creating mankind in his own likeness: "Then God said, 'Let
> *us* make man in *our* image, after *our* likeness' . . . So, God created man in His
> own image . . . male and female he created them" (Gen. 1:26-27). God
> made man a social being because the prototype for man—God himself—is
> a being in communion.[109]

The hallmark of being fashioned in God's image is having *relational person-*
hood imprinted on us as human beings. No other creature was given the image
and likeness of God as a person, and as John MacArthur so accurately stated,
personhood cannot be understood in solitude but only within relationships:

> The core of the image of God can be summed up by the word "person."
> We are persons. We live and move on the basis of relationships.
> Relationships! We understand fellowship. We understand love. We
> understand communion. We understand conversation. We understand
> sharing thoughts and sharing attitudes and sharing ideas and sharing
> experiences with others. And that is why when God created man, He
> immediately said, "It is not good for man to be alone." Why? Because the
> image of God is personhood, and personhood can only function in
> relationship. The image of God is the capacity for personal relationships
> and, most importantly, for a personal relationship with God.[110]

It is with this dramatic backdrop of the triune nature of God, the eternality
of love and relationship, and this relational fingerprint of God imprinted in the
creation of humans that the primacy of relationship ministry in the Church is

best understood.

God's Will Is Personal Sanctification that Transforms Relationships

As we have already shown, personal virtues are inseparable from relational virtues. In fact, every time in the New Testament you find "God's will" used to refer to personal spiritual growth, relationships are immediately discussed. For example, the Apostle Paul succinctly exhorted the Christians at Thessalonica: "It is **God's will** that you should be sanctified" (1 Thessalonians 4:3). Sanctification simply refers to the process of growing in holiness—how to live holy and godly in this present world.

It is with this dramatic backdrop of the triune nature of God, the eternality of love and relationship, and this relational fingerprint of God imprinted in the creation of humans that the primacy of relationship ministry in the Church is best understood.

But look closely at what it means to be sanctified? His very next line was this: "That you should avoid sexual immorality; that each of you should learn to control your own body in a way that is holy and honorable, not in passionate lust like the pagans, who do not know God; and that in this matter no one should wrong or take advantage of a brother or sister" (1 Thessalonians 4:3-6).

God's will for your life is all about how you live out agape love in your relationships. This includes personal virtues—how you set sexual boundaries and manage your own impulses, as well as relational virtues—how you act for the good of others and avoid wronging or taking advantage of anyone.

When we read in the Scriptures about the Spirit-filled life, we again find that it is manifested in loving relationships:

You, my brothers and sisters, were called to be free. But do not use your freedom to indulge the flesh; rather, serve one another humbly in love. For the entire law is fulfilled in keeping this one command: "Love your neighbor as yourself." If you bite and devour each other, watch out or you will be destroyed by each other. So, I say, walk by the Spirit, and you will not gratify the desires of the flesh.

But the fruit of the Spirit is love, joy, peace, forbearance, kindness, goodness, faithfulness, gentleness and self-control. Against such things there is no law. Those who belong to Christ Jesus have crucified the flesh with its passions and desires. Since we live by the Spirit, let us keep in step with the Spirit. Let us not become conceited, provoking and envying each other (Galatians 5:13-16; 22-26).

The "fruit of the Spirit" has been printed on posters, cards, bookmarks, t-shirts, and just about anything else you can imagine. But what few realize is that the entire passage, both the verses before and afterwards, is all about relationships!

Walking by the Spirit, being filled with the Spirit, being a "new creation" in Christ (2 Corinthians 5:17)—this is personal empowerment that is to transform relationships.

Over and over, the Scriptures define God's will for your personal spiritual development as the source of transformation in your relationships with others. Let me give you just one more example of this theme of God's will in another well-known passage by the Apostle Paul:

Therefore, I urge you, brothers and sisters, in view of God's mercy, to offer your bodies as a living sacrifice, holy and pleasing to God—this is your true and proper worship. Do not conform to the pattern of this world, but be transformed by the renewing of your mind. Then you will be able to test and approve what **God's will** is—his good, pleasing and perfect will (Romans 12:1-2).

The emphasis on personal character development ("renew your mind") is an integral part of spiritual growth. We wholeheartedly agree, for as the Proverb so aptly exhorted, "Above all else, guard your heart, for everything you do flows from it" (Proverbs 4:23).

However, true spiritual growth is equally and inseparably bound up with the transformation of your relationships. In your understanding of spiritual growth, it is thus vital to shift the emphasis from an *individualistic pursuit* of holiness to a holiness that includes healthy and godly relationships, especially within marriages and families.

So when the Apostle Paul offers step-by-step instructions to the Romans on exactly what "testing and approving God's will" entails, notice that all the major areas he emphasizes have a practical relationship focus and theme. These include:

- How to use your spiritual gifts to humbly serve others (12:3-16);
- How to love those who are unloving and hurtful (12:17-21);
- How to relate with those in authority over you (13:1-7);
- How to practice wise boundaries in relationships with unbelievers (13:8-14);
- How to be non-judgmental and build up those with whom you differ (14:1-23);
- How to use your strengths to support those weaker than you (15:1-13).

Virtues Are Essential in Marriages

I (John) recently reviewed a theory of a colleague I have known for over fifteen years—Jason Carroll, a professor of marriage and family studies and a prolific researcher of marital relations, having published over a hundred studies in peer-reviewed journals. He had proposed a multi-dimensional model of relationship health in a research study titled, *The Ability to Negotiate or the Ability to Love?*

After reviewing decades of research and theories about what is needed to make a high-quality marriage, he suggested that there must be a balance between interpersonal and intrapersonal competence.

Interpersonal competence within marriage is all about the relationship "between" spouses. It involves mastering the skills that are essential for maintaining a strong relationship with a spouse. These include good communication and intimacy skills, such as active listening, self-disclosure, and giving emotional support. Interpersonal competence also includes skills for engaging in solving problems, resolving conflicts, forgiving, and overcoming hurts.

Intrapersonal competence within marriage, on the other hand, is all about the "within" character qualities of each spouse. This includes a person's ability to control their own emotions and monitor their actions. Intrapersonal competence also includes the maturity of their conscience and their internal values and morals (essentially, what we have been calling personal and relational virtues).

This was the conclusion Jason and his co-authors reached:

> Defining marital competence in both interpersonal and intrapersonal terms facilitates a distinction between communicative skills and motivation. Defined in these terms, marital competence becomes as much about personal maturation and regard for others as it is about communication and problem-solving skills.[111]

Jason's work builds on the idea that what we are capable of in our relationships with others is yoked to our emotional capabilities and self-regulation. In the 1980s, Howard Gardner shattered the understanding of IQ by introducing the concept of multiple intelligences. He went on to claim that there are interpersonal and intrapersonal intelligences. Although some of these ideas had already been knocking around, Gardner organized them and introduced the world to EQ—emotional quotient, also known as emotional intelligence.

Assessment protocols were almost immediately designed to measure EQ, examining two major areas: First, how you manage yourself (intrapersonal intelligence); and second, how you manage your relationships with others (interpersonal intelligence). Up to this point, there had been a nagging mystery about IQ that puzzled researchers, and Gardner's discovery of EQ finally solved it.

The mystery was this: When evaluating performance on many different tasks, researchers had consistently found that those with the highest levels of IQ outperformed those with average IQs only 20 percent of the time, while those of average IQ actually outperformed those of high IQ 70 percent of the time.

What did the average IQ people have that the high IQ people were lacking?

The answer came from measuring their EQ. Many of those with a high IQ had a low EQ. They had difficulties with self-regulation and were socially withdrawn. They had not mastered personal or relational virtues and skills.

God's design for marriage is for virtue to drive how you handle yourself and your relationships with others. When your relationship loses strength; when trust is damaged; when needs go unmet; when commitment is weak; when touch has been neglected—in these times the virtue of agape love drives relational healing.

One of the most prolific researchers in the field of marital studies is an amazing Christian and beloved retired professor from Virginia Commonwealth University, Everett Worthington. I remember consulting with him back in the 1980s when I was working on my doctoral dissertation. We talked about the centrality of relationships, and how the maintenance of the bond within a marriage is pre-eminent. Not long after that, Everett devoted his remaining years of research to the study of forgiveness and the importance of blending a virtuous bond with the skill of relating well. In his article reviewing more than twenty years of research on marriage, he expressed hope concerning the elasticity of the bond that hold two people together in a marriage relationship:

Marriage research has flourished . . . changing our understanding of marriage. We know more about factors that promote or undermine marital success and happiness. We understand more about why some marriages deteriorate and others thrive. We know more about marriages that people call troubled—and have learned to our surprise that many find healing. Marital troubles are not the kiss of death for a marriage . . . Beneath these findings, we discover the buried treasure. The *emotional bond* between couples is the golden thread that holds partners together.[112]

Forgiveness is crucial to healthy marriages. Couples with long-term successful marriages identified forgiveness as one of the top three qualities that was responsible for their marital success... Forgiveness gives people a way to deal constructively with the almost inevitable disappointments that will occur in any relationship and thus heal the emotional bond . . . the last seven years of research on marital processes has suggested that it is not simple positive interactions but a strong emotional bond that holds marriages together.[113]

Two thousand years ago, long before any scientific studies of marriage relationships or emotional intelligence, Jesus captured the same two themes when He summarized all that is involved in fulfilling God's commandments. Love God with all your heart and with all your soul and with all your mind, and you will watch your *intrapersonal intelligence* grow in virtues of Christlikeness. And then, love others as yourself, and you will watch your *interpersonal intelligence* grow in virtues of agape love.

* * *

A QUICK RECAP

- Jesus answered the question about what the greatest commandment is by putting together two laws from the Scriptures previously considered unrelated: Love God and love others.
- Relationships are the vehicle in which we express the virtue of love. It is possible to have relationships without love, but not love without relationships.
- Personal virtues and relational virtues are intertwined in the Christian concepts of loving Jesus and walking in the Spirit.
- Love within relationships has existed within the Godhead from all eternity.
- God's will for the spiritual growth and sanctification of believers includes developing personal (intrapersonal) and relational (interpersonal) virtues.

CHAPTER 12

Healthy Relationships Engage with Proficient Skills

Christianity has it right when it comes to its emphasis on virtues in relationships.

My wife, Shirley, and I (John) love athletics. While our two girls were growing up, we coached over thirty of their sports teams—T-ball, softball, basketball, soccer, and cross country. One soccer player stands out in my memory from those many seasons. He was only twelve years old, but an amazingly talented player. His skill level put him in competition with the best of the high school team.

But his downfall was his lack of sportsmanship. He was the proverbial ball hog; he intentionally attacked opponents with aggressive and illegal kicks; he swore at the referees; and he couldn't control his tantrums whenever something didn't go his way. His skills were overshadowed by his lack of virtues.

We hope that you hear this loud and clear: The virtues of agape love are both individual and relational, and they are of the topmost priority in the life of a Christian. With that being said, there is a tendency to emphasize one truth while neglecting the other. And most Christian churches fail to offer relationship skill training as a counterpart to their emphasis on virtue development.

I have been in the field of marriage and family therapy since the 1980s, and the predominant explanation as to why marriages struggle has not been because of a lack of virtues but because of a deficiency in skills:

> Much of current marriage scholarship is based on the assumption that marital distress is caused by communication problems, which in turn are the result of spouses being deficient in communication skills.[114]

This emphasis has led relationship experts and therapists to practice a skills-based approach to helping couples with communication and conflict management techniques. Decades of research have provided clear evidence of the value of skill training in improving relationship quality. This secular approach is unquestionably valid, and offers a much-needed addition to the relationship content provided by most churches.

The irony, however, is that while the majority of secular marriage theories have emphasized skills to the neglect of virtues, the majority of Church ministries have emphasized virtues to the neglect of skills. As we emphasized in our last chapter, personal and relational virtues are pre-eminent in God's will for our lives. And yet, skill development is a vital pathway to living out God's will in practical, everyday relationship experiences. It is critical that your church find the balance of helping couples and individuals become proficient in their relationship skills so they can genuinely practice the virtues that emanate from agape love.

Poor Skills or Ill Wills

By differentiating skills from virtues, you clarify the value that each contributes to healthy relationships and are better able to incorporate both in your ministries.

> *By differentiating skills from virtues, you clarify the value that each contributes to healthy relationships and are better able to incorporate both in your ministries.*

This has been happening in the field of marriage theory, where a growing number of researchers are now emphasizing the important role virtues play in marriage. This idea was underscored in a landmark study by a pair of researchers, Brant Burleson from Purdue University and Wayne Denton from Wake Forest University. In their study, they found distressed spouses who had mastered relationship skills but were not using those skills in virtuous ways. They concluded that the marital distress experienced by these spouses was caused not by poor skills but by *ill wills*.[115]

Blaine Fowers, the author of *Beyond the Myth of Marital Happiness*,[116] is one of the researchers who have been pounding the gavel for decades for equal attention to be given to virtues and skills. "I argue that the successful exercise of communication skills is dependent on a set of virtues," he explains, "and that these virtues have been generally ignored in the professional literature."[117] Just as the field of marital research has tended to minimize the value of relationship virtues, church ministries and small-group studies have tended to minimize the value of developing relationship skills. I (John) was introduced to relationship skills-based training in the mid-1990s, just after I had assembled the content for a book I was writing, *How to Avoid Falling in Love with a Jerk.*[118]

Essentially, I proposed that my RAM chart could be used as an interactive tool for singles to pace the development of their romantic relationships. I had also organized into five categories hundreds of research studies about the pre-marital predictors of high-quality marriages which, when intentionally explored, would reveal the relationship potential of a prospective partner.

I tucked those five target areas into the *know* bond on my RAM as "windows" and "mirrors." They are windows to peer through to see the true character of a partner, but also mirrors that reflect one's own character and relationship potential. I had been presenting the content in daylong seminars, and, with my pastoral background, was following the usual style of the "sage on the stage." But then, in 1997, I attended the first Smart Marriage Conference,[119] a coalition of relationship experts who wanted to balance academic research with the importance of skill training in marriage programs. At that conference, I was immediately convinced that information alone is not sufficient—that changing lives requires *practicing how* to relate well in dating and marriage relationships.

So, I turned a corner and translated all the research that I had collected and organized for my book into a skills-based training program. Ten years passed before my book was published (some teased me that I had commitment issues). But those were invaluable years of road-testing the concepts and integrating content with practice and virtues with skills.

These three aspects of healthy relationships—bonds (as described in the RAM), skills, and virtues—can be better understood in a simple diagram.

This diagram (Figure 12.1) helps visualize how developing relationship skills and virtues will equip you with abilities to intentionally manage the bonds that comprise your relationships. As we saw in that amazing passage in Philippians 2, God works in you to cultivate Christlike virtues *as you work to master* relationship skills—and with the energizing power of the Holy Spirit, you are then able to live out Jesus in your relationships, thoughtfully managing the dynamic bonds of how you connect with others. *This* is how we fulfill our Lord's vision: *"By this everyone will know that you are my disciples, if you love one another"* (John 13:35).

Figure 12:1

An Integrative Theory of Relationships

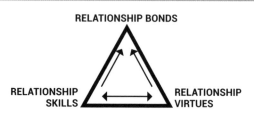

So let's explore relationship skills more deeply. A skill is defined as "the capacity to perform a task or activity with a given degree of proficiency."[120] Essentially, you begin with an activity and create a technique for mastering it.

Some skills are simpler to master because they only require an exact repetition, like addition, subtraction, or other math operations. Relationship skills, on the other hand, are complex because the techniques need to be able to work in different settings and with different people.

In marriage, there are many relationship activities, but communication has been the one most extensively studied and developed in skill training programs. What this means is that the components of positive communication are identified and organized in a standardized format that can be taught, modeled, practiced, and then generalized outside of the "classroom."

Does this sound familiar—teach, model, practice, and then commission? It should, because these elements of skill development were in the pedagogy of Jesus we commonly call *discipleship.*

He invited twelve men to follow him for three years, taught them every day, modeled how to handle just about every situation imaginable, had them practice by sending them out two-by-two and by processing their accomplishments and failures, and, finally, commissioned them to continue to exercise the virtues and skills He had shaped in them, empowering them with the gift of the Spirit of God.

This is the same approach taken by Moses with Joshua, Elijah with Elisha, Paul with Silas, and Barnabas with John Mark, and countless others. Teaching content was consistently followed by modeling that content, and then providing opportunities for the learner to practice the content. When it comes to dating, marriage, or other types of relationship, however, most churches only provide content without the subsequent skill training or practice. Incorporating these key elements into our relationship programs and studies will exponentially increase their effectiveness.

Relationship Skills Training Examples

Let me give you a couple of examples of skill training from two of my certified instructor-led relationship courses, PICK a Partner for singles and Couple LINKS (or for short, PICK® and LINKS®). These certification relationship courses are research-informed and evidence-based, and because they have Christian and secular versions, they have been taught in countless settings in addition to churches and faith organizations—high schools and universities, counseling and social work agencies, military and community settings, and more. (See www.LoveThinks.com for information on becoming certified.)

I adapted these courses in 2017 into video-based small-group studies and included them in a six-week, total churchwide healthy relationship series that includes a sermon series, lessons for children and youth, and two adult small-group studies. (See www.RAMseries.com for licensing this RAM Series in your church.) The RAM Singles Study is based on the PICK course while RAM Couples Study is based on the LINKS course. In both video-based, small-group studies, the RAM is used as a framework for understanding how individuals and couples can intentionally build and sustain their relationships.

In the RAM Couples Study, the main takeaway is for couples to have a regular check-in about their relationship, a meeting we call Couple Huddles. Couples use a small, interactive RAM chart to describe their present relational profile, and then are given general prompts to talk through each of the five dynamic bond areas of their relationship. They begin with 1) staying in the *know*, and 2) keeping a positive attitude of *trust*; then, they look forward by

3) planning ways they would like to have their meaningful needs and wants met (*rely*), and 4) identifying ways to support each other in their schedules (*commit*); they conclude with 5) checking in about their romance, affection, and sexual closeness (*touch*). This couple meeting is only meant to take thirty to forty minutes, and it is important to stay positive and encouraging. It gives a couple a chance to catch up on the recent past and serves as a planning meeting for the immediate future.

After couples learn the details of these concepts, they practice Huddles privately, and afterward share their challenges and benefits. Over the remaining weeks that couples are in the RAM Series for Couples small-group study, couples have homework, and one assignment is to continue having Huddles at home. The small-group leader is encouraged to review Huddles and have couples share the gains they are making from these brief and positively-focused check-ins. It is emphasized that couples are to approach each Huddle with the assumption that things are always a bit out of balance, and thus they should treat "slow leaks" as opportunities for growth rather than occasions for complaint.

The Huddle is an example of taking a concept—*"intentionally manage your relationship"*—and breaking it down to its essential steps, explaining those steps, helping couples practice the steps, and then following up to ensure that they are continuing to incorporate the steps in their routine at home.

Let me give another example from the RAM Couples Study. We emphasize that skills are a means to an end, and not an end in themselves. So, for example, communication skills must be motivated by a heart desiring to genuinely know a partner, wanting to understand what is meaningful and important to them. But what are the skills that help accomplish this end?

Obviously, the communication skills of active listening and restatement are essential. So we teach couples techniques for effective listening, and then they practice listening to each other and restating in their own words what their partner has discussed. But after this, we describe another skill that gets even closer to the heart of knowing your partner, which is called *"becoming your partner's connoisseur."*

A connoisseur is someone who is an expert on a subject. Take a connoisseur of fine wines, or *oenophile*—they know everything there is to know about wines. You can offer them a glass of wine and they will tell you every detail: type, acidity, sugar content, viscosity, grape varietals, region, vineyard, date the wine was bottled, and then, some insignificant story about the history of the winemaker. They are obsessed with the subject of their expertise.

> When you deeply know your spouse and maintain a positive trust, then you can truly fulfill the Golden Rule with your spouse.

The oenophile offers a picture of what it means to become the connoisseur of your spouse. For when you deeply *know* your spouse and maintain a positive *trust*, then you can truly fulfill the Golden Rule with your spouse. You remember the Golden Rule: *"Do unto others as you would have others do unto you."* Just to be clear, it does *not* mean to do for another *exactly* what you want them to do for you (e.g., giving your wife the DISH sports package you have been dreaming of buying). What it does mean is that you should treat others *in the same spirit* as you would like to be treated.

A skill-training activity for becoming your spouse's connoisseur is to have each spouse generate a top-ten list of their own personal needs and interests, and then exchange and discuss them. These lists are then incorporated into the third step of their Huddle (rely) when they talk about what they would like to be doing for and with each other in the following week(s), before their next Huddle.

When the RAM Couples Study is conducted with a large group of couples, the part where couples generate their personal top-ten lists is preceded by a highly energetic and interactive activity. The men and women are divided into two groups (one all-men and the other all-women), and each group is tasked with generating a top-ten list.

The twist comes when the group of women have to brainstorm what men want and need from their spouses, and the group of men must figure out what women want and need from their partners. The two groups create their top-ten list on a board, and when completed, they make a presentation to the other group.

The idea behind this exercise is to help men think like a woman and women to think like a man. And isn't this the design of true love! For love should move you out of your own world and into the world of the one you love, stretching you to become an expert on their needs and wants so that you can love that person in ways that are most meaningful to them.

Women have seemed to corner the market on the fun in this activity. I remember one group of women debating whether sex or respect should be at the top of their list. So, when they presented their findings, they lowered the page to their #1 item: *sexual respect*. And then, after some chuckles they lowered it again to #2: *respectful sex*. The men roared with laughter as well as with appreciation for the group of women recognizing areas that are important to them.

Interactive and skills-based exercises are common in relationship courses taught outside of church settings, but they are rare in small-group studies and marriage classes within church settings. However, they can be easily inserted and are essential for developing techniques to bring to life the virtues and principles upon which healthy marriage relationships depend.

Let me give two examples of how to integrate skills-based exercises into relationship classes, drawn from the RAM Singles Study that is based on my PICK program. For over twenty years, this program has been updated with current research and used with youth and adults of all ages, with divorced singles being some of the biggest fans. A major emphasis is on intentionally managing a relationship by pacing the bonds of a romantic relationship.

In the RAM chart, when all five bonds are at the top level, the feelings of attachment are strongest. But when even one bond dips low, attachment weakens, and feelings of closeness become mixed. You become easily confused, hurt, and doubtful. The *balance* of all five bonding dynamics determines the healthiness of your relationship and the clarity of your perspective on that person.

I want to review again one of the most important keys to building a new relationship, and, specifically, a dating relationship: *Never go further in the level of one relationship bond than you have gone in any to the left on the RAM chart.* This sequence suggests that the five bonding dynamics have a specific logic to them:

what you *know* about a person determines the degree you should trust him or her; this *trust* directs you in choosing what personal needs you can *rely* on him or her to meet; your *commitment* should only increase to the extent that you know, trust, and have proven reliability with that person; and finally, any degree of *sexual involvement* is safest when it matches or is lower than the context of the overall intimacy reflected in the levels of the other four dynamics (Figure 12.2).

Slipping out of the safe zone explains the most common mistake people make in romantic relationships. When the levels of the five dynamics are out of balance, the result is that the emotional bond becomes unhealthy, and people tend to overlook crucial characteristics of the other person that should be exposed and explored. Thus, their love becomes blind, and the bonds of their heart end up overriding the judgment of their mind.[121]

Figure 12:2

R.A.M.
Relationship
Attachment Model

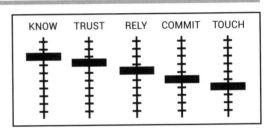

Figure 12:2 The pacing of a relationship in the "safe zone"

However, singles of all ages live in a mainstream culture that normalizes fast-paced sexual involvement with little to no guidance for evaluating character or discussing commitment (Figure 12:3). By helping singles have a self-directed plan for pacing their sexual involvement with the other four relationship bonds, you increase their skill level in building God-honoring and risk-minimizing dating relationships.

Another crucial concept that is taught in the RAM Singles Study is discernment. With the constant emphasis on never being judgmental,

> *Slipping out of the safe zone explains the most common mistake people make in romantic relationships.*

many singles have never learned how to discern the heart or character of a potential dating partner. In reality, trying to figure out what a partner is really like comprises much of what happens during a dating relationship. But who teaches techniques and skills for becoming more discerning in this dating process?

I mentioned earlier in this chapter that I collected hundreds of research studies that identified characteristics that existed prior to marriage that were

Figure 12:3

R.A.M.
**Relationship
Attachment Model**

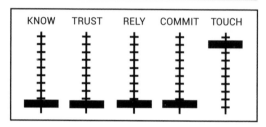

Figure 12:3 The pacing of a relationship in mainstream culture

found to predict the quality of that person's future marriage. (These areas are discussed in the RAM Singles Study, which is expanded upon in my book, *How to Avoid Falling in Love with a Jerk*). I categorized all these characteristics into five target areas that are invaluable sources of self-reflection (mirrors) as well as partner selection (windows). When they are all put together, you gain a fairly comprehensive understanding of a dating partner's relationship potential.

One of the five areas is family background: what happened during your upbringing and what experiences you are likely to repeat in your adult relationships. The Bible is rich with stories about families that illustrate the likelihood of family dynamics repeating unless intentional effort is made to change the trajectory of their impact. (A perfect example is how hard Joseph worked to change the impact of the previous generations of parenting favoritism.)

To help singles with the skill of considering their own family experiences, we have them first work in groups to design a family tree. As they imagine the marriage and family that they would like to someday create, they add to the tree three categories of experiences: what they want to repeat from their family background, what they do not want to repeat, and anything new that was not a part of their family experience but that they would want to be a part of their future relationships. Once they have completed these family trees, they share them with the other groups, and then individually map out their ideal marriage and family qualities by designing their personal family tree.

This exercise from the RAM Singles Study is a practical skill training for reflecting on one's own family of origin. Singles are then provided with twenty questions about family background along with twenty questions in the other four major areas to explore. (There are ninety-nine questions total in their RAM Singles Study Workbook.) To practice engaging in a conversation about family background (and the other four areas), a fun "speed dating" exercise is employed in larger group classes such as youth groups.

Essentially, singles form two parallel lines with each person in one line facing a partner in the second line. Every person in both lines has one question from the ninety-nine questions list. When you say go, everyone in line A asks their question to the partner in line B, who has thirty seconds to answer the question. Then you yell "switch," at which point those in line B ask their question to the partner in line A, who also has only thirty seconds to answer. You then shout "move," and line A moves over one partner (the member on the end of line A will have to run around to the opposite end of the line). Then it all starts over. In just five minutes, everyone has asked their one question to five partners, and answered five different questions from their five partners.

You can imagine the organized chaos of everyone talking at once, but this energetic activity is more than a fun game. Singles learn the power of the question—and that discernment must blend observation with conversation.

When processing this skill-building activity, many will tell you that they have wondered about some of these areas as they observed people they dated, but they were never fully sure what to think because they never discussed them directly. But now, after just a five-minute practice session with specific starter questions in these five major topic areas, they feel equipped to be significantly more discerning in their relationships. As they work through the RAM Singles Study, they learn details and Biblical principles related to the five key areas to explore about a partner,

Discernment must blend observation with conversation.

and they then practice skills of engaging in those relationships. The balance of teaching Biblical content with practical skill-building exercises greatly increases the confidence of singles in their relationship decisions.

Putting It All Together

Relationships are a vehicle for fulfilling the commandments of God—a vehicle that must be intentionally run with virtues and skills. In church ministry, our focus on discipleship is often to the exclusion of relationships, as if being discipled is only an "individualistic" spiritual journey. The major problem is not what we *are* doing, but rather what we are *not* doing.

Our concept of discipleship comes directly from Jesus, yet His emphasis on what it means to be a disciple includes becoming an expert on expressing agape love within relationships. Our definition of discipleship is too often framed only in the development of personal virtues *without any* emphasis on the development of the relationship skills needed to practice those virtues.

In the *Nicomachean Ethics*, Aristotle emphasized that virtue requires the cultivation of skills and habits practiced over time: "Anyone can get angry—that is easy . . . but to do this to the right person, to the right extent, at the right time, for the right reason, and in the right way is no longer something easy."[122]

Aristotle was correct when he implied that it takes *virtues* to regulate your anger along with *skills* to express it in the right ways. This is not a new idea. It's high time we update our concept and practice of discipleship to include relationship skill development! This means modeling relationship virtues in skillful ways, providing practical step-by-step techniques for engaging in relationships, and then creating activities and exercises in which these techniques can be practiced and mastered.

Larry Crabb, in his classic work, *Effective Biblical Counseling*, described his approach to integrating psychology and Christianity when he created a framework for Biblical counseling. He called it "Spoiling the Egyptians." When Moses led the children of Israel out of Egyptian bondage, there were some goods or "spoils" that God approved and others that were off limits.

This is similar to what we are suggesting: glean from science the *how-to's* for any Scriptural *ought-to's*. We have pointed out that there are techniques and insights from marriage research that can tremendously enrich the application of Christian principles and virtues. Many of the relationship courses and programs that have been validated in their effectiveness and facilitated outside of church settings have integrated this skill training in their content, and also offer Christian versions. There is no reason to "reinvent the wheel." Instead, you should consider and evaluate the best of these courses for implementation in relationship ministries. (And note that, as part of its subscription service supporting churches in building out a Full-Circle Relationship Ministry®, Communio has organized a searchable catalogue of skills-based Christian relationship programs that meet its gold standard.)

Jesus explained that the "greatest commandment" is the indivisible combination of two commandments: to love God and to love others. When it comes to our discipleship, we have tended to emphasize the first—love God, walk in the Spirit, become a new creation in Christ and express the fruit of the Spirit (virtues) in your life. However, we have given only scant attention to providing relationship skill training to fulfill the second commandment of loving others as yourself.

As Christians, we must give the same attention in discipleship to developing skills that are indispensable for healthy and godly relationships as we do to personal spiritual development. We must help our people dig in and "mine out" those relationship skills that then, with the power of the Holy Spirit, can be the vehicles of Christian virtue. In other words, true discipleship must combine the development of Christlike virtue and love for God with the development of the ability to intentionally manage relationships that express agape love with skillful proficiency.

A Theology of Relationships Demands a Paradigm Shift

In this book, we aim to convince you that the unmet needs of dating, marriage, and family relationships within our communities have created the opportunity for churches to step in and offer relationship content that improves those relationships, builds rapport, and ultimately, opens hearts to the Gospel and grows churches. But we want to be emphatically clear: This situation is not just an *opportunity* for churches, it is the *responsibility* of churches according to a Biblical theology of relationships.

In preceding chapters, we examined several Biblical mandates for the centrality of relationships. Now, I want to pull together those themes to make a case for a paradigm shift in our ministry priorities that moves relationship health to the top.

Let's first recall that God has existed for all eternity in relationship and in agape love. The Nicene Creed (AD 325) established that the doctrine of the Trinity was the centerpiece of Christian theology, as had been clearly articulated by the writers of the Gospels and Epistles.

We believe in one God, Father Almighty, Maker of all things seen and unseen; and in one Lord Jesus Christ, the Son of God, begotten of the Father, only-begotten, that is, from the essence of the Father, God of God, light of light, very God of very God, begotten not made, of one essence with the Father; by whom all things were made, both which are in heaven and which are on earth . . . and in the Holy Ghost. Those that say that there was a time when He was not, and that He was not before He was begotten, and that He was made of things that are not; or say that He is of a different hypostasis or essence from the Father, or that the Son of God is created, nourished, and capable of being changed, the Catholic Church anathematizes.[123]

This cannot be emphasized too strongly: Agape love through the vehicle of relationships has existed within the essence of God for all eternity. Truly, relationship is at the heart of the Godhead.

Moreover, God's very fingerprint of relationships is found throughout the universe. All that we know from science has affirmed this Scriptural concept of relationship systems as the template for the universe. There is no part or aspect of matter, neither small nor large, that exists in isolation; everything exists in relationship systems. One might say that God created a universe-masterpiece that mirrors the mysterious but defining characteristic of God—plurality within oneness.

An article titled, *The Beautiful Complexity of the Cosmic Web*, published in *Scientific American*, reviewed the research that supports the theory that all galaxies—groups, clusters, and superclusters—throughout the universe form an immense network that has been labeled the "cosmic web":

> Some people think that the universe is just a hodge-podge of various celestial objects, such as planets, stars and galaxies. But over the years, scientists have found more evidence that the universe may be anything but random and is actually more organized and interconnected—like an enormous spider web. [124]

Just as the macro-sciences affirm that this interconnectedness, or relationship, stretches into the farthest reaches of the known universe, the micro-sciences have found that every particle exists within a relationship, joined together, literally bonded with other particles.[125]

What is so important to observe is this: *Relationships are the essential threads that run throughout the fabric of our entire universe . . . everything relates and interacts in a network.* It is as if the universe is shouting, "Relationships hold together life."

God's plan of relationship was imprinted in the creation of humans even more dramatically than within the rest of creation. For if our universe is held together by the architecture of relational systems, then humans who are singularly created in the image of God are particularly designed to showcase the divine character of relationships. We observed much of this with our treatment of Scripture in Chapter 11.

Then, Jesus raised the priority of relationships to the very highest pinnacle when he joined together two commandments into the framework upon which hangs all the revelation of God through the law and Prophets (Mark 12:29-31).

Relationships must be a top priority in the ministries and outreaches of local churches because relationships are the fingerprint of God on all creation.

This means that true discipleship, true edification of the believers, and true ministry within the body of Christ must first and foremost build and sustain strong relationship skills and virtues that enable all relationships—but most importantly, marriage and family relationships—to fulfill the Great Commandment to love God and love others.

It bears repeating that every time in the New Testament you find "God's will" used to refer to personal spiritual growth, exhortations about relationships immediately follow. When it comes to spiritual growth, the personal and the relational cannot be severed.

Therefore, given the undeniably central importance of relationships to the divine plan, *developing strong relationships must be a top priority in the ministries and outreaches of local churches—because relationships are the fingerprint of God on all creation, and especially on humans who are created in the very image of a relational God, and because they are at the heart of the law of Christ and the will of God.* It is for these reasons that **churches must make a paradigm shift to elevate relationship ministry and infuse it within all other ministries.**

The last section of this book will provide you with a blueprint for making this paradigm shift in your ministry priorities. You will learn how to evaluate the relationship needs of your congregation and community; how to create relationship outreaches; and how to build the ladder that will bring people from your community into relationship ministries and ultimately, into an ongoing growth journey within your church.

*** *

A QUICK RECAP

- Both relationship skills and virtues are needed to equip a person to intentionally manage relationship bonds.
- Relationship skills are the tools that can express the virtues of relationships.
- Churches often overlook the development of relationship skills, even though skill development is at the heart of discipleship.
- The RAM Singles and Couples Studies provide useful skills-based content for this important ministry:
    o **The RAM Couples Study**: This study provides a tool and framework

for married couples to engage in regular meetings called Huddles that help them actively manage their relationship. In order to help identify ways to build the "rely" bond, participants create a top-ten list of needs and wants that they then exchange and use in their Huddles.

o **The RAM Singles Study**: Participants learn to identify the extent that they have progressed in each of the five relationship bonds—as well as how to keep a balance that ensures that they stay within a safe zone as they get to know a partner. To help build discernment, the study also explores five areas about a dating partner (and oneself) that help to reveal character and relationship potential. Singles learn about each of the five areas, and then practice skills and initiating conversations to explore those areas.

- A theology of relationships clearly challenges churches to make a paradigm shift that elevates relationship ministries and outreach to a top priority.

SECTION III:

A Comprehensive Strategy to Strengthen Marriage and Renew the Church

Chapters 13-16

We saw in Section I that parental marriage strongly predicts whether or not someone attends church as an adult. In 1960, just 28 percent of all adults were single. Today, that number is creeping toward 50 percent. As fewer and fewer people grow up in homes with married fathers, fewer and fewer people are open to the Gospel. In Section II, we looked at how the Gospel spread during the early Church because of the example of Christian relationships and, in particular, Christian marriage. We then looked more closely at the bedrock requirements of healthy relationships.

Here in Section III, we will provide a thorough overview of the key ingredients of an effective relationship ministry. *The harvest is plentiful but the workers are few.* Most marriage ministries remain a small side ministry that rarely reaches those who most need it. Just 28 percent of churches have a substantive marriage ministry. Less than 10 percent of churches have any ministry for singles that actively form them for relationship discernment and relationship success. To fill this gap, we will introduce a comprehensive strategy for animating relationship ministry with a proven model for church and community transformation.

CHAPTER 13

Key Ingredients for an Effective Relationship Ministry

A good friend of mine (JP), a priest whom my wife and I have known for years, had been trying to help a couple in crisis. From the outside as an observer, the situation was shocking. This particular couple had a bunch of beautiful kids and appeared to have it all together. They were a homeschooling military family and active in the parish, in church every Sunday. The kids were all sent to a faithful Christian college. The father was a guy that other men in the church looked up to and admired

But this couple's marriage had hit its "endgame."

Unbeknownst to friends, years of physical distance and stress from recurring deployments created an environment in which emotional distance became the norm. The wounds from tragically missed expectations and unmet emotional needs had finally culminated in an affair, and deep resentment set in on both sides.

Some close friends tried to step in, and the couple approached this pastor for help. He tried valiantly to counsel this couple and save their marriage.

It didn't work.

Certainly, there are effective interventions that can occur for couples in crisis, interventions which were not followed here. In this chapter, we'll touch on some of them. But anyone who works in this field will tell you that it is far easier to save a marriage by preventing it from ever falling into such a crisis in the first place.

In the survey that Communio partnered with the Barna Group on, we found that 93 percent of pastors reported that they do counseling for couples in crisis. But 57 percent of these pastors reported feeling either unqualified or only somewhat qualified for it. This finding held fairly consistently across both Protestant and Catholic pastors.

That statistic is shocking when you consider that your local pastor is perhaps the most commonly called "first responder" to a marital crisis. The fact remains that most are ill-equipped to handle it. Common training as a counselor is not sufficient.

Most pastors remain unaware of the most effective marital crisis ministry resources and strategies that are available. Many immediately refer couples to counseling. However, most professional counseling remedies are not evidence-based—meaning, they have not been subjected to outside independent evaluation to determine their efficacy in actually saving a marriage. Much of what passes for professional counseling is frequently shaped by the current relationship zeitgeist and focuses on "self-actualization" at the expense of the relationship. Christians are frequently surprised to find that even many Christian counselors are not primarily focused on helping a couple return to relationship health *as a couple*.

Simply put, most churches lack a "marriage 911" or an effective marriage emergency strategy.

But this critical gap is just one of many within church-based relationship ministry. To the extent marriage ministry might exist in a church, it frequently is comprised of 1) some basic marriage preparation path on the front end, and 2) inadequate crisis ministry on the other. If a church is among the current leaders in this field, it *might* once in a while host a marriage retreat. Now, some church leaders think that crisis ministry may only be needed a handful of times a year. After all, most churchgoers aren't facing a full-blown marriage crisis. With just three to six divorces occurring in a given community for every 1,000 adults in any given calendar year, they could be forgiven for making that conclusion.

But we know the crisis under the visible surface is many times larger than what pastors experience. As of this writing, Communio has helped churches conduct more than 20,000 surveys of their own active churchgoers. What we've found is that, regardless of the denomination, 24 percent of married people who are active members of a church report struggling in their marriage.[126]

The real number of total Christian marriages struggling is much higher, because churchgoing women in our surveying were 31 percent more likely than churchgoing men to report struggling in their marriage. Obviously, if one person in a marriage is struggling, then that marriage is struggling—regardless of whether both individuals are aware of it.

The data suggests what many instinctively know to be true: Men appear less aware of relationship challenges than women. It shows up in other data around divorce filings. Nearly 70 percent of all divorce filers are women.[127] Does this mean women cause 70 percent of divorces? No. Taken together with our survey data, we start to understand why women may often despair of being happy in their marriage. Statistically speaking, men are just less likely to report struggling and, as a consequence, are more likely to be unaware of their wife's struggles.

Our good friend Richard Albertson, the founder of Live the Life Ministries, likes to tell the story of when he and his wife attended a marriage class for the first time. They were to rate their marriage on a one-to-five scale. When he saw his wife's score, he said, "No, honey—five is the high score."

"I know," she replied.

Richard had no idea that his wife was highly dissatisfied. The encounter started him on a path to being, today, one of the national leaders in marriage ministry.

Any practitioner in marriage ministry will tell you that it is frequently a huge challenge to convince a husband to invest in his marriage before he perceives that it is in crisis. Even after he gets a sense that there is an initial challenge, getting him to show up for a program or a multiweek class is often about as hard as teaching a sixth grader advanced physics.

This is a huge obstacle.

A church must work creatively to overcome this important barrier for a relationship ministry to have any chance of success. Marriage and relationship ministry must be much broader than just prepping the engaged or doing sub-par work with those in crisis.

In this chapter, we'll explore the key ingredients in creating an effective relationship ministry, which should rest on the three strong legs of vision, community, and skills. When all of these elements are functioning in tandem, healthy decisions for those dating and married become the cultural norm of the church. This balance also ensures that people who enter your church for the first time, regardless of their romantic life stage, have a clear path for improving their relationship health and deepening their involvement in the life of the church community. After we lay out vision, community, and skills as a conceptual foundation, the next chapter will detail Communio's replicable framework for how a church can most effectively build out these three legs through the Data-Informed, Full-Circle Relationship Ministry.

Vision

"Where there is no vision, the people perish" (Proverbs 29:18 KJV).

The single biggest barrier to the success of a marriage and relationship ministry is the perception that the only people who attend or participate in such a ministry are people who have problems.

We addressed this *mis*perception directly in Chapter 9, which highlights how healthy relationships require intentional management. It is worth repeating: No relationship runs itself or fixes itself. We must therefore remove this barrier by elevating regular involvement in relationship ministry as a badge of a strong and healthy relationship rather than a sign of troubles.

In the 21st century, there aren't many homes with white picket fences anymore, but we do live in a world of Facebook, Instagram, and social media—where many of us want to project a life of unending happiness and success. We have pictures of lovely outings, delicious meals, and smiling kids.

For the most part, folks aren't posting as frequently about their real struggles at home. And we don't think that's a bad thing—we're not saying that we should be posting about deep struggles and challenges. Social media is a fairly public and oftentimes permanent forum where airing one's intimate laundry is unlikely to be healthy or productive. What we are saying is that any ministry must overcome the social media relationship culture where we project lives of endless rainbows and candy canes. This is where a church's vision for relationships comes into play.

For a church, a sound vision for relationship ministry begins from the pulpit and should be infused into all its ongoing hospitality, ministry, spiritual formation, and community outreach efforts. Put simply, the vision should communicate that:

> This is a church where all members, especially those with great marriages, regularly and intentionally invest in their relationship health. Marriage itself is an imitation and a sign of the relationship between Jesus and His Church (Ephesians 5) and so we celebrate it, invest in it, and encourage it.

Perhaps the most important phrase in that vision statement is "especially those with great marriages." We'll drill into this further in a moment.

To achieve this vision, you should think through how it is reinforced and repeated through sermons, announcements, and outreach run by the church. In the next chapter, we'll discuss the mechanics of Communio's Data-Informed, Full-Circle Relationship Ministry. But before getting there, we will recommend several practical tips you might consider employing at your church to advance a sound vision concerning relationship health.

Tip No. 1: De-stigmatize relationship enrichment.

If someone at your church announced that they had recently attended a marriage class or retreat, how likely is it that their fellow church members would immediately assume that the couple might be having problems?

Like it or not, marriage programs and marriage classes frequently and wrongly carry a stigma. It's the greatest misconception among singles and married couples. The Church's failure to fundamentally shift this mindset remains the biggest barrier to increasing participation in relationship enrichment of any kind.

Years ago, I (JP) was speaking with a pastor who was completely committed to marriage ministry—someone easily in the top 5 percent of pastors in terms of his investment in pastoral support for couples and for marriage. But a challenge this pastor faced was that interest in his church's marriage class had dried up. They were having a hard time finding any takers. When I asked him some of the ways he encouraged couples to attend their marriage class, he had an interesting take on it.

"I tell everyone in the church that if you don't love your spouse more today than you did one year ago, then you should join our marriage class," he said.

So, should we assume all those attending the marriage class loved their spouses less than they did before? How many people want to admit that publicly? How many people want to associate themselves with that thought? Ultimately, the pastor was inviting people to participate based on a negative motivation: If you don't love your spouse more today, you should come.

Here's our advice: When setting the vision before the entire congregation, go the other direction altogether. Make an entirely positive case for relationship enrichment.

If you have a great car, you don't wait to service it until it is breaking down, do you? No. You want it to keep running perfectly, so you bring it in regularly to have the fluids changed. In the same way, if you have a great marriage, today is a great time to attend relationship ministry. Just as long-term health requires good diet and exercise, so also does a healthy marriage require sustenance and activity. Relationship ministry is like strength training for your healthy marriage.

A Biblical example can be seen in our Lord's relationship with the Father. These two Persons in the Trinity are one (John 17). Yet, Jesus didn't take this for granted. He spent much time with His Father in prayer—you might say, He invested in that relationship regularly.

There is no way the Second Person of the Trinity, God the Son, could have needed to "work on" or "improve" His relationship with the First Person of the Trinity, God the Father. Yet still He invested in it. The time Jesus spent in prayer also drew in the apostles, who wanted to learn to pray like Him.

Remember that the Trinity is a model for a Christian marriage. No husband could ever have a better relationship with his wife than God the Son has with God the Father. And no wife could ever have a better relationship with her husband than do the Persons of the Trinity, either. So on what basis should someone with a great marriage *not* invest regularly in that relationship?

As we covered earlier, our survey data shows that one in four married people at your church are likely struggling right now in their marriage. By making a positive case for relationship ministry—that it's for everyone at this church, especially for people with great marriages—you allow those who are struggling in their marriage to attend without any shame. Participating won't mark them as having a troubled marriage. Additionally, those who have a great marriage can be better inculcated with the skills to help them navigate the inevitable challenges that come to all marriages, regardless of whether they are experiencing them now.

Tip No. 2: Keep in mind that every marriage has seasons.
Everyone struggles at different times in their marriage.

I (JP) like to joke that my wife, Christina, and I are extraverted extraverts. One of the hardest points in our marriage was when we moved to Virginia from Florida. Neither of us had any friendships in the area. We found ourselves often together and lonely. We love being together, but we also love being together with our friends. This was one of several hard stretches for us.

> *Our survey data shows that one in four married people at your church are likely struggling right now in their marriage.*

Through my work, Christina and I have had the chance to get to know Nicky and Sila Lee, the authors of Alpha's marriage course. They hosted us for lunch in their vicarage in Brompton on a trip a few years ago and we were blown away by their spirit of hospitality and their love for one another. One element they hit upon is that every marriage has its seasons. Some seasons are harder and more barren than others. This should not be a surprise to any of us. On this side of the eschaton, we will always experience suffering. Single people and married people alike—all experience suffering. So, advancing a message that marriage has different seasons (and some are more challenging than others) can help couples see their struggles as part of the norm of relationship life.

We emphasized this point when we explained in Chapter 9 that every relationship needs constant re-balancing, because life comes at us fast. There is a natural deflating that occurs from good experiences of life, not just the challenges. That is to be expected in every relationship, and especially in marriage.

Those who persevere through the most challenging seasons in their marriage report being happy again in their marriages afterwards. We referenced a study that bears repeating, *Does Divorce Make People Happy?*, that Shaunti Feldhahn also wrote about in her amazing book, *The Good News on Marriage: Debunking Discouraging Myths about Marriage and Divorce.* This study found that the vast majority of people who report being unhappy in their marriage subsequently report being happy in their marriage within five years. Feldhahn explained further that, among those unhappy couples who stick with their marriage, "the largest improvement [came] for those who were the most miserable." The report drew two conclusions:

- Two out of three unhappily married adults who avoided divorce or separation ended up happily married five years later.[128]
- Among those who rated their marriages as very unhappy, almost eight out of ten who avoided divorce were happily married five years later.

Every couple should be told and understand, through your preaching and teaching, that such ebbs and periodic unhappiness are normal for all marriages—including great marriages.

> Adult singles are some of the most underserved populations within relationship ministry.

Tip No. 3: Develop a game plan for singles.
Great marriages begin long before the wedding day! However, adult singles are some of the most underserved populations within relationship ministry. We already pointed out that our Barna study found that less than 10 percent of all churches in the United States have any ministry to adult singles, even though single heads of households comprise around 50 percent of our total population.

In this respect, creating a robust ministry to single young adults—and not just "young professionals"—is critically important. Recall that as many as 60 percent of millennials do not have a bachelor's degree. I (John) live in Southern California, in a town of around 65,000. Our family attends a church that has specifically targeted twentysomethings. It hosts a weekly gathering for them on Sunday evenings, using most of the building to engage around 300 singles. This church has a paid staff member whose ministry responsibilities are focused specifically on adult singles. As I sat down with him to talk about his ministry, he explained that so few churches offer anything meaningful for their singles that around 35 to 40 percent of those who attend are actually from other churches. Some come from close to an hour away, both to have relationships with other Christians within their age group and because this ministry has such relevance to their lives.

Now remember, I live in Orange County in Southern California—an area with a population of 3.1 million with many large and thriving churches. I was shocked to hear that so many singles feel overlooked in the churches they attend. But this matches the data from Communio's Barna study on the small number of churches providing ministries to singles. Perhaps a major barrier to this ministry type is that churches are not sure what the right relationship resources for singles are. They definitely lack meaningful outreach that invites singles into their communities. And yet, study after study on the millennial generation reveals that their *number one concern* is their relationships.

When such ministry exists, it often is geared to young professionals. Many churches seemingly forget that the majority of young adults never get a four-year degree. The programming and outreach designed by many churches oftentimes accidentally feeds into a class divide among young adults. Christina and I (JP) had this experience in helping a young, single mom in our area who had a GED and no further education. She shared with us that she felt out of place at young adult events in our area (Washington, DC-northern Virginia), because, she said, the substance always flew over her head.

For outreach to singles, one technique that works well is for churches to organize adult sports teams and even leagues as the outreach element of the ministry ladder. These teams and leagues can be co-ed. But they generally skew toward single, young adult men. An amazing ministry in Kansas City called City on a Hill, built by two former FOCUS (Fellowship of Catholic University Students) missionaries, has used this strategy to build effective outreach to single adult men.

Why do we emphasize single adult men? Because Communio's surveys of churchgoers show that 72 percent of all single respondents are women. Therefore, ministry to singles must focus on attracting men, as they are deeply underrepresented in nearly every church. (We will discuss this further in the next chapter.) I (JP) tell pastors that this basically means churches are like inverted night clubs. Night clubs are always trying to come up with ways to induce women to attend. Churches are in the same boat, but with the gender disparity reversed. Now, I wouldn't suggest breaking out velvet ropes and bouncers, but churches must think creatively about how to lure men via outreach. There is a general view among social scientists that sex-ratio imbalances can distort the behavior of getting married. In particular, when that number skews heavily where men are in the minority, they find marriage occurs less frequently. This is the central claim of Jon Birger's book *Date-onomics: How Dating Became a Lopsided Numbers Game*, and one that Mark Regnerus has made separately.

But from a ministry standpoint, when one says singles, one should include all those unmarried in this category: singles who are not dating or cohabiting, the unmarried who are dating, and those who are cohabiting. As we explained in Chapter 3, the world of singles has become increasingly complicated, as relationships have become less defined and commitments more ambiguous. Effective ministry must address the needs of unmarried people in a wide range of situations.

One example of helping to bridge the divide between singles who are not in any relationship and those who are, and even those cohabiting, is the RAM Singles Study. In this group study, all participants learn areas to explore in their own lives as well as with a dating partner. Those in a relationship can step back and evaluate the strengths and weaknesses of their present relationship, while those not in a relationship can discuss their friendships while they also learn a template of key areas to explore with a future dating partner. Presenting relationship resources that address the relevant and multifaceted needs of this large single population will enhance their relationships while validating their involvement in churches.

For the singles who are truly single (not dating or cohabiting), we recommend developing a separate Ministry Engagement Ladder that targets this group in particular. Given limited time and resources, the churches we advise normally begin with the couples' side of the ladder and then only add outreach for singles twelve to eighteen months after starting relationship ministry for couples. For those who are dating and those who are cohabiting, we encourage churches to be very intentional in their outreach to include them in anything being done to attract couples. Many of our church partners have been successful in pulling in those cohabiting in order to build relationships and help them to re-evaluate the "sequence" of their relationship bonds.

Tip No. 4: Infuse relationship ministry and content within ALL facets of your church.
This is the starting point of honoring the theological centrality of relationships: First and foremost, task all ministry leaders with finding creative opportunities to engage their people with relationship content. You do not have to "reinvent the wheel." Instead, infuse an ongoing relationship-focus within all ministries by having leadership consistently offer relationship content. This overarching focus allows those ministry leaders to contextualize that content to best meet the needs of those in their specific ministry.

> Ministry to singles must focus on attracting men, as they are deeply underrepresented in nearly every church.

This infusion will also greatly increase the impact and effectiveness of your efforts to help people grow in their relationship health. It will also rebrand the concept of building and sustaining healthy relationships from just being another "one of our many ministries," to a more Biblical mandate: *"Relationship health is the shared mission of all our ministries."* We will discuss the key ingredients of relationship health content when we get to skills further below.

Tip No. 5: Publicly recognize relationship milestones and new marriages.
Even before the COVID pandemic, in 2019, the total rate of marriages hit an all-time low. There were just 33.2 marriages per 1,000 women ages fifteen and older within the population. To put that in perspective, in the year 2000,

Are you still assuming that people will just get married and that you can begin to minister to them when they present themselves?

there were 48.2 marriages per 1,000 and in 1980 there were 68.8 marriages per 1,000 women ages fifteen and older. That number was 86 marriages per 1,000 women ages fifteen and older in 1970. The marriage rate has decreased 31 percent over the last twenty years, 48 percent over the last forty years, and 61 percent over the last fifty years[129] (Figure 13:1).

Unfortunately, there is no one-stop database for the total number of Christian marriages occurring each year that would help us understand the state of Christian marriage. But by looking at America's largest individual church body, we can see how sharp the decline has been. The last time that the Catholic Church in America reported more weddings than funerals was in the early 1970s, when Catholics had roughly 400,000 marriages and funerals alike. In 2019, there

Figure 13.1

The U.S. Marriage Rate Is at an All-Time Low

Number of newly married people per 1000 unmarried population age 15+

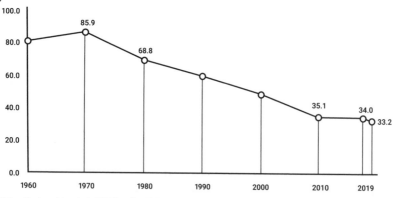

Notes: Marriage data prior to 2010 based on CDC/NCHS National Vital Statistics.
Unmarried population include those who have never been married, divorced or widowed.

were 392,277 funerals and just 137,885 marriages.[130] When you consider the absolute number of Catholics has increased by eighteen million, or 25 percent, over that time frame, you begin to grasp just how vast is the per capita collapse in marriage.

Use any metric you like for tracking such trends, and the story is the same: Marriage has been in a sharp decline.

So, what is your church doing to promote new marriages? Or are you still assuming that people will just get married . . . and that you can begin to minister to them once they present themselves? Perhaps you are counting on the culture around us to encourage marriages to take place? We hope this data disabuses you of that notion.

At the level of vision, every church in America should lean into the catastrophic decline in marriage by holding up and encouraging marriage in creative ways. For instance, Communio encourages churches to celebrate milestone anniversaries, and to offer to pray over those couples and renew vows at those milestones. The cost of a wedding has made it prohibitively expensive to include the entire church body in the celebration of a new marriage. So, we recommend that churches hold a quarterly churchwide celebration for all the weddings that took place among church members over the previous months.

At this celebration, newlyweds can be introduced to the whole church and invited to share their story of how they met. Those who have been married the longest can win a prize and share advice with the newlyweds and attendees. Attendees might be encouraged to bring a modest or no-cost gift such as a prayer bouquet for the newly married couples. You might even have newlyweds share their favorite part of their marriage preparation process or invite long-time married couples to share a key point that helped them from the church's relationship ministry. The objective here is to hold up and celebrate recently married couples, thereby encouraging marriage and making it more desirable to get married in and with the church.

Consider also publicly recognizing engagements. Those who have moved far enough through your church's discernment and marriage preparation process could be announced and welcomed.

> Do you see wedding fees in your church as a revenue generator? If so, please stop.

Tip No. 6: Reduce or eliminate fees and barriers associated with Christian weddings.

Most Christian weddings no longer occur on a church's campus. Some Evangelical churches won't even hold a wedding on their campus because it is always being used for other forms of ministry. If your church doesn't make its space available, consider changing that policy—and provide an inexpensive way for a couple to get married.

Finally, if your church does hold weddings on site, you should think through fees connected to weddings. Do you see these fees as a revenue generator? If so, please stop.

Setting aside the many great and obvious evangelical reasons for doing this, these fees are an outdated practice. Sometimes the fee served as a way for a church to get a couple to understand the weightiness of the decision. They were created in a time when couples felt the obligation to get married in a church and when weddings were very much the norm. This is no longer the case. They are justified only because the cost to operate the physical campus is a real expense. But if a church can't cover its costs without wedding fees, then that church probably has much larger challenges that can't be fixed through such fees.

As we have chronicled elsewhere in this book, Christian weddings are the key to the future health of the church. These fees put up unnecessary barriers at the very moment when someone is asking for marriage. The secular marriage industrial complex may behave as if they are forever hearing the sound of cash-registers cha-chinging—but the Church should not.

Besides, for those thinking about the effect of those lost fees on their church's ministries, consider that the long-term value of a married couple belonging to a church is many multiples of any transitory set of wedding fees. Waving such fees in conjunction with a marriage preparation strategy that forms real disciples—Witness to Love's program is atop this list of disciple-forming tools for the engaged—will expand the number of couples who actually become active members of your church.

To show you how this approach can work on a practical basis, let me tell you about a young man who my wife, Christina, and I (JP) knew many years ago through our days volunteering in youth ministry. He had graduated high school and worked as a barista at a nearby coffee shop. Like other young adults, he drifted in and out of church and moved in with his girlfriend. He eventually got her pregnant. Christina and I happened to see him and his twenty-plus week pregnant girlfriend one day at church. The social science will tell you church attendance is really unusual for cohabiting couples. This providential moment offered us a chance to reconnect. We invited them both over for dinner and began to build a stronger personal relationship. One day, I asked him, "Mike, I know you love your girlfriend—why aren't you married to her yet?" He said he just didn't feel like he had the money to give her a wedding. I was dumbfounded.

The barrier was the cost.

Christina and I called friends at our parish and we figured out a way for a group of us to organize a wedding reception for them. When we told him about our idea, he became excited. He ended up proposing to his girlfriend in front of friends at our annual Epiphany party. The reception was held at the nearby Knights of Columbus hall. Our friends got crafty on the decorations and we catered it with the finest Chick-fil-A had to offer. They remain happily married today and are closing in on a decade of marriage.

You and I can't easily imagine how much wedding expectations—and the costs associated with them—can form a barrier to encouraging marriage.

Tip No. 7: Ritualize relationship ministry throughout the calendar year.
Healthy relationship messaging and content should be peppered throughout a church's calendar. There should be "staple" relationship content that is offered regularly throughout the year. An example of this is a premarital course for engaged couples. This is mandatory in Catholic settings, and in many other church settings, for anyone seeking a church wedding. But, as valuable as premarital instruction is, it is not sufficient. So we recommend three other repeating content areas: dating; marriage; and parenting/family life.

Churches that have regular additions to their congregations can create a funnel system for new attendees to join a relevant relationship small group or class, along with whatever church orientation or membership class is offered.

Another approach to ensuring that relationship content is offered consistently is to integrate relationship content within the liturgical calendar. This relationship content would be related to the liturgical season and could be presented during the message or homily, or offered in another setting. This leads us to our next tip.

Tip No. 8: Preach regularly on marriage and relationship health.
Pastors have their own stories and their own testimony on marriage and relationships. Most have had their own struggles. Bearing authentic witness to those struggles is one of the very best ways for pastors to relate to other couples. There are always ways to take a message on marriage and relate it to those at any stage of relationship life.

Communio worked closely with Sun Valley Community Church in Phoenix and Chad Moore, its dynamic pastor. Through their partnership with Communio, Chad's team did substantial outreach and poured resources into their couples ministry. As a result, Chad's church experienced more than 20 percent growth during our 2016 to 2018 test phase with them. When asked for some key tips he'd share with other pastors, he didn't hesitate or miss a beat:

> The first thing that I would tell pastors in the realm of relationship ministry is this: anytime you have a sermon, you've got to ask yourself, *"Is this helpful?"* It's not just information that we're delivering. We're delivering an opportunity for application, and then with that, transformation. And people that show up to our doors could care less about our eschatology or ecclesiology or any of those kinds of things.
>
> The difference between a theologian and a pastor is the difference between a scientist and a medical doctor. What's the difference between a scientist and a medical doctor? People. As pastors we're called to reach, to love, and to lead people. And so, as we deliver our theology, we have to ask ourselves, *Is this helpful?* And people in our church week in and week out are going, *Is this going to help my marriage?* Is this going to help my

parenting? Is this going to help me—if they're a single adult—find the right kind of person? We have such a great opportunity to meet people right where they are with the unchanging truth of God's Word that is so practical, helpful, and life-changing. So I would say when you preach, "Is it helpful? Can any common person anywhere understand what you are saying and apply it to their life?"

Now, as a person who has an intense interest in eschatology and ecclesiology, I (JP) found myself raising some mental walls at Pastor Moore's comment. Obviously, Jesus told the Pharisees, "You shall love the Lord your God with all your heart, and with all your soul, and with all your mind" (Matthew 22:37 ESV). A key element of loving our Lord with all our mind means diving into the sacred Scriptures and grasping sound theology. However, I don't think Chad is dismissing the importance of this at all.

You see, his point is not that theology is not intensely important. Given the cultural storm around relationship health within our culture and the spiritual situation of the average church attendee, he is challenging pastors to ask the question that will help center their preaching on relationships and relationship health: "Is this helpful?" Chad had more to share:

The second thing: I would be very strategic about next steps. I believe preaching is catalytic. There are different parts to discipleship. And one-on-ten thousand is one aspect, but it's catalytic at best. And so, churches [must] provide opportunity, and very practical teaching, for people to take steps: "Go get in this group, it'll help your marriage . . . Go get in this group, it'll help you in your singleness . . . Go into this group, it'll help you with your parenting." Use those felt needs as opportunities to get people off of the weekend once you've helped them. It's catalytic and they're thinking to take a step and to actually follow Jesus.

Later, we'll review Communio's Ministry Engagement Ladder, which is part of our Data-Informed, Full-Circle Relationship Ministry to explore what practical next steps look like. As we saw in Tip No. 1 above, the stigma associated with relationship ministry is the single biggest barrier to success. Chad's final point is incredibly helpful to pastors as they think through ways to break down this barrier through preaching in a new way:

> The third thing is I would say is model your mistakes. One of the things we have leveraged here at our church is my weakness. The ways that I've been a relational idiot for most of my life. Pastors ask, "How can I preach a sermon that's relatable?" You can't. Because people don't relate to sermons. People relate to people. And so, when you put yourself in there—and when you preach out of weakness you never run out of material—but when you put yourself in there, and you talk about what you're learning, your failings, those kinds of things; and then talk about how this marriage class helped me, how this parenting thing helped me and it'll help you too . . . And by God's grace we're all in this together.

If we'll do that—preach, teach, model, and celebrate—that's how you build culture. So if the pastor will be very practical when they're preaching and teaching, and if they'll give really simple steps that people can take, that'll be helpful. And if they'll model it, through their own lives, through their own failures and what they've learned, and those kinds of things—that threefold strategy is really powerful in connecting with people, helping them relate to you, and helping them actually take steps that change their lives.

Chad's final point about being authentic in your weaknesses as a pastor is a powerful one. You might wonder if this advice is at odds with the positive suggestions in Tip No. 1. Not at all. Making sure everyone knows that relationship ministry is important for those in every marriage—especially those in great marriages—is an important message to communicate. Sharing your own personal struggles places any "negative" message within your own life experience, giving credibility and allowing others in the church to identify with it. Combining these themes is a powerful way to establish your vision.

Now, perhaps you are reading this book from a Catholic perspective, where pastors aren't typically married. As a Catholic with a priest for a brother, I want to tell Catholic pastors that they can still share their own relationship struggles and their own stories. Every priest had parents, and every priest has his own family of origin stories. In today's age, most of the ordained have "late vocations"—meaning they frequently dated or were engaged at one time in their lives. Following the Apostle Paul's encouragement of celibacy (1 Corinthians 7:32-35, 38) does not mean you cannot preach out of your own weaknesses. Let's just remember that God used the Apostle Paul, a single man, to pen some of the greatest Scriptural passages on the meaning and virtues of marriage in the New Testament.

Tip No. 9: Email, call, or write personal notes celebrating relationship milestones.

A personal note of encouragement from staff or clergy at your church celebrating specific relationship milestones is a great way to regularly reinforce a church's vision on marriage and relationships. In your church's existing database or CRM, do you have a place to register engagements, anniversaries, or deaths of a spouse?

> *Preach, teach, model, and celebrate—that's how you build culture.*

Could your staff divvy up the list to drop a handwritten note or call to congratulate a couple at key milestones, or to comfort a surviving spouse on the anniversary date of their husband or wife's death? Could your database be automated to send a personal email message from someone on staff to a member on their anniversary date?

If this seems too big a lift, could you start simply with messages or calls around the anniversaries of the weddings that clergy at your church personally officiated? I'll bet that even your insurance agent sends you a birthday card—so how much more should we celebrate the major relationship milestones of those in our church families.

In communications with couples, you could consider including a list of activities for couples your church is hosting over the next twelve months, along with an invitation to participate in a specific one.

And don't forget the singles you have within your church family. Many of them may be quiet, but they have relationship anniversaries too. There are those who have lost a spouse and continue to faithfully attend and engage in ministries, while no one remembers the anniversary of their beloved partner. And there are also those who have divorced who would be blown away if they received an email or note near the anniversary of their divorce, letting them know that they are being upheld in prayer.

Community

"Belong, Believe, Become."— *Mary Rose Verret, co-founder, Witness to Love*

When Christ set out to preach that the Kingdom of God was at hand, His first actions were not didactic. Instead, He invited the Apostles to enter into relationship with Him. Clearly his actions were deeply typological and ecclesiological in choosing the three—Peter, James, and John—as well as the twelve and the seventy. These weren't random numbers of coincidence.

Any effective relationship ministry must focus on creating easy on-ramps for people to belong.

It's important to understand that *communio*, or community with Christ, was the first step along the path to conversion for His disciples. When we are in an authentic relationship with someone, that person has the ability to influence us positively and help us grow as followers of Christ.

My (JP) friend Mary Rose Verret, the co-founder of the marriage ministry Witness to Love, put it very succinctly recently. Ultimately, she said, the steps toward transformation are threefold: "Belong, believe, become."

When we enter into authentic relationship with faithful Christians, we find a place where we *belong*. We experience the love of Christ through men and women in community. As we do this, we want to know why they love. We learn their love is animated by a person—the divine person of Jesus Christ and what He did for each one of us. This leads us to *believe*. The gifts of faith and love active in our life prompt us to *become* something more, changing how we live and who we are.

Following this model, any effective relationship ministry must focus on creating easy on-ramps for people to belong. This is why my organization is called Communio, because authentic Christian community is the first ingredient for encountering Christ. It is also an essential piece of any church-based relationship ministry.

But what pathways has your church developed that allow authentic relationships to form? In the next chapter, we will provide an overview of how Communio supports churches in the development of these pathways around relationship health through our Ministry Engagement Ladder. For now, we will provide just a few thoughts.

My current pastor, Fr. Alvero Montero, recently shared with me that behind the Iron Curtain in countries like Czechoslovakia, the Communist regime often allowed elements of worship like attending Mass. They were fine with that. What they didn't want was fellowship. So, they strictly controlled the life-giving elements of Christian community, knowing that such fellowship represented a huge threat to their regime.

As Christians, we know that life changes most powerfully through personal relationships. So what contexts, spaces, and opportunities does your church provide to make it easy for the people of God to form meaningful personal relationships with those who are not yet in your church, or with those who are not yet believers?

When Christians serve the poor, these opportunities frequently flow out of ministries that provide for basic needs, food pantries, or job ministries. When Christians go to third-world nations, we show up and dig wells, provide shelter, and give food. When the people see how we love, they want to know why. This sparks a curiosity that creates an openness to the Gospel.

At home, we live in the wealthiest nation on earth. Unlike in the Third World, very few live in absolute poverty, as measured by the number of people who live on $1.25 or less per day in the United States. But as Section I made clear, we do live with a tremendous poverty—a

Are our marriages and our homes as hospitable as the home in Bethany?

poverty in relationships.

Now, this poverty exists in every form of relationship, but here I want to draw us to the current nihilism surrounding the sexual embrace and our romantic relationships. As we showed previously, the majority of couples report having had sex with each other for the first time before a relationship formed. This immediate jump into the most high-intensity area of touch within John's Relationship Attachment Model—before knowing, trusting, relying, and committing—leaves a landscape of relationship wreckage, trauma, anxiety, and despair.

In church surveys we've completed, 62 percent of singles report "feeling weighed down from baggage from their past."

Kenny Comstock, the late executive pastor at Crossroads Church in Odessa (who tragically died with his wife in a car accident), attended our strategic planning session with his church leadership. When he listened to Communio's model, something clicked. He interrupted: "We already get this." Kenny said to his team with the fire and zeal of a missionary, "Relationship ministry is like digging wells for clean water!" He was comparing the service his church provides to the needy in the Third World with what it could bring to minister to the needs in the First World.

How many opportunities does your church create for couples, outside of and inside the church, to do something fun where they can encounter others in healthy relationships and invest in their own relationship? If you have these gatherings, how many of the less-churched or unchurched would find those opportunities actually attractive? How many non-Christians show up?

Let's face it, in our post-Christian world, most people are not yet ready to be invited to praise and worship on Wednesday night at an Evangelical church or Saturday family adoration hour at a Catholic parish. There is a natural barrier for the unchurched to such higher-intensity faith activities. What are your church's creative pre-evangelization relationship ministry on-ramps? You need them. And you need them in abundance. We'll go through some specific ideas and strategy in the section on the Data-Informed, Full-Circle Relationship Ministry.

My (JP) parish is run by an amazing group of men, the Disciples of the Hearts of Jesus and Mary, who focus their entire ministry on evangelization in and through the family. They place a great emphasis on what we can learn Biblically from the home in Bethany where Martha and Mary lived with Lazarus. This home was a home where Jesus was always welcome. He could come and go as He pleased because of His relationship with them. Because of their hospitality, our Lord was so close to Lazarus that He wept when He learned that he had died. It's the only occasion in the Scriptures where we see Jesus so overcome by sorrow.

Are our marriages and our homes as hospitable as the home in Bethany? Are you creating easy opportunities for your church to facilitate this hospitality for the less-churched or the unchurched? Are you creating the witness and the expectation among your people of such Christian hospitality? When someone comes to a gathering, do they encounter Christ through those they meet? This level of hospitality—especially when grounded in the family—is deeply attractive to a world badly lacking the security and safety of stable families and healthy relationships.

I (John) am so encouraged by the model of church planting that is being practiced throughout Latvia. Bill Hoyt is a former pastor, denominational executive with Converge Worldwide, and now President of NexStep Coaching and Consulting. I was sharing with him my vision for churches using home small-group marriage studies as a means for outreach, with those who attend the church inviting their unchurched friends or neighbors to also come.

Bill looked at me and said, "You have to meet Igors." Igors Rautmanis helped establish the Baltic Pastoral Institute (BPI) in Riga, Latvia. Through his involvement at BPI and a personal ministry of coaching leaders, Igors influences key leaders throughout Latvia. His full-time work is the European Regional Director for the International Fellowship of Evangelical Students. Igors is one of the most focused church planters I have ever met.

Bill has taught leadership courses at the Baltic Pastoral Institute for years. He arranged a week with Igors in Latvia, where we provided relationship-focused training and support for Latvian students, pastors and church planters. You see, their primary approach to outreach and evangelism involves establishing small-group marriage studies in homes and inviting the unchurched to attend. They have received overwhelming interest, and the most common request when the marriage study is completed is, "Okay—what's next?"

Infusing mission outreach through relevant relationship-focused small-group studies held in homes is not just an approach that works in Eastern European settings. Regardless of geography and despite cultural differences, it is one of the best ways to build deeper relationships while addressing an essential need. That's why it's so prominent in Communio's Ministry Engagement Ladder as the growth journey rung. Everyone seems to know someone outside of their church family, either an individual or a couple, that is hungry for relationship content. Some need to be reached through big events that have small commitments (such as attending a three-hour event). But there are others who would gladly step into a six-week small home group if it is hosted by a good friend.

Skills

Enhancing spiritual growth and Biblical knowledge.

The hard work of putting ideas into daily practice is the area where many churches fumble when they consider marriage and relationship ministry. In the second section of this book, we offered a thorough overview of relationship health and provided examples of how teaching relationship content should be combined with practicing the virtues *and* skills. This was our Lord's model of discipleship—teach, model, practice, and then commission—and it is essential for church leaders to understand and implement.

A singular focus on relationship skills without any emphasis on virtue is dangerous.

At times, there appears to be a view within church leadership and Christian circles that spiritual growth, theological knowledge, and Biblical depth is all that is needed for people to have a healthy marriage. But good teaching on marriage is not enough—no matter how compelling a sermon, homily, or spiritual reflection might be.

Of course, a singular focus on relationship skills without any emphasis on virtue is dangerous and can create manipulative people who leverage skills without virtuous motives. But the failure to teach skills while teaching virtue is equally problematic, often resulting in individuals and couples who know *what* God wants them to do but who lack the skills and habits for *how* they should do it.

The good news is that there are many skills-based resources that both teach and practice the skills necessary for healthy relationships. The two categories of virtues and skills previously outlined—interpersonal and intrapersonal—are helpful ways to organize and evaluate the relationship courses and programs your church provides.

There are two important points to clarify before giving examples of skills-based topics. The first point is that some relationship courses cover many of these areas in a global approach to relationships, while others focus on just one main area of relationships. For instance, the RAM Series for Couples is a global approach to working on a marriage relationship and will cover many of the skills listed below. In contrast, a small-group study on forgiveness might be just as valuable but will tend to only focus on a few of the skills.

Second, many of these *intra*personal skills have an *inter*personal skill counterpart. Let's take a course on forgiveness as an example. Of course, learning to forgive requires that you internalize Scriptural principles about forgiveness, while also relying on Jesus to cultivate a forgiving spirit in your heart. But then you also need to grow in knowing how to express your forgiveness to others, particularly the one you have forgiven. So, it is fair to say that an effective course will provide practical spiritual exercises and skills for letting go of the thoughts and emotions related to an offense (intra-skills) while also teaching and practicing skills of apologizing, talking through hurts, and expressing forgiveness to one another (inter-skills).

Therefore, these two categories often overlap when they address a common relationship area, and it is vital that our relationship content provide Biblical teaching along with opportunities to model and practice skills in both categories.

1. *Interpersonal Skill Building.*

As we previously explained, *interpersonal competence* refers to the skills and virtues that are used to manage a relationship and the ways you interact with one another. It involves mastering the skills that are essential for maintaining a strong relationship—with a spouse, with a friend, or within a family. Some of the primary skill areas that need to be taught, practiced, and developed are:

- Communication skills: e.g., active listening, self-disclosure, and restatement; [131]
- Conflict resolution skills: e.g., apologies, forgiveness, conflict resolution plans;
- Emotional intimacy skills: e.g., giving and receiving support;
- Togetherness skills: e.g., sharing roles and responsibilities ;
- Relationship management skills: e.g., regular couple check-ins and planning meetings for mutual need fulfillment.

2. *Intrapersonal Skill Building.*

Intrapersonal competence, on the other hand, is all about the thoughts, feelings, and attitudes within each person in a relationship. It takes personal skills to regulate your own thoughts and emotions and how you view another.

In a marriage, for instance, we could say that every spouse lives with a partner in the home and a partner in their head. The attitudes and feelings that they hold toward their spouse in their head will filter the ways that they act and react with their spouse in the home.

This is not just true of marriage, but of all our relationships—with our children, our friends, our faith communities, and even God. We must develop skills to manage the relationship "within" our heads in addition to the skills to handle the relationship "between" ourselves and others. Developing an interior life of prayer centered on Christ is one practical skill area that should be built in our minds and hearts. Churches should encourage this form of spiritual growth inside and outside of relationship ministry. Some of the other primary skill areas that need to be taught, practiced, and developed are:

- Discernment skills: e.g., discerning the marriage potential of a dating partner;[132] Appreciation skills: e.g., focusing on the strengths of a spouse

in marriage;[133]
- Self-control skills: e.g., managing anger and sexual boundaries;
- Expectation skills: e.g., cultivating realistic expectations for marriage;[134]
- Commitment skills: e.g., maintaining a priority of marriage.[135]

Many churches are unaware of the extensiveness of the Christian skills-based relationship content that is already available to them, but these resources are both plentiful and easily accessible. Communio has compiled a comprehensive catalogue of more than eighty effective resources in relationship education that allow church leaders to sort materials by a number of different criteria including: type (plug-and-play, facilitator-led, group study, event-based), faith tradition (Evangelical, Protestant, Catholic), audience (singles, engaged, married, crisis ministry, parenting), venue (online versus in-person), and costs. There is no reason for a church leader to be wondering where to find effective resources for relationship ministry.

Communio-subscribing churches can access this catalogue, and a host of other support services, at Communio.org.

*** *

A QUICK RECAP
- Most churches simply lack a 911 or an effective marriage emergency strategy.
- Communio's surveys of active churchgoers shows that one in four people at any given church are likely struggling in their marriage.
- Adult singles are some of the most underserved populations within relationship ministry. Moreover, the singles in churches are overwhelmingly female. Attracting single men must be a priority for every church and relationship ministry.
- Marriages have decreased 31 percent over the last twenty years, 48 percent over the last forty years, and 61 percent over the last fifty years. Are you still assuming that people will just get married, and that you can begin to minister to them once they present themselves? And if so, why exactly?
- When we are in an authentic relationship with someone, that person has the ability to influence us positively and help us grow as followers of Christ.

- Any effective relationship ministry must focus on creating easy on-ramps for people to belong and form real relationships. So, what are your church's creative "on-ramps" for relationship ministry?
- Relationship skills devoid of virtues are dangerous and can create manipulative people who leverage skills without virtuous motives. But the failure to teach the skills while teaching virtue is equally problematic.
- Some relationship courses cover many of these areas in a global approach to relationships, while others are focused on just one main area of relationships.
- Interpersonal skill-building and intrapersonal skill-building: these two categories often overlap when they address a common relationship area. It is vital that our relationship content provides Biblical teaching along with opportunities to model and practice skills in both categories.
    - o *Interpersonal competence* refers to the skills and virtues that are used to manage a relationship, the ways you interact with one another. It involves mastering the skills that are essential for maintaining a strong relationship.
    - o *Intrapersonal competence*, on the other hand, is all about the thoughts, feelings, and attitudes within each person in a relationship.
- Many churches are unaware of the extensive Christian skills-based relationship content that is available for them, but these resources are both plentiful and easily accessible. Communio has compiled a comprehensive catalogue of more than eighty effective resources in relationship education that allow church leaders to sort by a number of different criteria.

CHAPTER 14

Growing the Church Through Relationship Ministry: The Data-Informed, Full-Circle Relationship Ministry

What Do We Mean by Data-Informed?

Can you imagine a doctor jumping in to perform major surgery without first running an MRI or any other scans? What kind of orthopedic surgeon would start working on someone's knee with his arthroscope before diagnosing the problem?

Now, I (JP) am less medically inclined, more of a sports and football guy. (Gator football is the other religion in the De Gance home.) So let me try to make this point a different way: Can you imagine a college football coach at the highest level heading into a game without breaking down film of his opponent? A coach needs to prepare by knowing the quarterback's tendencies, or what kind of plays and key personnel groupings the offensive coordinator goes for on certain downs and distances. To answer these questions, the coach needs to really dive into the data.

You saw in Section I that the collapse of marital and relationship health is creating a crisis across the world and in the Church. In the last chapter, we noted that the marriage rate has collapsed 31 percent since 2000 and 48 percent since 1980. This is no ordinary problem. It is historic in scope and threatens the health and vitality of the Church and the entire planet.

In other words—to stick with my football analogy—for the Church, this undertaking is far bigger than coaching any title game in the College Football Playoff. So why on earth would any church attempt to develop a "game plan" for their congregation or community without first analyzing and looking at the data to identify the problems in their relationships?

On this point, I sometimes get some pushback. There appears to be a sense among many pastors that doing analysis and looking at data goes against trusting in the Holy Spirit. An approach that sounds like something pulled from the business world is often viewed as profane.

In defense of this "unworldly" position, some may point to an example from the Gospel. When the disciples were sent out two by two, Christ asked them simply to bring their walking stick and to rely on the hospitality of those open to the Gospel (Mark 6:8; Luke 9:3). There were no provisions made for this initial group of missionaries—so why should we be any different today?

The Gospel is not somehow opposed to people using the mental capacities God has given them to create plans to leverage the best techniques and tools available.

I would hesitate to draw such a conclusion from the commissioning of this special group during the time Jesus walked among us, however. Missionaries to foreign countries today certainly make the habit of ample planning before heading out. And did not even our Lord instruct his disciples to be "as shrewd as serpents and as innocent as doves"? (Matthew 10:16) The Gospel is not somehow opposed to people using the mental capacities God has given them to create plans to leverage the best techniques and tools available. It's my argument that it is a moral imperative to welcome a data-informed approach.

Let's consider the Parable of the Talents, from Matthew 25. Before departing, the master gives three servants a differing number of talents to be used in his absence. Each servant is held responsible for how he stewards the talents to produce a return.

Should those servants invest their master's talents without spending time for adequate planning? That seems risky and imprudent.

For the good servants to follow the master's wishes, they would have to plan and measure. Not doing so would be little different from gambling. They have to move their resources in the direction that will produce the highest possible yield. When the master returns, he measures their output. Those servants who invested their talents wisely are rewarded by the master. They are the faithful ones praised at the end of the parable.

And what does our Lord say of the man who sets out to build a tower in Luke 14, but who does not plan and measure his resources accordingly? He only has enough provisions to lay the structure's foundation. Those who see the partially-completed project mock the man who built it for failing to plan and measure properly. With His disciples, Christ uses this fool as a negative example of imprudence.

Clearly, Christ wants us to best use the talents and the resources that He has placed in our hands to become disciples and build up the Kingdom of God. As good stewards of the talents and the resources of the King, we must therefore act with great faithfulness and diligence to complete the task He has placed before us. To me, this means that taking a data-informed approach to advancing the Gospel is nothing less than a moral imperative.

Survey Says

So when we use the term "data-informed" at Communio, we mean getting an accurate measure of the current state of relationship health of your own congregation and community. That entails diagnosing the challenges your particular community is facing. Communio performs this diagnostic in two ways:

1) We start with a brief but informative survey of everyone in a relationship and everyone who is currently single. If you're in a relationship, we want to know: Are you married, engaged, seriously dating, or cohabiting? If you're single, we want to know: Are you never married, divorced, separated, or widowed? We then inquire into what you perceive the quality of your relationships to be.

2) Separately, we apply data modeling from consumer product purchasing habits to a church's surrounding community. If a church is willing, we also apply this consent-based modeled data to their membership, thereby generating reports on the overall church body but no data on individual members. This is the same thing large companies use to plan new locations or to inform their own product marketing.

Let's begin by discussing Communio's survey.

We typically have a church deliver the survey through a mobile link or text feature. The sermon or homily on that Sunday should be focused on marriage and relationships, and ideally, the pastor incorporates the survey into that message. The sermon is informed by many of the points outlined in the vision section above.

I (JP) recently wrapped up a strategic planning meeting at a majority-minority Evangelical church in a very working-class community in West Texas. It is an incredibly loving church, one which is serious in its theology and in which hospitality is central. Our Communio survey found that 79 percent of their never-married singles under age forty reported "feeling weighed down by baggage from their past." In spite of having run tens of thousands of surveys, I had never seen that question come back at such a high percentage. If this church is going to encourage new marriages and healthy relationships, it is going to have to minister to its people in ways that help them wrestle with and overcome their past. As we saw in Section I, loneliness and relationship hardship is far more the norm than the exception today.

Now, we also had this working-class church in West Texas survey its couples. The design of the question comes directly from the academy, such that the structure of the question and the way it is answered offers an accurate predictive look at those couples most likely to be trending toward divorce. We found that three in ten, or 29 percent, people surveyed admitted that they were struggling in their marriage. But when we dug a little deeper, we found that 31 percent of the married women age forty-nine and younger admitted to struggling, in contrast to just 20 percent of the men. That means married women in the church were more than 50 percent more likely to report struggling in their marriage than men were. That's a massive gap. Identifying this gap in the responses of the congregation is helping the church inform its preaching, outreach, and the rest of its strategy.

Model Builder

Data modeling has become an incredibly common tool across business sectors and politics. Anyone who suggests otherwise is either deeply ignorant of the field or is being intentionally manipulative to mislead you into downplaying its importance.

Now, there are many different ways to model, and many different data sources with which to inform modeling. When Communio uses modeling, we use data from the largest consumer product data warehouses. It's all consent-based data and is compliant with the California Consumer Protection Act. An example of a large player using this kind of data is Experian, a name you probably recognize because of its credit reports.

Why shouldn't the Church have access to the same resources that Fortune 500 companies or political campaigns have? Is the Church's mission less important?

Tens of thousands of companies license credit data every day to help them develop insights to improve advertising or determine where to build a new store location.

In 2012, I had begun to see the use of this technology proliferate in the political and public policy arenas. That led me to ask, why shouldn't the Church have access to the same resources that Fortune 500 companies or political campaigns have? Is the Church's mission less important? Indeed, the Church's mission is the most important. We wouldn't stand aside and let the secular world claim exclusive rights to use the television, radio, computers, mobile phones, or the internet.

In 2015, there was no data warehouse and analytics shop that worked in ministry. So we licensed data from analytics shops that worked in the political world and asked them to create models to help us target the Church's focus on those who were experiencing serious needs. If a business such as Amazon or Walmart can use models to determine what group of consumers is the most likely to purchase a product, or if the Obama campaign could use models to determine what group of voters were most likely to be undecided on which candidate they might vote for in November, then why couldn't the Church use models to understand things like who in the population is most likely to be struggling in their marriage or in their finances? Once the local church knows these felt needs, it can step in and provide support and care in a way that allows it to best utilize its scarce resources.

Data-informed insights allow us to use information to become better stewards of the limited resources God has provided us.

But before going further, here's a crash course on modeling.

To create what's called an algorithmic model that gives you insights into someone's likelihood to buy something or engage in any other behavior, you begin with what's called a "super sample" of people who engaged in the specific behavior you are seeking to understand.

For example, if you are using this sort of consumer data to sell a type of sneaker or a new Wi-Fi-enabled doorbell or any other product, you first start with a large group—5,000 to 10,000 people who have purchased that sneaker or doorbell. This group becomes your super sample. Next, the modeler scoops up and licenses all the consumer spending habits of everyone in the super sample from one of the many data warehouses that have proliferated in recent years. A data scientist then looks at the thousands of data points that arise from the super sample and finds the most commonly occurring consumer behaviors. These commonly occurring behaviors form the model. The data scientist then applies the model to everyone else in the large data file and attempts to determine who fits this model with a 70 or 80 percent (or greater) match rate. Your company can subsequently improve its advertising spending by buying advertisements or mailing coupons to those people who fit the model most closely.

Does this sound strange or exotic? Consider that anytime we go to the grocery store and use a shopping "club card"—or any plastic such as a debit card or credit card—we allow those purchases to be linked to us and then repackaged and sold through various large-scale data warehouses. Whether we like it or not, data has become the new resource of the 21st century.

Now, I want to point out that the data and insights drawn from consumer spending habits are not determinative. We are not automatons. This isn't the old Tom Cruise movie *Minority Report* with its Center for Future Crime. Fitting a model just means you are more likely to engage in a given behavior than those who do not fit the model. It doesn't mean you will engage in the behavior.

These data-informed insights allow us to use information to become better stewards of the limited resources God has provided us. The alternative is for churches to continue to spend those precious resources on sending a mailer to every single home within a three-, five-, or ten-mile radius of their church. How often is that done—and how many of those resources are wasted?

In the case of relationship ministry, Communio equips a church with several models and identifies trends in the data that will help it diagnose challenges and take action. The first is a model on marital hardship. We help a church understand how many people in their membership and in their community resemble, in their consumer spending habits, those who recently divorced. A second model we use allows a church to identify all those in their community who look like those who most recently have married.

A third model we employ relates to pregnancies or an expected baby in the home. Having eight kids myself, I can tell you that for many years my wife frequently received coupons in the mail for diapers, wipes, and various maternity and feminine products. So, if diaper companies can sell wipes to my wife, how might a church use the same information to creatively invite first-time parents into its community?

I like to point out that there are three commonly occurring life events that cause people to rethink the importance of faith: the moments of hatch, match, and dispatch—a.k.a. births, weddings, and funerals. Why not develop outreach and evangelization strategies to invite folks in at each stage and equip them to have a healthy relationship? Communio helps churches do just that.

We also like to look at the number of households where two adults are likely cohabiting—couples both with and without young kids. Now, contrary to some in the Church who see opposition to cohabitation as a throwback from the 1950s, it's critical to understand this relationship status as the threat it truly is. In Chapter 5, we walked through some of the science around cohabitation. Research continues to show within the social sciences that women in cohabiting relationships are the most vulnerable to domestic violence. Moreover, a child living in a home with a man who is not her father is the most vulnerable to abuse. This grim fact makes intuitive sense: A child living in a cohabiting home is either living with a man who is not her father or is living in a home with a father who is a flight risk. 40 percent of children conceived with an unmarried father are without a dad by age five and 70 percent are without their dad in their lives by age twelve.[136] Everyone in the Church needs to know these statistics. Communio works with churches to develop outreach and engagement strategies to reach these fragile couples.

Helping a church get a good sense of relationship ministry challenges and opportunities can assist it in thinking through and designing the most effective outreach into the community. It also quickly gets a church's leadership team to understand the great challenge facing *their church*.

It's one thing to know about relationship crisis issues in the abstract. It is altogether different to know that 39 percent of your married people fit the model of a struggling marriage. That was the case for the working-class church in West Texas I (JP) referenced earlier. In fact, within five miles of their church campus, there were 9,698 married people who fit into the struggling marriage model. Just as alarming for the church's leadership, there were 4,434 cohabiting adults with kids and 5,908 cohabiting adults without kids within five miles. Communio has been supporting this church in the immense and vital task of designing an outreach ministry to engage these couples and transform the entire community.

Setting Mission Outcomes and Mission Activities

Once a church has a handle on the relationship health of its congregation and community, Communio works with each church to prayerfully discern what the desired end point of their ministry should be. Under our framework, this means setting clear and measurable Mission Outcomes for married individuals and singles. We typically cap a church's Mission Outcomes at three for marrieds and three for singles.

Then, we want the church to think about each individual Mission Outcome and begin working backwards to develop three clear Mission Activities for each Mission Outcome they can execute that would enable the church to achieve that particular Mission Outcome.

Examples of Mission Outcomes include:
• Growing Sunday attendance by Y before DATE;

- Moving 50 percent of all couples in the church through a skills-based growth journey by DATE;
- Increasing the self-reported relationship health of the membership by 50 percent by DATE;
- Increasing the number of weddings celebrated within the church by DATE.

Ultimately, any strategy that a church develops must be informed by what it hopes to achieve. What is the end goal? Once that is made clear, the church can develop a comprehensive plan to make it happen.

But before we go any further, we ought to flesh out in greater detail what Communio means by a Full-Circle Relationship Ministry model.

The Data-Informed, Full-Circle Relationship Ministry: What Do We Mean by Full-Circle?

Recall that in the Barna Survey we commissioned, 85 percent of churches reported spending zero percent of their annual budget on marriage and relationship ministry. Just 8 percent of churches had ministry for singles to help them form healthy relationships.[137] And for those who are divorced, few churches offer any ongoing support or care. Also recall that the marriage rate sits at an all-time low.

As the Church, we must go beyond what we currently call marriage ministry. Churches must do much more than offer basic marriage preparation for the engaged (such as running

The collapse of relationship health facing the Church is an existential threat.

a relationship inventory, meeting a few times with engaged couples, etc.). The Church must do much more than offer a once-a-year retreat or an occasional class for married people. And pastors must do more than meet with couples only when they are struggling or in crisis.

We've chronicled that the collapse of relationship health facing the Church is an existential threat. The Church's response ought to be proportionate to the threat. That's why we use the term Full-Circle Relationship Ministry—because we support churches in applying cutting-edge ministry strategies for each stage of relationship life (Figure 14:1):

- For those who are single: This group includes never-married singles and those who are single again through death or divorce. It should also include care for single parents;
- For those who are engaged or seriously dating: This group is now less clearly delineated than in prior generations;[138]
- For those who are married: 67 percent of all regularly attending churchgoers are married.[139] This is the largest segment in any typical church's membership;
- For those in crisis: Although not every couple will reach a crisis where a divorce attorney is called, every couple *will* struggle at some point in their marriage. Your church must have a clear strategy for any couple experiencing significant challenges.

Figure 14.1

Data-Informed, Full-Circle Relationship Ministry®

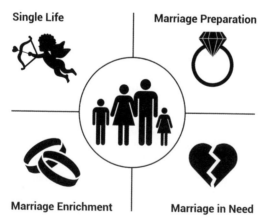

Single Life   Marriage Preparation

Marriage Enrichment   Marriage in Need

Some folks are surprised that my organization, Communio, does not actually author skills-based content for couples or for singles. We recognize that there is an abundance of effective resources readily available for churches in different theological and community contexts. The academic research shows that if the core skills for living a healthy relationship (summarized previously in the Skills Section) are included, a church has solid grounds for confidence in the efficacy of the resource for boosting relationship health.

I (JP) believe that John Van Epp's resources are among the most effective. The reason I was so excited to write this book with John is because he is one of the rare content authors who truly understands the interrelationship between all stages of relationship health. His RAM Series is the first church-based enrichment resource Communio has found that provides a coherent application to *every* member of the church at each stage of life. The RAM Series speaks to both singles and couples through a six-week sermon series, while simultaneously engaging elementary kids, youth, young adults, singles, and married couples with complementary relationship content.

When the Communio team consults with a church, we work with them to build out a ministry strategy for each phase of relationship life. That task obliges a church to tackle the following questions:

- How do we develop strategies to attract single young adults—many of whom are unaffiliated in faith and disconnected from their community?
- How might we craft a community of singles discerning whether or not they are called to marriage and what the best practices are for happiness in their relationships?
- How can we better engage men? Over the more than 20,000 completed Communio surveys, we see that churches have a large gap between men and women. Men make up just 37 percent of the surveyed. Search your own pews on any given Sunday, and you'll likely see that those numbers aren't far off. Getting to greater balance is necessary to reach men with the Gospel and strengthen their relationship health.
- How can we develop on-ramps and ongoing engagement for each state of relationship life, so that folks build community and increase their engagement in skills-based resources?
- How can we equip ourselves to understand what skills-based resources to use? Should we select plug-and-play content or get teams trained in a

facilitator-led resource? Both have a role and purpose in these ministries.

Many churches begin their marriage or relationship ministry with a focus first on getting the right program or skills-based content in place. But before you go down this path, consider that in the entire country, only a small minority of Americans are motivated enough to go out and purchase content or participate in a ministry to improve their relationship health. Those who do attend typically fit into one of two camps:

1) The small number of marriage champions who are highly motivated to attend every marriage program that they can;

2) The even smaller number of those struggling in their marriage who are actually willing to admit it, and are motivated enough to work on their relationship.

I (JP) tease my wife that we are the weirdo highly-motivated marriage champions with eight homeschool kids traveling around in the fifteen-person van. But you don't need to have eight kids or be a homeschool family to fit into this group. If you are reading this book, you probably belong in this highly-motivated group.

However, the vast majority of couples do not fit within either group. Those with relatively strong relationships are most often *not* in the champion camp and just dismiss the marriage ministry because they believe it is only for couples with problems. And those who do have problems perceive attendance as an admission of their issues, which they are resistant to doing. Always keep in mind that the single greatest obstacle for any relationship ministry remains the perception that relationship enrichment is just for people with problems. All too

Always keep in mind that the single greatest obstacle for any relationship ministry remains the perception that relationship enrichment is just for people with problems.

frequently, life-changing, skills-based resources sit on the shelves of church staff or volunteers and never reach those who need them most.

So, how do you reach your entire church with relationship ministry? How can you attract the larger community outside of your church who would benefit from a relationship ministry and who need Jesus?

These questions, we know now, are really asking this: How do you build the Data-Informed, Full-Circle Relationship Ministry? In the next chapter, we'll show you how to do just that as we introduce you to the Ministry Engagement Ladder (see Figure 15:1 on page 225) and dive into practical ways to bring a Full-Circle Relationship Ministry model beyond the walls of your church and its membership.

* * *

A QUICK RECAP

- Could you imagine a doctor jumping in to perform major surgery without running an MRI or any other scans? For the Church, the outcome and consequence of investing in relationship ministry is even bigger than surgery—it affects our ability to invite more souls to relationship with Jesus and eternal life. So, why would churches attempt to provide help and healing to relationships without first analyzing and looking at the data to diagnose the relationship problems in their congregations and communities?
- The Gospel is not somehow opposed to men using the mental capacities God has given to create plans that leverage the best techniques and tools available.
- When we use the term "data-informed," we mean getting an accurate measure of the current state of relationship health of your own congregation and community. This entails diagnosing the challenges of your particular community. We do this in two ways:
  1. We start with a brief but informative survey of everyone in a relationship and everyone who is currently single. We want to know everyone's relationship status, and how they view the quality of their relationships.
  2. Separately, we apply data modeling from consumer product purchasing habits to a church's surrounding community. If a church is willing, we also apply the modeled data to their membership, thereby generating

reports on the overall church body and no data on individual members. This is the same thing large companies use to plan new locations or to inform their own product marketing.

- The crisis of relationship health facing the Church is an existential threat, so the Church's response ought to be proportionate to the threat. That's why we use the term Full-Circle Relationship Ministry—because we support churches in applying cutting-edge ministry strategies for each stage of relationship life: single (and single again), engaged, married, and those in marital crisis.

- Consider that in the entire country, only a small minority of Americans are self-motivated to take action steps to improve their relationship health. If you are reading this book, you probably belong in that group. Finding effective ways to reach the rest of the people (not just the highly-motivated) with relationship ministry is mission critical.

- The single greatest obstacle for any relationship ministry remains the perception that relationship enrichment is only for people with problems. Too frequently, these life-changing resources sit on the shelves of church staff or volunteers and never reach those who most need them.

CHAPTER 15

Going on Mission: The Ministry Engagement Ladder

Let's consider a church with a traditional, cross-shaped architecture as a metaphor for evangelization.

The sanctuary has a long vertical central aisle, or nave. The door at the entrance of this traditionally-built church is the best one to enter, because the building was constructed with this user experience foremost in mind.

When done well, the architecture of such a church is designed in such a way as to raise our eyes above to God and create a sense of awe. In this analogy with evangelization, we will call this the Jesus door.

The Jesus door is always the best one to enter when seeking a relationship with Christ. It is the most direct.

But in our modern world, many of us are simply unready to enter this door. In today's post-Christian and perhaps even pre-Christian world, many don't yet know that they need to enter it and are hostile to the unique claim of Jesus being the only way to heaven. Returning to our church architecture analogy, when we enter such a church in this secular frame of mind, we are little more than gawking tourists snapping pictures—unable to be raised in mind and heart to heavenly things. And so, the experience will impart to us little enduring impact.

The other doors to this church are the lateral doors, or side doors. When entering such cruciform-shaped churches, these side doors rarely have the same immediate impact on our senses. But, when we enter them, we are inside the church all the same. In this analogy, these are the doors we like to refer to as the relationship doors. So many of us today are hungry and longing for meaningful relationships. Many who are lost recoil from the claims of the Gospel on an initial hearing, but still want to slake their thirst for meaningful relationships. This is where we as a church must build our focus on evangelization in the 21st century.

During Communio's multi-year experiment in Jacksonville, the biggest mistake we made was trying to connect members of the churches and the community *too rapidly* with skills-based relationship ministry (a.k.a. couples' education programs).

We had spent all of 2014 and 2015 studying the landscape in this space. Research consistently shows that an eight-hour or more dosage of skills-based education produces measurable improvement in outcomes in relationship health.[140] So, my team thought we could leverage a data-informed approach to immediately invite people into a skills-based ministry at a church. Our team spent literally hundreds of thousands of dollars in the first year trying to promote church-based couples education programs. We developed digital ads and ran a multilayered funnel to get people to sign up for eight-hour, ten-hour, and sometimes fourteen-hour classes.

An eight-hour or more dosage of skills-based education produces measurable improvement in outcomes in relationship health.

What did we learn?

Well, we learned that *didn't* work.

About six months into our test, we finally recognized that getting someone to join a program—such as the phenomenal Marriage Course created by Nicky and Sila Lee with Alpha, or another skills-based class—is a huge bar for any couple to hurdle *unless that couple has already formed some real relationship with the church or someone from the church.* While data is great, you need to develop the person-to-person bonds between those in your church and the community that allow you to invite people to climb one step higher in their own journey.

In year one of our Culture of Freedom Initiative, we succeeded in moving 47,000 people through four-hour or longer skills content across our multi-city pilot—largely through churches, but not exclusively so. But we reached that number at a cost of $261 per person. We began to restructure our initiative based on what we'd learned, and we found that we could drive down our costs considerably while increasing our yield. Over the last two years of the initiative, we engaged just shy of 150,000 people in four-hour or longer programs at an average cost of approximately $40 per person, for a savings of 85 percent. We did this by focusing on "warming up" audiences by attracting them to lower intensity engagements with the church. This increased the number of personal relationships within the church. We also focused on helping churches leverage their already existing personal relationships within the church.

This period of learning helped our team create Communio's strategic framework to equip churches to reach both those in their congregation and those in the surrounding community. We call it the Ministry Engagement Ladder, and it has four rungs (Figure 15.1).

Figure 15.1
Ministry Engagement Ladder™

4
Growth Journey

3
Ongoing Engagement

2
Outreach

1
Invitation

1. Invitation

We made this point earlier, but it bears repeating: Life changes most fundamentally through personal relationship. The Ministry Engagement Ladder is designed to help churches create a step-by-step plan to scale the number of meaningful, life-changing personal relationships that can exist within the local church. It replaces neither relationship nor authentic discipleship; instead, it seeks to scale the ability of your church to form discipling relationships.

The first rung of the ladder is an Invitation designed to encourage people to take a small step. That small step—the second rung of the ladder—skews toward the fun and engaging, but still has some substance. I'll get to that step in a moment.

But first, consider this: The number one reason someone joins a cause or becomes involved in anything is that they're asked.

Communio has developed an entire suite of church support services that allow churches to combine grassroots person-to-person invitation techniques with digital marketing, email prospecting, person-to-person texting, direct mail marketing, and other strategies. We help a church systematically leverage insights gathered from consumer product data to maximize its ability to run outreach. Put simply, we put cutting-edge marketing techniques to work to help churches reach far more people than they otherwise would.

Our teams work with a church to develop a multichannel Invitation strategy that extends over eight weeks ahead of an outreach event, so as to drive participation both within the church's membership—lapsed and active—as well as in the surrounding community. Many large churches already know how to run sophisticated campaigns. But because the Communio team runs hundreds of church-based campaigns annually, we remain on the cutting edge of what works best—which changes frequently, particularly within digital platforms.

As a nonprofit ministry, Communio provides masterclasses on Invitation and Outreach strategies, consults with a church's existing team to share our knowledge, and runs large elements of these campaigns on behalf of church clients—soup to nuts. In digital outreach, this assistance includes creative design, revision, ad placement, ad spending optimization, and all reporting. We also help churches plan and successfully execute person-to-person texting campaigns, door-to-door block-walking campaigns, and direct mail outreach. Our goal is to transform what churches can do to drive turnout within their community.

Taking a data-informed approach allows a church to craft an invitation built around a relationship health opportunity and felt need. For example, it might involve helping a church to target invitations to all parents within five miles that have kids under the age of ten by offering a date night event with childcare provided. When our kids were small and we didn't have the spare cash for babysitters, our parish could have asked us to come and hand copy the book of Leviticus on a Saturday night. So long as they promised to watch our toddlers for a couple of hours, we would have jumped at the chance!

Within the digital space, our team designs an entire multilayered marketing funnel to help a church cultivate an initial digital or brand relationship with folks from the community. The funnel gradually increases engagement, moving a person to accept an invitation to the church's outreach. When we use the term marketing funnel, what we mean is using several different marketing devices to move a person from a cold contact into a lukewarm and then warm contact. When Communio does this work alongside of a church, we do this either through a two-to-three step Facebook advertising campaign or through an Invitation campaign that includes delivering marketing that engages a prospect through email, Facebook, text, direct mail, and door-to-door prospecting. Marrying a pastoral approach with marketing best-practices, Communio both provides advice to a church to build this Invitation funnel or our staff works alongside a church to provide this as an entire turnkey service on behalf of the church.

Now, if all of this sounds far too businesslike for your liking, I want to emphasize just how massive the collapse in marriage and relationship health has been over the last sixty years. As we covered in Section I, the decline in marriage has taken a huge toll on the Church, on our communities, and on the world around us. In ministry, doing more of the same thing—or a slightly more improved thing—is woefully insufficient for addressing the crisis.

It's absolutely critical that churches advance beyond last century's basic invitation techniques of blanket mailers or canvassing an entire neighborhood. *There is no Gospel mandate to be unsophisticated.* Cooperating with the Holy Spirit, the Church must marshal its limited resources and deploy them in the way that will produce the highest yield.

But Invitation alone is obviously not sufficient. One needs the invitation to lead to relationship.

2. Outreach

There is no gospel mandate to be unsophisticated.

In the post-COVID era, we think of Outreach in a newly multifaceted way. Traditionally, Outreach would be for an in-person event that a church would host for couples, where most of the event was designed to be fun and engaging. Think 90 percent "popcorn," or fun, and just 10 percent "spinach," or education. In other words, a small portion of the overall event should fit into some element of couples enrichment. Today, we also consider digital and virtual events to be an effective component of a church's larger Outreach menu.

Communio has built a large menu of Outreach concepts drawing on the many examples of Outreach events our church partners have found most effective, as well as insights into the Outreach concepts that have proven to be ineffective.

We consider our framework to be just that—a framework, or form if you will. Ultimately, the matter or substance of each event is up to the individual church. What works in Fort Worth, Texas, won't necessarily work in Boston, Massachusetts, or Belle Glade, Florida. It's important to consider each community's unique culture in designing these events.

At these gatherings, the individual church must showcase the most effective norms of Christian hospitality. Every Full-Circle Relationship Ministry should have a task force of volunteers and their responsibility must be to model good hospitality. They should not be seen at these functions socializing together, but instead finding ways to meet and authentically engage with those whom they do not yet know. A great pointer for these individuals is to ask them to gather as many stories as they can from newcomers on how they first met. Then, when the task force meets again, see who can recount the most stories. Nearly every couple enjoys sharing their own story and taking an interest in someone else's story is a tremendous way to build trust.

Taking this approach will maximize the number of individuals from your surrounding community who will enter into meaningful personal relationship with those in your church. More on this in a moment.

First, when we help churches set up Outreach events for relationship ministry, we want them to consider these events as part of their larger strategy working towards their Mission Outcomes. Generally speaking, this means most churches will try to schedule three relationship Outreaches for their church and community on an annual basis. Now, Outreach events should not be held until you have also planned the third rung of the ladder—the Ongoing Engagement events—and until you have selected a skills-based Growth Journey (the fourth rung). Let's take a look at the Ongoing Engagement events.

3. Ongoing Engagement

In the Ministry Engagement Ladder framework, every rung of the ladder is set up strategically to lead into the next step of engagement. We never want a church to hold an Outreach event without determining the next couple of rungs of the ladder and how they plan to invite people to take those steps.

> *In the Ministry Engagement Ladder framework, every rung of the ladder is set up strategically to lead into the next step of engagement.*

The big difference between Outreach and Ongoing Engagement is the amount of spinach in the program. At this stage, it goes from 90/10 (popcorn/spinach) in Outreach to 75/25 in Ongoing Engagement. We typically work with churches to place communications skills questions creatively into the program. This can be done through cards on tables, event programs, slides, or prompts from the event stage. For a couples event, the key is to allow individual attendees to converse with their date. We often try to "gamify" these questions to encourage couples to participate. I would strongly discourage group sharing at this stage. Remember, many of the people in attendance won't yet have a strong relationship with others in attendance and may be embarrassed or fearful of what their partner might share.

Communio has developed a manual and training module for churches on structuring these events. Any time individuals come to an Outreach or Ongoing Engagement, you need to come up with creative ways to share the dates and times your community will be meeting for their next activities. Some of our partner churches create refrigerator magnets with all the events for the year. A common mistake is not finding electronic ways to quickly capture contact information for all attendees at Outreach and Ongoing Engagement events. Paper sign-up sheets frequently have penmanship errors, are lost, or are never entered into a database. Communio helps churches set up electronic systems to make sure no one falls through the proverbial cracks.

If you are familiar with college campus ministry, the following example will be one you recognize. Most campus ministries have some sort of semester kickoff event. Effective campus ministries will capture the names and contact info of all who attend and have a hospitality team intentionally work the event to build relationships. Next, everyone who attends will be invited back to the weekly free dinner at the student center. There, students are still really investing in community more than spiritual growth, but a short talk will frequently occur that provides some spinach. Ultimately, the campus ministry leaders are working to move those who attend these ongoing engagements into small groups in order to grow spiritually and deepen their relationship with Jesus. The Ministry Engagement Ladder in relationship ministry works in a very similar way.

4. Growth Journey

There are more difficult things than getting a married man to attend a couples relationship education program. Splitting the atom and landing a robot on Mars come to mind, for instance, as two items that have a *slightly* higher level of difficulty.

Too frequently, churches begin relationship ministry by going right to offering skills-based programs. They offer what we call a growth program and make some announcements to promote it. Maybe it's a great plug-and-play resource or facilitator-led resource. In any case, churches are regularly disappointed by how few people participate, and so they give up on their relationship ministry shortly thereafter.

The reason these ministries fail so frequently is that the church has simply not laid the groundwork for them, either through person-to-person relationship development or through establishing your church's compelling vision for relationship ministry. At Communio, we see small groups as a very effective way—but not the only way—to organize and deliver the skills-based Growth Journey.

To understand why, think back to Section I on the loneliness crisis—our society is starving for community. Individuals will thus come for the community and, if the programming is well designed around building relationships, they will stay for the growth.

Consider having each member of your task force or hospitality team organically build a group through the Ongoing Engagement event attendance that he or she can then invite into his or her home for a weekly small group. You can select a plug-and-play resource that can be delivered as a weekly "date night," such as the Marriage Course by Alpha or CouplesTalk by Don and Alexandra Flecky. Or you can use a great video-based group resource like the RAM Couples or Singles Studies.

We like including a witness talk during Ongoing Engagement activities or when you are promoting this skills-based programming, in which the couple sharing their own journey might note that they recently began participating in the church's Growth Journey. "We joined a small group and met some amazing people. We've had

> The church has simply not laid the groundwork for relationship ministries.

lots of fun. If you haven't yet done it, I'd encourage you to go see Bob and Julie in the back and make sure to sign up for one." The repetition of inviting people both collectively and individually through person-to-person encouragement, over time, will funnel more and more individuals into your church's skills-based, couple relationship education programing (the Growth Journey).

Your church should look to build up a facilitator-led Growth Journey and deliver it at least twice annually. Many of these programs can be delivered through small groups—with the only barrier being the challenge of getting a large group of small-group leaders trained and licensed as facilitators. To that end, most churches we partner with seek to hold larger marriage retreats. Adventures in Marriage by Richard Albertson, Van Epp's courses, Couple LINKS, PICK for singles, or Our Home Runs (see www.LoveThinks.com for certification information) are some phenomenal facilitator-led resources.

It is absolutely critical that the leaders of your relationship ministry model fully participate in the resource.

In all of these resources, it is absolutely critical that the leaders of your relationship ministry model fully participate in the resource. If your staff, pastors, and leading volunteers aren't making use of this, why should anyone else?

To reiterate the points raised in Chapter 14, your church must destroy the notion that relationship ministry is either for the troubled or for those perceived as Christian-commandos— i.e., those endeavoring to be faithful Christians to whom your "typical person" cannot relate. You know who I'm talking about: The hyperbolic Ned Flanders character from *The Simpsons* comes to mind, or those strange homeschool families . . . like mine.

For our part, my wife and I love to host folks to build community. We watch sports, socialize, or run our kids ragged with other families so our crew will pass out early. When we organize a skills-program (i.e., a Growth Journey), we draw on these personal relationships to invite friends. I make it a point to target the husbands. I'll tell my guy friends that my wife and I personally have gotten a lot out of it, and, besides, it'll be a fun-time to grab a beer together. We make sure every growth journey or couples program has plenty of *communio*—community—built in so folks can socialize together and receive the blessings of a life-giving Christian community.

Beyond the Church: Bringing Relationship Ministry to Our Communities

The Ministry Engagement Ladder itself is a system for churches to reach out to both their membership and their surrounding community to draw people into the Church, strengthen marriages and relationships, and facilitate encountering Christ. When churches embrace healthy relationships, it often creates additional avenues for services and outreach in the community beyond Communio's model. Take, for example, Celebration Church—one of our early partner churches in Jacksonville, Florida.

Celebration Church pastor Wayne Lanier had developed such a deep bench of marriage mentors, trained by Live the Life Ministries, and these mentors had developed such a reputation in the community for their service to couples, that secular authorities began to seek out their help. The local public school system asked for ways that Celebration Church marriage mentors could provide and support couple relationship education for the parents of their students. Teachers know that the most critical factor in a child's performance in school is their home life. If parents get along better and home life is more stable, children tend to perform substantially better. To meet this need, there are examples of evidence-based, secular couple relationship education curricula that can be suitably deployed in more secular settings.

We raise this possibility here because after an individual church removes the plank from its own eye in relationship ministry—and develops a real skill set in championing and strengthening marriages and relationships—it is well-equipped to find additional creative avenues to bring its mission of relationship health to the surrounding community. For instance:

- Churches can work with area businesses to bring relationship education through human resource departments, offering communications skills classes that improve relationship health of employees and their families;
- The same can be done through schools and secular nonprofits such as the Boys and Girls Club or the United Way;
- First Responders—police, firefighters, and health care workers—frequently work difficult hours in very high stress and even traumatic situations. Offering couples relationship education, either directly through employers or by inviting those in these professions to the church, addresses a critical area of need.

In Chapter 1, I (John) shared about the amazing impact that "Mr. Randy" (how his students knew him) had in facilitating the PICK course (a.k.a., *How to Avoid Falling for a Jerk or Jerkette*) to more than 20,000 students in public schools. This is an evidence-based course with a secular version that clearly promotes values consistent with our Christian faith but drawn from psychosocial scientific research. During those years of teaching healthy dating relationships, Randy helped to reshape the culture of relationships among those high school students. Churches have the opportunity to offer relevant and educational relationship content in secular settings that will build a rapport with their community and influence cultural trends with Judeo-Christian values. In Chapter 8, we reviewed just a few of the major ways that Christianity has been a culture-changer, and continuing that mission in this area of ethical relationship education is the primary need of our time.

The U.S. Military has learned how important relationship health is for military readiness. One faith-based organization that has modeled the relationship mission that churches should implement is the Army chaplaincy. As I (John) mentioned in Chapter 1, the Army has invested hundreds of millions of dollars in training their chaplains to step out of the chapels and into their Army communities to offer relationship courses to singles and couples,[141] transforming countless lives in the process. I have been honored to be included in this mission, called Army Strong Bonds, for over twenty years with three of my evidence-based courses (PICK, LINKS, and Our Home Runs®), along with similar relationship initiatives conducted by the Air Force and Navy chaplaincy.

One of the side benefits that chaplains have identified is that these offerings of relationship courses have radically improved the perception of chaplains by soldiers and their families. They have won the hearts and respect of many in a generation that is skeptical of religion. And the relevance and practicality of their skills-based relationship courses have increased openness to conversations about faith and God. One chaplain represented this consensus of experience when he said to me, "Our Strong Bonds relationship events are the best outreaches we have ever conducted . . . because we go to our community, talk together about their most meaningful relationships, build a strong rapport, provide information and skills that they love, and establish a relationship that opens the doors for subsequent conversations about life and faith that would have never occurred otherwise."

But what the military chaplaincy has been doing, churches have not been doing. Relationship ministry acts as a magnet to attract massive numbers of people who would never previously have considered stepping into a faith setting.

They establish trust and provide a platform from which to share the Gospel message.

As your church cultivates a larger community of individuals and couples investing in their relationship health, you will find that many of your members will feel increasingly called to serve in new and creative ways. Ultimately, the Church is called to be salt and light. So, after successfully deploying and running a Data-Informed, Full-Circle Relationship Ministry, you will be in a position to establish creative ways to bring ethical relationship education to secular settings.

* * *

A QUICK RECAP

- Research continues to show that a minimum eight-hour dosage of skills-based education produces measurable improvement in outcomes in relationship health.
- While data is great, you need to develop the person-to-person bonds between those in your church and the community that allow you to invite people one step higher in their own journey.
- Our experimental period in Jacksonville helped our team create a strategic framework to equip churches to reach both those inside their church and those in the surrounding community. We call it the Ministry Engagement Ladder, and it has four rungs: Invitation, Outreach, Ongoing Engagement, and Growth Journey.
- Taking a data-informed approach allows the Church to craft an invitation built around a relationship health opportunity and felt need.
- *There is no Gospel mandate to be unsophisticated.* Cooperating with the Holy Spirit, the Church must marshal its limited resources and deploy them in the way that will produce the highest yield.
- We consider our framework to be just that—a framework. Ultimately, the matter or substance of each event is up to the individual church. What works in Fort Worth, Texas, won't necessarily work in Boston, Massachusetts. It's important to consider each community's unique culture in designing these events.

- When churches set up Outreach events for relationship ministry, they should consider them as part of their larger strategy and Mission Outcomes. Outreach events should not be held until you have also planned the third rung of the ladder—the Ongoing Engagement events—and until you have selected a skills-based Growth Journey.
- The big difference between Outreach and Ongoing Engagement is the amount of educational content in the program. At this stage, it goes from 90/10 (socialization/education) in Outreach to 75/25 in Ongoing Engagement.
- Churches must plan strategically to attract more married men to attend couples relationship education programs.
- Too frequently, churches begin relationship ministry at the skills-based program stage—announcing some sort of growth program or resource. But churches often are disappointed by how few participate, and then give up their relationship ministry shortly thereafter.
- These programs fail so frequently because your church has not laid the groundwork—either through person-to-person relationship development or through establishing your church's vision for relationship ministry.
- As your church cultivates a larger community of individuals and couples investing in their relationship health, you will be in a position to establish creative ways to bring ethical relationship education to secular settings.

CHAPTER 16

A Model Church for Prioritizing the Mission of Relationship Health

Coming Together in Lancaster

JP: When Communio came out of its testing phase in Jacksonville at the end of 2018, we began to look for cities and individual churches in which to replicate our approach. My travels began to accelerate as I met with pastors and business leaders from across the country.

The first citywide project Communio launched was in Billings, Montana. Then, four months later, business leaders invited us to get started in the Permian Basin: Midland and Odessa, Texas. Five months after that, funders asked us to serve churches in Denver and Fort Worth.

In the meantime, individual churches contacted Communio from cities as diverse as Detroit, Palm Beach, Philadelphia, and Spokane, Washington. It was at this time in early spring, 2019, that I met John Van Epp by way of Luke Nelson, Communio's national director of city strategy. John and I had lunch and spent much of a day discussing our common passion for relationship health and our interest in working through the Church to bring it about. It became immediately clear that we shared approaches which, when combined, could be transformative in the life of a church and community.

JOHN: For the past twenty-some years, I had been working extensively with the military and community nonprofits in their attempts to provide relationship education to lower divorce rates and other relationship risks, and to increase the quality of marriages, families, and dating relationships. Many of those working in this field were motivated by their faith and were taking these resources out to their communities rather than asking the communities to come to them.

During those years, I trained and certified over ten thousand instructors in my Love Thinks relationship programs—and witnessed lives being changed by the classes they offered. One nonprofit in Evansville, Indiana—Community Marriage Builders (CMB)—had taught my course for youth and single adults, PICK (*How to Avoid Falling for a Jerk or Jerkette*), and my course for couples, LINKS, for ten years. Data that CMB collected over those years indicated that their tri-county outreach of relationship education had decreased the divorce rate by 20 percent. However, a major downfall for the community marriage movement has been the dependency on government funding . . . and as soon as CMB's grants were not renewed, they had to close their doors. While this is heartbreaking, it signals the unsustainability of government-run programs.

> We need a paradigm shift in our conceptualization of discipleship and local missions that significantly increases our emphasis on relationship health in dating, marriages, and families.

As I worked with so many parachurch organizations, it became clear that churches were missing one of the greatest opportunities to do something essential for their communities while also building networks of relationships that could lead to evangelism. I became convinced that this is an outreach model that churches could and should incorporate—first, because of pragmatic... people in their communities are struggling in their relationships and these resources could meet those needs in relevant and rapport-building ways.

The second reason that this is a vital outreach model for churches is because of the centrality of relationships in the Bible's description of discipleship and true spiritual development. As we have pointed out in the preceding chapters, we need a paradigm shift in our conceptualization of discipleship and local missions that significantly increases our emphasis on relationship health in dating, marriages, and families.

JP: One of the first people I called for advice to begin replicating Communio's model was my good friend Dave Travis, who had been the president of the Leadership Network. The Leadership Network worked with the largest

Evangelical churches in America and helped them share best practices and collaborate on new initiatives. Dave had worked closely with Communio (then called the Culture of Freedom Initiative) on implementing our pilot projects by organizing a series of meetings, called accelerators, with participating large churches. LN, as we called it, was a tremendous partner in helping us find ways to use a data-informed approach to relationship ministry. During this phone call in January of 2019, I explained that Communio needed to find dynamic pastors to serve on our new advisory committee at a national level.

Dave immediately thought to introduce me to David Ashcraft, the founding pastor of LCBC in Lancaster, Pennsylvania. LCBC, which stands for Lives Changed by Christ, is an amazing Christ-centered community that helps tens of thousands of souls encounter Jesus. With 17,000 weekly attendees across fifteen different campuses, it has become the largest church in the Keystone State.

By virtue of this introduction, I contacted David and spoke about Communio's vision and need to find innovative pastors to partner with us on our advisory board. David was interested, but more interested in understanding whether our model could help bring more souls to Jesus at LCBC.

So, I made the two-hour drive to LCBC's main campus in Lancaster (best pronounced Lank-ester, or else everyone knows you aren't a local). When I walked him through the data on family structure and faith practice (see Chapter 2), David and his leadership team became convinced that relationship health had to be the next big focus of his church.

Communio's Data-Informed, Full-Circle Relationship Ministry seemed to track well with them. They had just finished a churchwide series on financial wellness offered through Financial Peace University, and wondered if there was a churchwide series that they could use to kick off their new goals for relationships. Jason Mitchell, one of the church's teaching pastors and a key senior member of LCBC's leadership team, wanted to understand how Communio's model incorporates those who are not married—the never-married singles, those divorced, single parents, and the widowed. Because I could show him how Communio's approach provides a focus on every stage of relationship life, we were able to get rolling.

JOHN: One of the major challenges that pastors face with addressing relationships is that the content is almost always *relationship-type specific*—designed for marriage, or dating, or parenting, or some particular type of relationship. So what happens is, when pastors conduct a marriage series, the singles feel overlooked; and when they conduct a dating series, the married couples feel uninterested (hopefully, not jealous).

I knew that my RAM was the perfect framework for a series on healthy relationships that could address singles and couples at the same time, and in every message. This is a big deal for pastors who want a relationship series to be all-inclusive. But because I am a big believer in skills-based training, I wanted this series to be more than just a sermon series.

So, in 2017, Morgan Cutlip, Ph.D., (my oldest daughter and partner at Love Thinks) and I adapted my instructor-led courses into two video-based small-group studies for singles and for couples. We worked with many exceptionally talented people to make corresponding video-based curricula for elementary and youth.

I then wrote six sermon manuscripts that could be contextualized by pastors for their own churches. The first message introduced the RAM and used it as a framework for understanding our relationship with God, the foundation for all other relationships. The five subsequent messages developed one component of the RAM per sermon and applied it primarily to dating and marriage and secondarily to relationships within families and faith communities. The result was a sermon series that addressed all relationships while the small-group studies and classes focused on the specific relationship most meaningful to those involved.

Developing a Strategic Plan

JP: We held the strategic planning session with LCBC in mid-September of 2019 for their church staff of more than 200 people. This is a church with both a huge heart for their community, and—by virtue of their fifteen campus sites across central and southern Pennsylvania—the means to produce real movement on relationship health across much of their state.

At the meeting, we dove into the survey data that came back from his church's fifteen campuses:

- 25 percent of couples reported struggling in their marriage;
- 37 percent of singles said they wanted the church to provide teaching on how to build lasting relationships and opportunities to discuss this subject further. LCBC had one of the highest rates of single men participating in their survey at 32 percent. But this still reflected a sizable gap between the sexes in terms of participation;
- 184 individuals said they were engaged—the church staff had only known of sixty or so engaged people in the church. But of the survey respondents, only 20 percent had started any formal process of preparing for marriage.

Laying out the vision of a Full-Circle Relationship Ministry approach to the LCBC team, Communio helped them design a Ministry Engagement Ladder that would be feasible given the staff's incredibly full workload. This church was already accustomed to doing outreach. The question was, how could they think about it through the lens of relationship health? How could they construct each stage of their Ministry Engagement Ladder without creating an unrealistic load of new work for their staff, while still equipping their church to transform their community?

They anchored themselves to three large-scale Outreach events and six Ongoing Engagement experiences for their church and the community. We encourage churches to consider Christmas and Easter to be natural Outreach events that should be leveraged as part of relationship ministry.

David Ashcraft decided to center the Christmas message that December on Jesus and the God-honoring idea of relationship health. The birth of Christ would become the official kickoff for this new ministry. Communio's team recommended the RAM Series as their churchwide Growth Journey. The Christmas sermon announced this new focus and invited everyone to participate in their six-week relationship series starting in January.

JOHN: David Ashcraft and the staff at LCBC did everything right! They contacted me in early fall 2019 and, over a Zoom call with their ministry staff, I explained the details of the RAM Series. They were convinced that the RAM provided them the framework to speak to marrieds and singles at the same time, and they were especially impressed with the way that the RAM provided a logical sequence for growing in healthy and godly dating relationships.

They engaged with me on a couple more Zoom meetings with ministry groups, and then invited me to come and personally meet with staff. They had scheduled a series of conference room meetings with each major ministry team to hammer out details about contextualizing the materials to their fifteen campuses and vast diversity of small groups. They also set up a meeting with their entire staff and lay workers where I could make a presentation to address their own relationships prior to encouraging others to work on theirs.

I have worked with churches that do not put this same amount of time or organizational energy into the RAM Series. Their people end up missing out on the degree of transformation that comes from this relationship series that offers singles and couples, kids and parents, young and old—essentially everyone—a universal tool for evaluating and talking about their relationships.

When we license a church to conduct the RAM Series, we allow them to come up with their own title. LCBC chose to call the RAM Series, *Winning at Relationships*. They created a short video promo that would bring just about anyone to tears, with moving music and a video collage of various relationship scenes with corresponding subscripts: "Win at romance . . . win at quality time . . . win at friendships . . . win at bedtime . . . win at growing up . . . win at growing old . . . win at being there. Relationships aren't just built . . . they are won."

A good pastor knows that the process of forming a great marriage begins many years before the wedding day.

I think the other major benefit from my involvement with the ministry leadership was the contagious excitement that grew over those months leading up to the kickoff of the RAM Series in January. They got it right when their leadership actively and intentionally worked on their own relationships as a prerequisite to helping others in their respective relationships. I believe God honors that priority in ministry.

Engaging the Entire Church

JP: The LCBC team planned to first engage their church with the RAM Series through January 2020, and afterwards, to launch their larger Ministry Engagement Ladder in the community in February. We had encouraged them to consider their Christmas services as the starting point. Jason Mitchell told us that during the RAM Series they had the highest retention of seasonal Christmas attendees into January with the largest number of people coming to their nonholiday services in their entire history. Jason Castelli, the pastor overseeing their small groups, added that they also had the highest volume of group participation in their church's history.

David preached the first sermon on the RAM on the first Sunday in January. This also kicked off the RAM Series with elementary schoolers, youth, and adults in their respective small groups. The plan was for the six-week series to be followed by an Outreach event kicking off LCBC's invitation to the community to focus on strengthening their relationship health. That Outreach would then be followed by a series of Ongoing Engagement events—offsite date nights for couples facilitated by the LCBC team on a nearly monthly basis.

"We've got about every group size you can imagine at LCBC," Castelli said. "So, we have 'on-site groups' that can be up to 500 people who meet together at the church—all the way down to small groups that are just a few couples meeting in someone's living room. The RAM Series small-group studies for singles and couples worked well across all of those environments . . . What I love about it is that you can watch each video lesson in segments, or you can watch it straight through. And it gives groups ultimate flexibility to choose what works best in the right size environment."

Communio frequently recommends the RAM Series because it is an example of relationship health content that can equip a church to address every stage and type of relationship. A good pastor knows that the process of forming a great marriage begins many years before the wedding day. With this in mind, LCBC now has a path to get to youth and singles.

"What the RAM Series gives us is a comprehensive package," Castelli said. "We not only use the material with our adults on the weekend, but it's also going from the elementary kids up to middle school students through high school, and then on to adults. So, we're hitting every audience with the same relationship language across our entire church."

The survey data we conducted at LCBC found that singles demonstrated a deep interest in learning how to navigate single life well. And that demand was validated after this series began: "At our Manheim locations [LCBC's main campus], our young adult population has about doubled through the course of the RAM Series. If we compare the numbers of singles going through this series versus last semester when we were just doing other group curriculum—our numbers have about doubled."

JOHN: Relationships are the need of the hour. The lockdowns of 2020 increased isolation, resulting in dramatically increased cases of depression, anxiety, and suicide. We are created in God's image, and that means personhood and living in relationships. So it's not surprising that when churches like LCBC have conducted the RAM Series, they have witnessed record numbers in attendance.

The first church that conducted the RAM Series in 2017 was the Northview Christian Church in Carmel, Indiana. Lead pastor Steve Poe and Derek Irvin, the director of small-group ministry, were instrumental in helping shape the messages and small-group materials for the RAM Series.[142] They planned the series around the time they traditionally kicked off their nine months of small groups. They had a 30 percent increase in the number of groups formed (from 336 to 425 small groups) and were able to involve over 80 percent of their congregation in groups. These numbers are stunning—and affirm the tremendous desire for relationship content.

The success of a relationship series is not just evidenced by the immediate improvement of relationships but also by the increased motivation to heal unresolved relationship issues.

Derek Irvin shared an email with me at the conclusion of their RAM Series that had been sent to Pastor Poe from the director of a local Christian counseling center.

Although this center was unrelated to the church, they had an unprecedented number of couples from Northview initiating counseling over the previous six weeks. The staff at the counseling center said that these couples consistently brought in their discussion guides and RAM charts to explain what they were learning in the series. The success of a relationship series is not just evidenced by the immediate improvement of relationships but also by the increased motivation to heal unresolved relationship issues.

Channeling the Momentum

JP: LCBC followed the six-week RAM Series with the launch of their community Outreach, which they called A Great Date. The event included a Christian comedian, dessert reception, couples games, and conversation questions. LCBC's communications team collaborated with Communio's digital outreach team to develop a six-week promotional campaign for their campus locations.

The results were huge. They had more than 6,200 people show up for it, 32 percent of whom were not members of their church. Before every guest left that night, the LCBC team handed out a small bag of treats with a card that included date night dates for the ongoing engagement activities throughout the year—thereby leveraging the Ministry Engagement Ladder.

"One of the things our partnership with Communio has done specifically has been to give us a strategic framework for thinking about how to move people into more relational health," Jason Mitchell said. "We've been able to take some existing programs and be a little bit more strategic [with] how they funnel in and work together. From the Ministry Engagement Ladders that Communio has pushed us towards, what we're seeing now is strategic movement—starting with outreach events and then moving people to ongoing engagement with our church."

For the Ongoing Engagement events, LCBC set up a childcare program so that parents could drop off their kid(s) and enjoy a date night experience on them. This made the workload of the Ministry Engagement Ladder more manageable for their team. Their staff pulled together content for the date to facilitate good conversation. This rung of the ladder would move to the next rung—the Growth Journey.

"We want to move [couples] from their date night experience into more group environments where now they're talking about Biblical content," Mitchell said. "Now they're talking about maybe God's intent for their relationships. So Communio has just pushed us to think more strategically . . . and been a guide to really help us put the pieces together to make sure we are leveraging our energy in the best possible way to move people forward."

COVID-19 disrupted many of LCBC's in-person plans in 2020. However, they worked to deliver each rung of their ladder digitally and virtually through Outreach, Ongoing Engagement, and Growth Journey experiences. The big win for them has been in the number of folks who completed eight-hour or longer Growth Journeys.

Despite the pandemic, LCBC moved a huge number of people through their Growth Journey level. In all, 6,649 signed up for the RAM Series and 4,111 complete at least five out of the six RAM small-group meetings. Think about that: That number is the equivalent of reaching more than a fourth of their Sunday adult attendees with this relationship skills-based Growth Journey. LCBC is following up this series with an in-person Ministry Engagement Ladder in 2021 that will again include Outreach, Ongoing Engagement, and Growth Journeys.

Leading People to a Relationship Growth Journey

JOHN: One of the most exciting aspects of working with LCBC was that they wanted to establish ongoing small-group classes of the RAM study for couples and the RAM study for singles. They made this a staple in their calendar, and these studies will be used in their Ladder outreach to their communities. As singles and couples become introduced to LCBC through relationship events, they are offered the opportunity to dig deeper in their relationships by attending the six-week studies. This also sets the trajectory of relationship health as a central feature of discipleship.

I have attempted to cast this vision to other churches—to use the church-wide RAM Series to initiate regular offerings of the RAM Singles and Couples Studies as an outreach to their communities and an introduction of relationship content to new members. I think that many churches have an insatiable appetite for asking, "What's next?" However, when churches work with Communio, they become convinced of the need for a paradigm shift to make relationship ministry and skills content central in the discipling and spiritual growth focus of their people, as well as in their outreach to their communities.

JP: LCBC continues to design relationship-focused Outreach programs and Ongoing Engagements to maximize participation in their skills-based trainings. But their lead pastor recognizes the subtle ways that the focus on relationships can be disrupted both by expediency and by other priorities. David Ashcraft explained:

> *Too many churches have an insatiable appetite for asking, "What's next?"*

The connection with Communio has been great for us. Whenever you're working on a project, you always think you can do it yourself without any outside help. But what we've learned over the years is that having somebody from the outside who's an expert at what they're doing not only gives expertise but also gives accountability. The accountability, to my mind, is just as important as the expertise because it causes us to say, okay, we need to go and pull this off. We're going to trust you guys at Communio that you know what you're doing because of your history. So, let's go ahead and follow the plan even though we might prefer to bail out or to do it differently ourselves or take short cuts. What I think oftentimes hurts initiatives like this is, you start taking shortcuts and then all of a sudden it doesn't work out the way you'd hoped that it would but it's because you ended up cutting a lot of the important things. So direction is important, guidance is important, expertise is important.

LCBC has a world-class team focused on the mission of the Gospel. While the partnership started just months before the life-altering and church-altering event of the pandemic, they have leaned into the serious headwinds and produced some major movement within their community. So far, more than 4,000 people in southcentral Pennsylvania have received life-changing relationship health support.

Learning from a Model Church

So, what do we learn from LCBC? If we circle back to the Barna Survey data we described in Chapter 2, then you will remember that 85 percent of all churches reported spending zero dollars annually on marriage ministry; and just 28 percent had a substantive marriage ministry. But now, as one of the largest 100 churches in America, LCBC has begun to close this gap in its church and is running effective outreach in its community that is focused on strengthening dating relationships and marriages. Now, LCBC is capable of influence in its community that goes far beyond the scope of your average church. But, what if every church in America, appropriate to its own unique capacity and community, began to focus strategically on ministering to these two key relationships. What change would follow?

* * *

A QUICK RECAP

- Churches can follow the example of LCBC and make relationship health a major priority in both ministry and outreach.
- When churches warm up people from their community with relationship resources, hearts are opened up to the Gospel.

CHAPTER 17

The Endgame for the Church in America

When I (John) was the founding pastor of an Evangelical church in northern Ohio, there was a lay leader who always insisted that the church sing his favorite Bill Gaither "contemporary hymn." I can still see him smiling ear to ear as he belted out the first line: "I'm so glad I'm a part of the family of God."

JP and I suspect that there are only a few churches that even remember this song. However, those words, "I'm a part of the family of God," will forever ring true. Have you ever wondered why God chose the symbolism of marriage and family to be the preeminent portrayal of His relationship with His people? Take a moment to meditate on the following Scriptures.

> I will betroth you to me forever;
> > I will betroth you in righteousness and justice,
> > in love and compassion.
> I will betroth you in faithfulness,
> > and you will acknowledge the Lord
> > (Hosea 2:19-20).

> The Spirit you received brought about your adoption to sonship. And by Him we cry, "Abba, Father." The Spirit himself testifies with our spirit that we are God's children (Romans 8:15-16).

God's love, the greatest love imaginable, is best portrayed through the language of marriage and family. Why? Because the most intimate cry of a child to Abba, Father, and the faithful love of a bridegroom for his bride are the only human experiences that even come close to describing the matchless love that God has for us.

So, what happens in a culture where marriages are broken, families are frag-

As we witness Christianity declining, we find the new religions of transhumanism, scientism, technocracy, and nihilism growing in its place.

mented, and children are fatherless? You find a generation that is blind to the love of the Heavenly Father because they have been denied the love of an earthly father.[143] You find a generation that avoids marriage and is plagued with the fear of commitment because they have been disillusioned by decades of divorce. You find that the pain of widespread family disintegration has sowed seeds of narcissistic individualism. Ultimately, you find more and more hearts hardened to the Gospel because those whose life choices depart from marriage and family resent being accountable to the God of Christianity. So, as we witness Christianity declining, we find the new religions of transhumanism, scientism, technocracy, and nihilism growing in its place.

In the name of humanism, *society is becoming de-humanized.*

* * *

Loving and lasting marriages, and secure and stable families not only provide human beings with a foretaste of Divine love—they also serve as the beltway to transmit faith from one generation to the next. The "Family Factor," as Mary Eberstadt calls it, is the "irreplaceable transmission belt for religious belief." We have presented overwhelming evidence throughout the previous chapters of this book that the collapse of the family over the last sixty years is the major driver of America's collapse in faith. And yet, there is hope, for we agree with Eberstadt that this trend of declining Christianity can be reversed.

What might a family revival mean for Christianity? If the argument presented here is correct, and people come to religious practice much of the time, or even just some of the time, because of their experience of the natural family rather than vice versa, then a very different verdict about the fate of religiosity might yet be written on the decades and centuries to come. If there is a family renaissance, there may be a religious renaissance too.

And a religious renaissance in turn would make that family renaissance stronger for the same reasons already seen—because strengthening one spiral cannot help but reinforce the other.[144]

We have emphatically proclaimed that the content of evangelism will always be the Gospel. But in this world of family brokenness, the *platform* of evangelism will be built with the practical resources for marital and family health. *If we want to see an explosion of evangelization, then churches must launch a marriage and family renaissance!*

Churches cannot continue as they have done throughout the last sixty years if they want to turn the tide of a declining Christianity. They must radically shift their pri-

> *If we want to see an explosion of evangelization, then churches must launch a marriage and family renaissance!*

orities for both ministry and outreach. They must build intentional communities anchored in championing healthy relationships that lead to and revitalize God-affirming marriages.

"Marriage ministry" and "relationship outreach" must become normative line items to the fiscal budgets of churches. No longer can marriage ministry be pawned off on lay volunteers. Pastors and staff must lead the charge!

They must re-align their vision statement to prioritize marriage and family health. They must clearly assess the relationship strengths and weaknesses within their own congregations and communities. They must institute skills-based relationship supports that address the most relevant needs of their people. They must build outreach ladders to their surrounding communities that offer relationship-friendly outreach events that will become a beacon of hope to individuals and couples. They must redesign their calendars to provide ongoing relationship courses for those who are new to their church. And they must engage all their people in a growth journey that regularly strengthens the skills and virtues needed for God-honoring dating and lifelong marriages.

* * *

Time is not on our side. The hardening of hearts from six decades of high divorce rates, unwed childbearing, hook-ups and breakups, failed cohabitations, and fatherlessness is metastasizing into a defiant and lonely self-centeredness.

However, there remains a sliver of hope. With the empowerment of the Holy Spirit, churches can rebuild the structure of society—faithful marriages and loving families.

> Sustained marriage ministries will only happen when pastors and leaders do their part... their vision sets the trajectory of the future of their churches.

But this will only happen when pastors and leaders do their part. They are the shepherds who lead the flock. Their vision sets the trajectory of the future of their churches. Only when they commit to a paradigm shift of prioritizing marriage ministry and outreach will this hope ever be realized.

Imagine what the next ten years could look like if pastors and churches band together under this common vision.

First, Christian dating and marriage would once again become a sharp contrast to the relationship practices of the surrounding world. The numbers of those waiting until marriage, living separately until marriage, marrying first and then having children, staying together through the storms of life—all these numbers would begin trending away from the trajectories of mainstream society.

Second, churches would become known as centers of relationship health, and Christians would become known for their commitment to building and sustaining secure marriages and families. We would reclaim our heritage in which the Gospel of Christ, which reconciles us to God, would become known to the world as the transforming power that reconciles estranged spouses and heals fragmented families. Churches would produce the fruit of Christ-centered marriages that would transform the world.

We do not overlook the reality that "all have sinned and fallen short of the glory of God." We admit that Christians are fallible and struggle with every temptation known to mankind. The enemy can be relentless, but greater is He who is in you than he who is in the world!

If churches would greatly increase their ministry resources for those who are dating (from youth through single adults) and for those preparing to marry, for marriages that are strong and for those that are struggling, then they would clearly transform the health of relationships within their congregations and their surrounding communities. Churches would become society's standard-bearer of sexual purity, sexual fidelity, and flourishing marriages and families. When the messages from the pulpits of churches are matched with practical and life-changing ministries for healthy and godly relationships, then churches can certainly birth a family renaissance across America.

* * *

Our Lord intended marriage on earth to point to the New Jerusalem.

Think about this: *Your eternal salvation will be celebrated as a wedding feast* (Revelation 19:7-10) *and your relationship with Christ is most accurately described as a marriage union* (Ephesians 5). What more do churches need to read in the Scriptures or witness in their communities before they decide to seriously invest in the marriages of their people and communities?

As we said before--the Church in America is running out of time. *What is your endgame?* It bears repeating that the message of the Church is the Gospel of Christ, but in our current epidemic of relationship disintegration, the *platform* for drawing souls to Christ will be constructed with relevant and accessible resources for their most significant relationships.

Churches *do* have the power and resources to revitalize a belief and love for marriage and family across America. Churches *can* leverage the best in ministry strategy, technology, and skills-based practices. And churches *will* heal a generation that has lost its way while leading hearts back to Christ, but only when they unite together with this common mission!

> For the Church in America and throughout the West, we must decide our endgame.

We wholeheartedly believe that Jesus will build His church, and the gates of Hell will not prevail against it. We clearly know how the Biblical story ultimately ends. But between now and then, the story for our children and our children's children will be written by the choices we make today. For the Church in America and throughout the West, we must decide our endgame.

Chapter Notes

Chapter 1: The Church's 21st Century Opportunity and Responsibility

1   We want to emphasize, first and foremost, that practitioners want to help couples live in a healthy marriage. Where there is intimate partner violence, like JP's sister experienced, the first priority is the health and safety of the spouse and children. A huge part of what Communio now calls Full-Circle Relationship Ministry® includes a focus on single life. This means helping those who are unmarried develop the relationship skills and habits to discern whether someone would make a good spouse and to avoid a marriage that could become dangerous. In addition, this is a core focus of John's book and program, *How to Avoid Falling in Love with a Jerk or Jerkette.* We work to equip churches to imbue singles with the skills and discernment to make wise partner choices, as well as discern when a marriage is unhealthy and dangerous and how to provide assistance to endangered spouses to find the support they need.

2   Jeffrey M. Jones, "U.S. Church Membership Falls Below Majority for First Time," *Gallup,* March 29, 2021, http://news.gallup.com/poll/341963/church-membership-falls-below-majority-first-time.

Chapter 2: Fighting the Smoke Instead of the Fire

3   "Most Teenagers Drop Out of Church When They Become Young Adults," *Lifeway Research,* January 15, 2019, http://lifewayresearch.com/2019/01/15/most-teenagers-drop-out-of-church-as-young-adults.

4   2019 Communio-Barna Report on Relationship Ministries, 5, accessed June 2, 2021, http://communio.org/wp-content/uploads/2021/06/Communio-Barna-Report_Relationship-Ministries.pdf.

5   2019 Communio-Barna Report on Relationship Ministries, 7, accessed June 2, 2021, http://communio.org/wp-content/uploads/2021/06/Communio-Barna-Report_Relationship-Ministries.pdf.

6   "Fast Facts about American Religion," Hartford Institute for Religion Research, accessed May 14, 2021, http://hirr.hartsem.edu/research/fastfacts/fast_facts.html.

7   David Masci and Gregory A. Smith, "7 Facts about American Catholics," *Pew Research Center,* October 10, 2018, http://www.pewresearch.org/fact-tank/2018/10/10/7-facts-about-american-catholics.

8   The Cru expenses excludes their spending through Family Life Ministries.

9   "America's Changing Religious Landscape," *Pew Research Center,* May 12, 2015, http://www.pewforum.org/2015/05/12/americas-changing-religious-landscape.

10   Daniel Cox and Robert P. Jones, Ph.D, "America's Changing Religious Identity," *Public Religion Research Institute,* September 6, 2017, https://www.prri.org/research/american-religious-landscape-christian-religiously-unaffiliated.

11   Pew Center Research, "Landscape."

12   Robert J. McCarty and John M. Vitek, *Going, Going, Gone: The Dynamics of Disaffiliation in Young Catholic,* (Winona: St Mary's Press, 2017), 42.

13   McCarty and Vitek, *Going, Going, Gone,* 41.

14   Mark Regnerus, Discussion on 2018 American Political and Social Behavior Survey, interview by JP De Gance, December 2018-January 2019, record on file with Communio. A summary of key findings are on page 256.

IN THE 2018 DATA:

Q8. Were your biological mother and father ever married to each other? <u>BOOMERS who attend 2x/mo or more (percent)</u>:

Yes, still married or were until death... 35%
No, divorced/separated, or never married... 25%

Q8. Were your biological mother and father ever married to each other? <u>GEN-X who attend 2x/mo or more (percent)</u>:

Yes, still married or were until death... 35%
No, divorced/separated, or never married... 24%

Q8. Were your biological mother and father ever married to each other? <u>MILLENNIALS who attend 2x/mo or more (percent)</u>:

Yes, still married or were until death... 32%
No, divorced/separated, or never married... 18%

15 Regnerus, interview.
16 "In General Social Survey, declining share of Christians and growth of religious 'nones,'" *Pew Research Center*, October 16, 2019, https://www.pewforum.org/2019/10/17/in-u-s-decline-of-christianity-continues-at-rapid-pace/pf_10-17-19_rdd_update-00-011/; "How the American Family Has Changed," *Pew Research Center*, accessed June 1, 2021. https://assets.pewresearch.org/wp-content/uploads/sites/12/2014/12/FT_Family_Changes.png.
17 Tyler Daswick, "Have Christians Turned Marriage into an Idol?" *Relevant*, May 2, 2019, https://relevantmagazine.com/love-and-money/christians-turned-marriage-idol/.
18 Katherine Weber, "Jefferson Bethke to Christian Singles: Don't Make Marriage an Idol," *The Christian Post*, April 26, 2016, https://www.christianpost.com/news/jefferson-bethke-to-christian-singles-dont-make-marriage-an-idol.html.

Chapter 3: The Decoupling Effect

19 The findings in these bullet points about loneliness are from an Ipsos poll conducted from February 21 to March 6, 2018, on behalf of Cigna. For the survey, a sample of 20,096 adults ages 18 and over from the continental US, Alaska, and Hawaii was interviewed online, in English. The precision of Ipsos online polls is measured using a credibility interval. In this case, the poll has a credibility interval of ±0.8 percentage points for all respondents surveyed.
    The study's questionnaire is based on the UCLA Loneliness Scale, a twenty-item questionnaire developed to assess subjective feelings of loneliness or social isolation. An index was created based on these twenty statements, which include a balanced mix of positive (e.g., how often do you feel outgoing and friendly?) and negative (e.g., how often do you feel alone?) statements, and respondents were assigned a loneliness score based on their responses to these questions. Higher scores indicate increased loneliness. Individual respondent scores were combined to obtain a total average loneliness score both nationally and across different cities throughout the US.

Ellie Polack, "New Cigna Study reveals Loneliness at Epidemic Levels in America," *Cigna Newsroom*, May, 1, 2018, https://www.cigna.com/newsroom/news-releases/2018/new-cigna-study-reveals-loneliness-at-epidemic-levels-in-america.

20 Ceylan Yeginsu, "UK Appoints a Minister for Loneliness," *New York Times*, January 17, 2018, www.nytimes.com/2018/01/17/world/europe/uk-britain-loneliness.html.

21 J. Twenge, et al., "Age, Period, and Cohort Trends in Mood Disorder Indicators and Suicide Related Outcomes in a Nationally Representative Dataset, 2005–2017." *Journal of Abnormal Psychology* 128, no. 3 (2019): 185–199.

22 W. Wang and W.B. Wilcox, "The millennial success sequence: Marriage, kids, and the 'success sequence' among young adults," *Institute for Family Studies*, June 14, 2017, https://www.aei.org/research-products/working-paper/millennials-and-the-success-sequence-how-do-education-work-and-marriage-affect-poverty-and-financial-success-among-millennials/. "A record 55% of millennial parents (ages 28-34) have put childbearing before marriage, according to a new analysis of Bureau of Labor Statistics' Panel data by the American Enterprise Institute and the Institute for Family Studies"(3). However, this statistic may change as more women from the millennial generation have children.

23 Steve Camarota, "Births to Unmarried Mothers by Nativity and Education," *Center for Immigration Studies*, https://cis.org/Camarota/Births-Unmarried-Mothers-Nativity-and-Education. Data from the National Center for Health Statistics, 2017.

Chapter 4: The Decoupling of Sex from Marriage

24 Stephanie Coontz, *The Way We Never Were* (New York: Basic Books, 1992), 185.

25 Mark Regnerus, "Mating Market Dynamics, Sex-Ratio Imbalances, and their Consequences," *Society* 49, (2012): 500-505; Mark Regnerus, *Cheap Sex: The Transformation of Men, Marriage and Monogamy*, (New York: Oxford University, 2017).

26 Regnerus, *Cheap Sex*, 34-35.

27 Regnerus, *Cheap Sex*, 7.

28 Nicholas Wolfinger, "Counterintuitive Trends in the Between Premarital Sex and Marital Stability," *Institute of Family Studies*, June 6, 2016, https://ifstudies.org/blog/counterintuitive-trends-in-the-link-between-premarital-sex-and-marital-stability.

29 Laura Kann, et al.," Youth Risk Behavior Surveillance — United States, 2017," *Surveillance Summaries 67*, No. SS-8 (2018): 1-114, https://www.cdc.gov/mmwr/volumes/67/ss/ss6708a1.htm.

30 David Popenoe and Barabra Dafoe-Whitehead, "Sex Without Strings and Relationships Without Rings: Today's Young People Talk About Dating and Mating," *The State of Our Unions 2000: The Social Health of Marriage in America*, June 2000, http://moralissues.web.fc2.com/mi/NMPAR2000.pdf.

31 The Next Generation Study builds on 40 years of data already collected by the Dunedin Multidisciplinary Health and Development Study, which has followed a cohort of 1,037 children since birth in 1972/73. This study has accumulated an extraordinary amount of information on almost every aspect of the study members' lives.
"Next Generation Study," *The Dunedin Multidisciplinary Health and Development Research Unit*, accessed May 14, 2021, https://dunedinstudy.otago.ac.nz/studies/sub-studies/next generation-study.

32 Popenoe and Dafoe-Whitehead, "Without Rings," 9.

33 Popenoe and Dafoe-Whitehead, "Without Rings," 11.

34 Regnerus, *Cheap Sex*, 97.

35 Scott Stanley, "Motivated Ambiguity: 'Is This a Date or Not?'" *Sliding vs Deciding,* January 27, 2014, http://slidingvsdeciding.blogspot.com/2014/01/motivated-ambiguity.html.

36 Alex Williams, "The End of Courtship?" *New York Times,* January 13, 2013, https://www.nytimes.com/2013/01/13/fashion/the-end-of-courtship.html.

37 Dan Slater, *Love in the Time of Algorithms: What Technology Does to Meeting and Mating* (London: Penguin Books, 2013), 234.

38 David Ayers, "Current Sexual Practices of Evangelical Teens and Young Adults," *Institute for Family Studies,* August 2019, https://ifstudies.org/ifs-admin/resources/final-ifsresearchbrief-ayers-evangelicalsandsex8819.pdf. David J. Ayers also wrote an excellent and extensive book, *Christian Marriage: A Comprehensive Introduction* (2018), in which he summarizes data from the 2014-2016 National Survey of Family Growth (Bellingham, WA: Lexham Press).

39 Ayers, "Current Sexual Practices."

40 Ayers, "Current Sexual Practices."

Chapter 5: The Decoupling of Romantic Partnerships from Marriage

41 This name and any others from counseling cases have been changed in order to protect identities and maintain confidentiality.

42 A. Jose A, D. O'Leary, and A Moyer, "Does Premarital Cohabitation Predict Subsequent Marital Stability and Marital Quality? A Meta-Analysis," *Journal of Marriage and Family* 72 (February 2010): 105–116.

43 J. Teachman, "Premarital Sex, Premarital Cohabitation, and the Risk of Subsequent Marital Dissolution Among Women," *Journal of Marriage and Family* 65: 444-455.

44 David Ayers, "Cohabitation Among Evangelicals: A New Norm?" *Institute for Family Studies,* April 19, 2021, https://ifstudies.org/blog/cohabitation-among-evangelicals-a-new-norm.

45 Ayers, "Cohabitation Among Evangelicals."

46 Ayers, "Cohabitation Among Evangelicals"; David Ayers, in his excellent and extensive book, *Christian Marriage: A Comprehensive Introduction,* summarized data from the 2014-2016 National Survey of Family Growth in which the majority of Evangelicals disagree with the statement, "A young couple should NOT live together unless they are married." This indicates that the majority have not become convinced of the benefits of not cohabiting until married, nor the risks that are associated with cohabitation.

The tables on page 259 show that the majority of Evangelical singles also agree with the statement, "Living together before marriage may prevent divorce." This indicates that the majority of singles in churches believe something that is both unscriptural and contrary to a vast body of scientific studies. The church is clearly not presenting accurate and convincing information to their singles, even within the strictest of Christian churches.

47 David J. Ayers, "Cohabitation Among Evangelicals." Among the currently cohabiting, only 55 percent of cohabiting Evangelicals were certain they would marry their partners—less than mainline Protestants (59 percent), but more than other religious groups. Of these Evangelicals, 13 percent were living with partners they had no clear intention of marrying; about the same as for Catholics (12 percent).

48 David J. Ayers, "Cohabitation Among Evangelicals," 7.

TABLE 5.1:

Singles, by Age Group, Religious Affiliation, and Church Attendance, Who Disagreed with the Statement, "A Young Couple Should NOT Live Together Unless They Are Married" (NSFG 2014 and 2016). Cited from *Christian Marriage: A Comprehensive Introduction*, by David Ayers.

	15-22	23-32	33-44
Males			
Evangelical	59%	64%	67%
Other	75%	79%	75%
Evangelical Weekly Church Attenders	47%	41%	57%*
Other Weekly Church Attenders	57%	60%	53%
Females			
Evangelical	60%	71%	45%
Other	78%	83%	80%
Evangelical Weekly Church Attenders	51%	53%	37%**
Other Weekly Church Attenders	59%	57%	66%

* This percentage is based on only 37 of 65 respondents who fit all the criteria and must be interpreted with caution.
** This percentage is based on only 16 of 43 respondents who fit all the criteria and must be interpreted with caution.

TABLE 5.2:

Singles, by Age Group, Religious Affiliation, and Church Attendance, Who Agreed with the Statement, "Living Together Before Marriage May Prevent Divorce" (NSFG 2014 and 2016). Cited from *Christian Marriage: A Comprehensive Introduction*, by David Ayers.

	15-22	23-32	33-44
Males			
Evangelical	55%	65%	63%
Other	71%	76%	76%
Evangelical Weekly Church Attenders	45.5%	39%	53%
Other Weekly Church Attenders	56%	60%	61%
Females			
Evangelical	49%	56%	57%
Other	64%	72%	68%
Evangelical Weekly Church Attenders	38%	36%	46%
Other Weekly Church Attenders	47.5%	58%	58%

Chapter 6: The Decoupling of Parenting from Marriage

49 Sara McLanahan, Irwin Garfinkel, and Maureen Waller, "The Fragile Families and Child Wellbeing Study," *Public Policy Institute of California*, 1999.

50 Warren Farrell and John Gray, *The Boy Crisis* (Dallas: BenBella Books, 2018), page 402.

51 Martin Daly and Margo Wilson, "Child Abuse and Other Risks of Not Living with both Parents," *Ethology and Sociobiology* 6 (1985), 197-210. See also: Fourth National Incidence Study of Child Abuse and Neglect, Report to Congress, 2010, U.S. Department of Health and Human Services. "Children living with their married biological parents universally had the lowest rate, whereas those living with a single parent who had a cohabiting partner in the household had the highest rate in all maltreatment categories."

52 Marite P Thompson, JB Kingree, and Dorian Lamis, "Associations of Adverse Childhood Experiences and Suicidal Behaviors in Adulthood in a US Nationally Representative Sample," *Child Care Health Dev*, 45 (January 2019): 121-128, https://doi.org/10.1111/cch.12617.

53 W. Wang and W.B. Wilcox, "The millennial success sequence: Marriage, kids, and the 'success sequence' among young adults," *Institute for Family Studies*, June 14, 2017, https://www.aei.org/research-products/working-paper/millennials-and-the-success-sequence-how-do-education-work-and-marriage-affect-poverty-and-financial-success-among-millennials/. This report is part of the Home Economics Project, a research effort of the American Enterprise Institute and the Institute for Family Studies that explores if and how strong and stable families advance the economic welfare of children, adults, and the nation as a whole. The project also examines the role, if any, that marriage and family play in increasing individual opportunity and strengthening free enterprise at home and abroad, as well as their implications for public policy.

54 W. Bradford Wilcox, "How Focused on the Family? Evangelical Protestants, the Family, and Sexuality," in *Evangelicals and Democracy in America, Volume 1: Religion and Society*, ed. Brint, Steven, and Jean Reith Schroedel (New York: Russell Sage Foundation, 2009), 251-275. David Ayers discusses Wilcox's research in *Christian Marriage*, page 91.

55 W. Bradford Wilcox and Nicholas Hs Wolfinger, "Then Comes Marriage? Religion, Race and Marriage in Urban America," *Social Science Research* 36, no. 2 (2007): 569-589.

56 David J. Ayers. *Christian Marriage: A Comprehensive Introduction* (Bellingham, WA: Lexham Press, 2018).

57 Mary Eberstadt, *How the West Really Lost God: A New Theory of Secularization* (West Conshohocken: Templeton Press, 2013), 20-21.

58 Steve Camarota, "Births to Unmarried Mothers by Nativity and Education," *Center for Immigration Studies*, https://cis.org/Camarota/Births-Unmarried-Mothers-Nativity-and-Education. Data from the National Center for Health Statistics, 2017.

Chapter 7: The Flight from Marriage Produces Bad Fruit for the World and the Church

59 "About Us," MARRI Research, accessed May 14, 2021, https://marri.us/about.

60 Patrick Fagan and Althea Nagai, "Feels Thrilled, Excited During Sexual Intercourse by Family Structure and Religious Practice," *Marriage and Religion Research Institute*, accessed May 14, 2021, https://marri.us/wp-content/uploads/MA-116.pdf.

61 "Census Super-PUMAs (1-percent sample) comprise areas of at least 400,000 people and are aggregations of the smaller 5-percent Public Use Microdata Areas. These page sized state-based maps depict Super-PUMA boundaries and codes, state boundaries, and county boundaries and names." www.census.gov From "Census 2000 PUMA Maps," United

States Census Bureau, accessed June 9th, 2021, https://www.census.gov/geographies/reference-maps/2000/geo/2000-pumas.html.

62   Henry Potrykus, "Correction of Bias in the Index of Family Belonging and Rejection," *Marriage and Religion Research Institute*, February 12, 2014, https://marri.us/publications/correction-of-bias-in-the-index-of-family-belonging-and-rejection/.

63   Henry Potrykus, "U.S. Social Policy Dependence on the Family Derived from the Index of Belonging," *Marriage and Religion Research Insitutute*, February 14, 2013, http://marri.us/publications/page/15/.

64   Pat Fagan, Anne Dougherty, and Miriam McElvain, "164 Reasons to Marry," *Marriage and Religion Research Institute*, January 2, 2014, https://marri.us/wp-content/uploads/164-Reasons-to-Marry.

65   Fagan, Dougherty, and McElvain, "164 Reasons to Marry."

66   Fagan, Dougherty, and McElvain, "164 Reasons to Marry."

67   Gaby Galvin, "U.S. Marriage Rate Hits Historic Low," *U.S. News & World Report*, April 29, 2020, https://www.usnews.com/news/healthiest-communities/articles/2020-04-29/us-marriage-rate-drops-to-record-low.

68   Amanda Barroso, Kim Parker, and Jesse Bennet, "As Millennials Near 40, They're Approaching Family Life Differently Than Previous Generations," *Pew Research Center*, May 27, 2020, https://www.pewresearch.org/social-trends/2020/05/27/as-millennials-near-40-theyre-approaching-family-life-differently-than-previous-generations.

69   Laura Tach, Ronald Mincy, and Kathryn Edin, "Parenting as a 'Package Deal': Relationships, Fertility, and Nonresident Father Involvement among Unmarried Parents," *US National Library of Medicine National Institutes of Health* 47, no. 1 (February 2010): 181–204, https://www.ncbi.nlm.nih.gov/pmc/articles/PMC3000012/#b7-dem-47-0181.

70   Paul Florsheim and David Moore, *Lost and Found: Young Fathers in the Age of Unwed Parenthood* (New York: Oxford University Press, 2020), 35.

71   Council of Europe Committee of Ministers, "European Population Committee: The Demographic Characteristics of Linguistic and Religious Groups in Switzerland," October 27, 1999, 38, https://rm.coe.int/16804fb7b1.

72   Emily Badger, "The Unbelievable Rise of Single Motherhood in America over the Last 50 Years," *The Washington Post*, December 18, 2014, https://www.washingtonpost.com/news/wonk/wp/2014/12/18/the-unbelievable-rise-of-single-motherhood-in-america-over-the-last-50-years/.

73   This chart is a combination of data from two sets of data from Pew Research Center:
"In General Social Survey, declining share of Christians and growth of religious 'nones,'" *Pew Research Center*, October 16, 2019, https://www.pewforum.org/2019/10/17/in-u-s-decline-of-christianity-continues-at-rapid-pace/pf_10-17-19_rdd_update-00-011/;
"How the American Family Has Changed," *Pew Research Center*, accessed June 1, 2021, https://assets.pewresearch.org/wp-content/uploads/sites/12/2014/12/FT_Family_Changes.png.

74   Paul C. Vitz, *Faith of the Fatherless: The Psychology of Atheism* (San Francisco: Ignatius Press, 2013), 76.

75   Vitz, *Faith of the Fatherless*, 76.

76   Vitz, *Faith of the Fatherless*, 77–82.

Chapter 8: The Church's 21st Century Mission: Relationship Health to Evangelize the World

77 Rodney Stark, *The Triumph of Christianity: How the Jesus Movement Became the World's Largest Religion* (New York: HarperCollins, 2012), 95.

78 Rodney Stark, *The Triumph of Christianity: How the Jesus Movement Became the World's Largest Religion*, (New York: HarperCollins, 2012), 207 (Apple Version).

79 Stark, *The Triumph of Christianity*, 98.

80 Stark, *The Triumph of Christianity*, 101.

81 Stark, *The Triumph of Christianity*, 99.

82 William Jurgens, *Faith of the Early Fathers*, The Order of St. Benedict, Inc., Volume 1, 2.

83 Stark, *The Triumph of Christianity*, 102.

84 Joyce Ellen Salisbury, "Perpetua: Christian Martyr," *Encyclopedia Britannica*, last modified March 3, 2021, https://www.britannica.com/biography/Perpetua-Christian-martyr.

85 St. Augustine of Hippo tells us, "Those likewise are to be detested who deny that our Lord Jesus Christ had Mary as his mother on earth. That dispensation did honor to both sexes male and female and showed that both had a part in God's care; not only that which he assumed but that also through which he assumed it, being a man born of a woman.... Nor should our faith be lessened by any reference to 'a woman's internal organs,' as if it might appear that we must reject any such generation of our Lord because sordid people think that sordid. 'The foolishness of God is wiser than men'; and 'to the pure all things are pure.'" Augustine, "Faith and the Creed," IV, 9, trans. John H. S. Burleigh, *Augustine: Earlier Writings* (Philadelphia. Westminster Press, 1953), 358.

86 "Marriage Ministry and the Cost of Divorce for Churches," *Lifeway Research*, July 23-28, 2015, http://lifewayresearch.com/wp-content/uploads/2015/10/Healthy-Marriages-Report.pdf

87 St. Jerome—one of the foremost biblical scholars in the early Church—wrote, "The whole world groaned, and was astonished to find itself Arian." Arianism and other Trinitarian heresies were extinguished by the Church in council.

88 Karl Zinsmeister, *What Comes Next? How Private Givers Can Rescue America in an Era of Political Frustration* (Washington, D.C.: The Philanthropy Roundtable, 2016), 64.

89 Zinsmeister, *What Comes Next?*, 50.

90 Zinsmeister, *What Comes Next?*, 80.

91 W. Bradford Wilcox, Spencer James, and Wendy Wang, "Declining Divorce in Jacksonville: Did the Culture of Freedom Intiative Make a Difference?" *Institute for Family Studies*, https://ifstudies.org/ifs-admin/resources/ifscofjacksonvillereportfinal.pdf.

92 Wilcox et al., "Declining Divorce in Jacksonville."

93 "Sunday Attendance Grows by 23% After Churches Use Donor-Provided Data Tool," The Philanthropy Roundtable, accessed May 14, 2021, https://www.philanthropyroundtable.org/home/programs/culture-of-freedom/donor-developed-data-insights-platform-helps-churches-boost-attendance-increase-weekly-collections.

Chapter 9: Healthy Relationships Require Intentional Management

94 James Strong, *The New Strong's Expanded Exhaustive Concordance of the Bible*, (Thomas Nelson, 2010).

95 Philippians 2:1-4.

96 William Barclay, *The Letters to the Philippians, Colossians, and Thessalonians* (Louisville and London: Westminster John Knox Press, 2003).

Chapter 10: Healthy Relationships Consist of Strong Bonds

97 A relationship is defined on dictionary.com as: "1. a connection, association, or involvement. 2. connection between persons by blood or marriage. 3. an emotional or other connection between people." Accessed June 9, 2021, https://www.dictionary.com/browse/relationship?r=75&src=ref&ch=dic.

98 For licensing information and downloadable sample materials of the RAM Series see www.RAMseries.com.

99 Gerhard Kittel, ed., *Theological Dictionary of the New Testament*, Vol. I, pages 689-714 (Grand Rapids: Eerdmans Publishing Co., 1976).

100 John Gray, *Men Are from Mars and Women are from Venus* (New York: First Quill, 1992).

101 Emerson Eggerichs, *Love & Respect: The Love She Most Desires; The Respect He Desperately Needs* (Nashville: Thomas Nelson, 2004).

102 Gary Chapman, *Love Languages: How to Express Heartfelt Commitment to Your Mate* (Chicago: Northfield Publishing, 1992).

103 Linda J. Waite et al., "Does Divorce Make People Happy? Findings from a Study of Unhappy Marriages," *Institute for American Values*, 2002, http://www.americanvalues.org/search/item.php?id=13.

104 Waite et al., "Does Divorce Make People Happy?" page 5.

105 Heather Dessinger, "Seven Reasons to be Skin-to-Skin with your Baby after Birth" *Mommypotamus*, accessed May 14, 2021, https://www.mommypotamus.com/benefits-of-sskin-to-s.

Chapter 11: Healthy Relationships Express the Virtues of Agape Love

106 John MacArthur, "The Great Commandment: Sermon on Matthew 22:34-40," recorded on February 5, 1984, https://www.gty.org/library/sermons-library/2358/the-great-commandment.

107 "What Does it Mean that the Trinity is God in Three Persons?" Got Questions, accessed May 14, 2021, https://www.gotquestions.org/God-in-three-persons.html.

108 John Paul II, *Theology of the Body: Human Love in the Divine Plan*, (Boston, MA: Pauline Books & Media, 1997), 46.

109 Philip Ryken and Michael LeFebvre, *Our Triune God: Living in the Love of the Three-in-One* (Wheaton: Crossway, 2011), page 92.

110 John MacArthur, "Creation Day 6, Part 2: Sermon on Genesis 1:26-27," recorded on July 18, 1999, https://www.gty.org/library/sermons-library/90-218/creation-day-6-part-2. This concept is expanded in: John MacArthur, "Creation Day 6, Part 3: Sermon on Genesis 1:26-31," recorded on July 25, 1999, https://www.gty.org/library/sermons-library/90-219/creation-day-6-part-3.

111 Jason Carroll, Sarah Badger, Chongming Yang, "The Ability to Negotiate or the Ability to Love? Evaluating the Developmental Domains of Marital Competence," *Journal of Family Issues* 27, no. 7 (July 2006): 1001-1032.

112 Everett Worthington, "Repairing the Emotional Bond: Marriage Research from 1997 through Early 2005," *Journal of Psychology and Christianity*, Vol 24(3), Fall 2005, 259-262.

113 Everett Worthington (2005), 261.

Chapter 12: Healthy Relationships Engage with Proficient Skills

114 Carrol, Badger, and Yang, "The Ability to Negotiate or the Ability to Love?" 1001-1032.

115 Brant R. Burleson and Wayne H. Denton, "The Relationship between Communication Skill and Marital Satisfaction: Some Moderating Effects," *Journal of Marriage and the Family* 59, No. 4 (November 1997): 884-902.

116 B.J. Fowers, *Beyond the Myth of Marital Happiness* (San Francisco: Jossey-Bass, 2000).

117 B.J. Fowers, "The Limits of a Technical Concept of a Good Marriage: Exploring the Role of Virtue in Communication Skills," *Journal of Marital and Family Therapy* 27, no. 3 (July 2001): 327-340.

118 John Van Epp, *How to Avoid Marrying a Jerk* (New York: McGraw-Hill, 2007). The paperback was retitled, *How to Avoid Falling in Love with a Jerk*... although I always wanted McGraw Hill to add "or Jerkette," which I added every time the title was referenced and to all my programs by the same title.

119 The Smart Marriage Conference and Coalition was established by Diane Sollee in 1997 and became the spearhead of the Community Marriage Education movement during its formative years. She brought together developers of relationship education programs for every aspect of dating, marriage, and family with nonprofit and community-based organizations, academics, key political figures, and recipients of state and federal grants. Diane was a major leader and visionary within the relationship education movement.

120 Dictionary, https://www.yourdictionary.com/skill.

121 John Van Epp, *How to Avoid Falling in Love with a Jerk: The Foolproof Way to Follow Your Heart Without Losing Your Mind* (New York: McGraw-Hill, 2007), 25-28.

122 Aristotle, *Nicomachean Ethics*, trans. Martin Ostwald (Indianapolis: Bobbs-Merrill, 1962), 214.

123 Alexander, cited in Systematic Theology, Lewis Sperry Chafer (Dallas Seminary Press, Dallas, TX), Vol. I, 297.

124 Amanda Montañez, "The Beautiful Complexity of the Cosmic Web," *Scientific American*, April 14, 2016, https://blogs.scientificamerican.com/sa-visual/the-beautiful-complexity-of-the-cosmic-web/; "Missing Matter of Universe Found; Cosmic Web Discovered," *ScienceDaily*, May 20, 2008, https://www.sciencedaily.comreleases/2008/05/080520152013.htm; H. Umehata et al., "Gas Filaments of the Cosmic Web Located around Active Galaxies in a Protocluster," *Science* 366, no. 6461 (October 2019): 97-100, https://science.sciencemag.org/content/366/6461/97.

125 Glenn Roberts Jr., "Preparing for a New Tool to Study the 'Glue that Binds Us All,'" Berkeley Lab, February 8, 2019, https://newscenter.lbl.gov/2019/02/08/preparing-for-a-new-tool-to-study-the-glue-that-binds-us-all.

Reporter Roberts explains, "There is another exotic force called gluon that is truly the glue that binds us all." Berkeley Lab researchers participated in science review of a planned next-gen electron-ion collider. This glue (i.e., gluon), the mediator of subatomic particle interactions within atomic nuclei, is responsible for most of the visible universe's matter and mass. To learn about this glue, scientists are proposing a unique, high-energy collider that smashes accelerated electrons into charged atomic nuclei.

Also see in this article Tom Hartsfield. He explains this glue or interconnectedness of the smallest known particles. According to him, there are two exotic forces, called the strong and the weak, that are active within the nucleus. "While the electromagnetic force can attract and repel at large distances, the strong and weak forces within the nucleus are negligible at any distance larger than a few femtometers (a femtometer is a millionth of a billionth of a meter, which is 100 billion times smaller than the width of a hair). But at distances smaller than a few femtometers, these nuclear forces dominate." It is this strong force that holds particles together.

Chapter 13: Key Ingredients for an Effective Relationship Ministry

126 "The Relationship Health Report," Communio, accessed on May 27, 2021, https:// communio.org/the-state-of-marriages-relationships-in-the-church-download/, 2.

127 "Women More Likely Than Men to Initiate Divorces, But Not Non-Marital Breakups," *American Sociological Association*, August 22, 2015, accessed June 1, 2021. https://www.asanet. org/press-center/press-releases/women-more-likely-men-initiate-divorces-not-non-marital-breakups.

128 Shaunti Feldhahn, *The Good News About Marriage: Debunking Discouraging Myths about Marriage and Divorce* (Colorado Springs: Multnomah Books, 2014), 52.

129 Wendy Wang, "The US Divorce Rate Has Hit a 50-Year Low," *Institute for Family Studies*, November 10, 2020, https://ifstudies.org/blog/the-us-divorce-rate-has-hit-a-50-year-low.

130 "Frequently Requested Church Statistics," Center for Applied Research in the Apostolate, accessed May 14, 2021. https://cara.georgetown.edu/frequently-requested-church-statistics.

131 There are many aspects to communication that can be practiced in a skill-focused exercise. This includes skills for active listening, restatement, self-disclosure, depths of openness and intimacy. And then, there are skills related to problem solving and conflict resolution. There are many programs and studies that both teach *and* provide skill development in these areas of communication.

Worldwide Marriage Encounter teaches written dialoguing designed around practicing and eliciting empathy. John's RAM Series and his instructor-led course Couple LINKS use what he calls a Couple Huddle where spouses can practice all the core elements of communication skills and get back in balance. His instructor-led course, PICK, also creates skills-based exercises for single individuals. Couple Talk by Don and Alex Flecky is another resource geared toward helping couples develop communication skills. Some resources include question cards to help practice effective communication.

132 This is a major focus of the instructor-led course, PICK, based on the book, *How to Avoid Falling in Love with a Jerk or Jerkette*. It is also covered extensively in the RAM Series for Singles Study that is designed for youth groups and all adult ages.

133 Ken Fremont-Smith, "How to Change Your Own Contempt," *The Gottman Institute*, September 8, 2020, https://www.gottman.com/blog/how-to-change-your-own contempt. Resentment and contempt are emotions that can poison any relationship. This is frequently fueled by a misalignment in expectations. Dr. John Gottman has called contempt the "sulfuric acid of love." He has written that "there needs to be a path that leads to a culture of appreciation, and that is by expressing your feelings and longings." A good skills-based program will help couples practice habits that let each member share their wants and needs.

134 Oftentimes, conflicts arise because our experiences in a relationship do not line up with our expectations. Unfulfilled expectations are one of the most common sources of conflict in the first two years of marriage. Addressing this in premarital classes while also providing relationship courses for newlyweds that identify these common unrealistic expectations and provide skills-based plans for discussing and revising them will strengthen relationships and void future conflicts.

135 The RAM Series for Couples is based on the instructor-led relationship course, Couple LINKS. Published research on this course had found that the commitment of couples that went through the course more than doubled in strength compared to increases in commitment for couples who went through other relationship courses. The RAM provides a clear understanding of the relationship bonds that need to be regularly strengthened, but it also emphasizes that the virtues of commitment need to pull couples through conflicts and challenges they face in marriage. Whatever skills-based tool you utilize, a focus on reinforcing commitment and providing practical skill exercises to enhance commitment should be included.

Chapter 14: Growing the Church Through Relationship Ministry: The Data-Informed, Full-Circle Relationship Ministry

136 Sara McLanahan, Irwin Garfinkel, and Maureen Waller, "The Fragile Families and Child Wellbeing Study," *Public Policy Institute of California*, 1999, https://www.ppic.org/wp-content/uploads/OP_1199MWOP.pdf.

137 2019 Communio-Barna Report on Relationship Ministries, 4, accessed June 2, 2021, https://communio.org/wp-content/uploads/2021/06/Communio-Barna-Report_Relationship-Ministries.pdf.

138 Scott Stanley uses the phrase "sliding verses deciding" to describe the path many couples take toward cohabitation and commitment.

139 Mark Regnerus, sociologist and professor at the University of Texas, discussions with JP De Gance, June 2, 2021, regarding the 2018 American Political and Social Behavior Survey, email record of conversation on file at Communio.

Chapter 15: Going on Mission: The Ministry Engagement Ladder

140 Alan J. Hawkins, Scott M. Stanley, Victoria L. Blanchard, Michael Albright. "Exploring Programmatic Moderators of the Effectiveness of Marriage and Relationship Education Programs: A Meta-Analytic Study," *Behavior Therapy* 43 (2012): 77-87.

141 Scott M. Stanley et al., "Decreasing Divorce in US Army Couples; Results from a Randomized Controlled Trial Using PREP for Strong Bonds," *Journal of Couple and Relationship Therapy* 9, no. 2 (April 2010): 149–160, https://www.researchgate.net/publication/45200564_Decreasing_Divorce_in_US_Army_Couples_Results_from_a_Randomized_Controlled_Trial_Using_PREP_for_Strong_Bonds.

Chapter 16: A Model Church for Prioritizing the Mission of Relationship Health

142 Steve Poe, Lead Pastor at the Northview Christian Church in Carmel, Indiana, was the first pastor to preach through the RAM series. When churches license the RAM Series, they are allowed to design their own title for the series, and Steve chose *Relationship Goals*. John is indebted to Steve for his thoughtful organization of the Scriptures and illustrations used in those messages. The sermon manuscripts now included in the RAM Series have incorporated with Steve's permission some of those salient points.

Chapter 17: The Endgame for the Church in America

143 Paul Vitz. Discussion about his book *Faith of the Fatherless*, interview by J.P. De Gance, March 9, 2020, record on file with Communio.

144 Mary Eberstadt, *How the West Really Lost God: A New Theory of Secularization* (West Conshohocken: Templeton Press, 2013), 187-188.

Subject Index

1920s: Roarin' Twenties
47, 60

1960's: Sexual Revolution
19, 32–33, 42, 45, 47, 48, 53,
60, 61, 89, 94, 179, 192

**Adverse Family Experiences
(AFEs) or Adverse Child
Experiences (ACEs)**
78, 79, 84

Agape Love
125, 139, 147–159, 161, 162, 172,
173, 174

Albertson, Richard
11, 111, 183, 231

Alpha or the Marriage Course
111, 112, 187, 224, 231

Montero, Alvero
201

Appreciation Skills
206

Aristotle
172

**Army Chaplaincy Strong
Bonds Program**
14–15, 234

Ashcraft, David
239, 241, 242, 247

Barna Group or Barna Study
26, 27, 33, 105, 106, 165,
181, 188, 189, 217, 248

Birger, Jon
190

**Burgess, Ernest and Wallen,
Paul**
47

Carroll, Jason
156

Castelli, Jason
243, 244

Christ
3, 8, 10, 16, 17, 19, 27, 33,
34, 35, 36, 37, 38, 89, 96, 97,
102, 104, 108, 110, 113, 123,
124, 126, 127, 139, 140, 141,
142, 145, 149, 155, 173, 174,
176, 200, 201, 203, 206, 207,
210, 211, 223, 232, 239, 241,
243, 252, 253

City on a Hill
186

Cohabitation
57, 64, 65, 67, 68, 69, 70, 71,
72, 84, 91, 215, 252

Commitment Skills
207

Communication Skills
162, 166, 206

Communio
11, 26, 27, 30, 33, 90, 105,
113, 114, 116, 132, 152, 153,
181, 182, 184, 185, 189, 190,
193, 196, 201, 207, 208, 211,
212, 215, 216, 217, 219, 224,
225, 226, 227, 228, 229, 230,
232, 237, 239, 241, 243, 245,
246, 247

Community Healthy Marriage Initiative
13, 22

Comstock, Kenny
202

Conflict Resolution Skills
206

Connoisseur of a Spouse
166–167

Coontz, Stephanie
47

Crabb, Larry
172

Data-Informed, Full-Circle Relationship Ministry, or Full-Circle Relationship Ministry
173, 184, 185, 197, 209–222, 228, 235, 239, 241

Date or Dating
17, 19, 20, 22, 41, 42, 47, 51, 52, 54, 55, 56, 57, 58, 65, 66, 82, 83, 84, 96, 97, 107, 112, 114, 118, 119, 131, 134, 135, 136, 143, 144, 163, 165, 167, 168, 169, 170, 171, 173, 177, 183, 190, 191, 195, 199, 206, 211, 218, 224, 226, 227, 228, 231, 239, 234, 237, 238, 240, 242, 243, 245, 246, 247, 248, 251, 252, 253

Date-onomics
190

Decoupling effect (general references)
23, 39, 41–46, 47

 from parenting
23, 39, 41, 43, 44, 45, 46, 57, 71, 75–85, 96, 99

from romantic partnerships
23, 44, 57, 63–73, 78, 81, 99

from sex
23, 44, 45, 47–61, 62, 68, 78, 81, 83, 84, 99, 105

Discernment Skills
206

Disciples of the Hearts of Jesus and Mary
202

Eberstadt, Mary
82, 83, 85, 250

Economic Mobility and Marriage
60, 84

Emotional Intimacy Skills
130, 156, 206

EQ--Emotional Quotient
157, 158

Evangelicals, Protestants, & Catholics
20, 27, 29, 57–60, 69–72, 81–84, 105, 106, 107, 109, 115, 192–193, 207

Expectation Skills
207

Family Background of Dating Partner
170–172

Farrell, Warren
77

Fatherlessness
75, 77, 84, 94, 95, 252

Feldhahn, Shaunti
188

Fowers, Blaine
162

Fragile Families Study
75

Fruit of the Spirit
155, 173

Gardner, Howard
157

God's Will
176

Gospel
11, 19, 22, 34, 91, 96, 97, 99, 101,
102, 104, 105, 109, 113, 116, 173,
174, 179, 201, 210, 211, 219, 221,
223, 227–228, 235, 248, 250, 251,
252, 253

Good-enough Relationship
120

Health Relationships
117–177

**How to Avoid Falling in Love
with a Jerk**
14, 16, 56, 136, 170

Huddles for Couples
165, 166, 176

**Interpersonal Competence
or Skill**
156, 157, 159, 205, 208

**Intrapersonal Competence
or Skill**
156, 157, 159, 205, 206, 208

Irvin, Derek
244, 245

Jesus
3, 8, 10, 19, 20, 33, 35, 96, 108,
110, 113, 124, 139, 141, 142, 145,
147, 149, 155, 159, 164, 172, 173,
174, 175, 185, 186, 197, 200, 202,
203, 205, 210, 221, 223, 230, 239,
241, 253

John Paul II
43, 152

Know-Quo or 3Ts
134, 135, 144

Lanier, Wayne
233

LCBC
114, 237–248

Lewis, C.S.
149

LINKS or Couple LINKS
165, 231, 234, 238

Live the Life Ministries
11, 183, 233

Loneliness
39, 41–43, 45, 141, 212, 231

MacArthur, John
149, 153

Ministry Engagement Ladder
114, 190, 197, 121, 204, 221,
223–236, 241, 245, 246

Mitchell, Jason
239, 243, 245

Moore, Chad
196

**National Survey of
Children's Health**
78–79

National Survey of Families and Households
139

Nicene Creed
174

Lee, Nicki and Sila
187, 224

Northview Christian Church
244, 245

Ogg, Kate, David and Jamie
140

Opportunity and Responsibility
1–22, 41, 84, 99, 174

Vitz, Paul
93

PICK or PICK a Partner or How to Avoid Falling for a Jerk or Jerkette
14, 165, 168, 231, 233, 234, 238

Poe, Steve
244–145

Poor Skills or Ill Wills
162–165

Popenoe, David and Barbara Dafoe-Whitehead
51

RAM
114, 129-145

RAM and Relationship with God
141-142

RAM Series (6-week Churchwide Series)
114, 219, 237-248

RAM Series for Couples
165-168, 176-177, 205, 231

RAM Series for Singles
163, 168-172, 176-177, 190, 231

Regnerus, Mark
30, 33, 52, 110, 190

Relationship Bonds, Skills, Virtues diagram
164

Relationship Bonds: Know... Trust... Rely... Commit...Touch...
133-141

Relationship Management
117-127, 206

Relationship Ministry
23, 97, 132, 176, 228-229, 251

Relationship Outreach
23, 97, 132, 176, 228-229, 251

Relationship Skills
8, 15, 118, 143, 161-177, 204-207, 246

Relationship Virtues
15, 118, 138, 149, 163, 164, 172

Roundtable
7, 11, 30, 93, 110, 113

Safe Zone with RAM
143, 145, 169, 177

Sanctification
154-156